which fill out my obsessions
with D.R. & his world. You
mentioned you'd be interested
in reading them for their own
sake. I hope to see you soon —
liked your article on Woodstock
in "Midwest".

Thank you,
Mart Siegel

Scorsese
by Ebert

OTHER BOOKS BY
ROGER EBERT

An Illini Century

A Kiss Is Still a Kiss

Two Weeks in the Midday Sun:
A Cannes Notebook

Behind the Phantom's Mask

Roger Ebert's Little Movie Glossary

Roger Ebert's Movie Home Companion
annually 1986–1993

Roger Ebert's Video Companion
annually 1994–1998

Roger Ebert's Movie Yearbook
annually 1999–

Questions for the Movie Answer Man

Roger Ebert's Book of Film: An Anthology

Ebert's Bigger Little Movie Glossary

I Hated, Hated, Hated This Movie

The Great Movies

The Great Movies II

Awake in the Dark: The Best of Roger Ebert

Your Movie Sucks

Roger Ebert's Four-Star Reviews 1967–2007

With Daniel Curley   The Perfect London Walk

With Gene Siskel   The Future of the Movies:
Interviews with Martin Scorsese,
Steven Spielberg, and George Lucas

DVD Commentary Tracks   Beyond the Valley of the Dolls

Casablanca

Citizen Kane

Crumb

Dark City

Floating Weeds

(Roger Ebert)

Scorsese
by Ebert

FOREWORD BY *Martin Scorsese*

THE UNIVERSITY OF CHICAGO PRESS

Chicago and London

Roger Ebert is the Pulitzer Prize–winning film critic of the *Chicago Sun-Times*. Starting in 1975, he cohosted a long-running weekly movie-review program on television, first with Gene Siskel and then with Richard Roeper. He is the author of numerous books on film, including *The Great Movies*, *The Great Movies II*, and *Awake in the Dark: The Best of Roger Ebert*, the last published by the University of Chicago Press.

The University of Chicago Press, Chicago 60637
The University of Chicago Press, Ltd., London
© 2008 by The Ebert Company, Ltd.
Foreword © 2008 by The University of Chicago Press
All rights reserved. Published 2008
Printed in the United States of America

17 16 15 14 13 12 11 10 09 08   1 2 3 4 5

ISBN-13: 978-0-226-18202-5 (cloth)
ISBN-10: 0-226-18202-9 (cloth)

LIBRARY OF CONGRESS CATALOGING-IN-PUBLICATION DATA
Ebert, Roger.
    Scorsese by Ebert / Roger Ebert ; foreword by Martin Scorsese
    p. cm.
    ISBN-13: 978-0-226-18202-5 (cloth : alk.paper)
    ISBN-10: 0-226-18202-9 (cloth : alk paper) 1. Scorsese, Martin—Criticism and
interpretation. I. title.
    PN1998.3 .S39E33 2008
    791.430233092—dc22
                                                        2008015418

The interview in part 4 between Martin Scorsese and Roger Ebert was conducted in February 1997 at the Wexner Center for the Arts at the Ohio State University in Columbus, Ohio, as part of the Wexner Prize ceremonies. Courtesy the Wexner Center for the Arts with the permission of Martin Scorsese.

♾ The paper used in this publication meets the minimum requirements of the American National Standard for Information Sciences—Permanence of Paper for Printed Library Materials, ANSI Z39.48-1992.

All previously published reviews, essays, and interviews originally appeared in the *Chicago Sun-Times*, and are reprinted with permission. © Chicago Sun-Times, Inc., 1967–2008.

Note of 3/12/70 reproduced on endpapers couresy of Roger Ebert and Martin Scorsese.

Dedicated to Marty, obviously.

... New talents abound these days —
Bogdanovich, Coppola, Friedkin — but
I would propose, as an educated hunch,
that in ten years Martin Scorsese will be a
director of world rank.

He's not only that good but he's that
adept at taking the stuff of real life and
handling it at the realistic level while
somehow informing it with deeply affecting symbolism. He does it as fluently (although not yet as stylishly) as Fellini; and
because his obsessions seem more deeply
felt, I think his work will turn out to have
greater gut impact. Fellini's genius has
always been in his broad strokes, in his
showmanship; Scorsese goes for the in-
sides. If it seems premature or reckless to
mention Fellini (by my notion, one of the
handful of living directorial geniuses) with
Scorsese, who is a kid from Little Italy,
then let it sound that way: I stand on it.

Roger Ebert
Chicago Sun-Times
November 1973

Contents

Foreword

By Martin Scorsese

Movies, like any other works of art—or presumptive art—don't change. DVD "director's cuts" aside (and there are, I think, legitimate debates to be had about them), most movies are destined to live their lives in the form in which they were first released. But the people who watch movies do change. They grow up—or at least grow older—and their perceptions of a particular movie change. Movies we loved as young people sometimes seem less lovable when we revisit them years later. The opposite is also true; sometimes we need more experience to appreciate fully the subtlety of movies we saw for the first time in the distant past. What's true of us, as individual moviegoers, is also true of the world at large. It changes, too, and it is sometimes true, especially of visionary films, that they have to wait for their time to come.

Because movie critics are obliged to go on the record during the heat and haste of a movie's initial release, they are pretty much stuck with their first impressions, even though, as time goes by, they, too, may well have a radically changed opinion of a film. It is therefore brave of Roger Ebert to publish this collection of pieces unedited, to set whatever revisionary ideas he has about the films he discusses apart from his original texts. It is also brave of him to confine this collection of reviews, interviews, and reflections to a single director. That's an implicit and inherently controversial endorsement of that director's style and sensibility—food for the critic's critics to feast on.

Since my work is the subject of this book I'm deeply flattered by the careful attention Roger devotes to it, though in all modesty I must wonder if it is worthy of such an extensive treatment. But Roger is a first-rate reviewer—observant, knowledgeable, forthright, and deeply serious about the movies. He is always worth reading, no matter what you think of his subject.

We have known each other since 1967, when I took my first feature, *Who's That Knocking at My Door*—it was then entitled *I Call First*—to the Chicago Film Festival and he wrote a very positive review of it. It was a modest little film, shot on a shoestring, by a group of us who were no more than semiprofessionals at the time. It was not widely released or reviewed, but Roger saw something in it that most people did not. He made a personal connection with it, based on the fact that we were both marked by our relationship with the Catholic Church, in which we had both been raised. His was the Irish church, mine, the Italian. But we had both, at one point in our young lives, aspired to a priestly vocation and we had both failed in that ambition. We were also marked, as Harvey Keitel is in that film, by another sort of torment, which is a sexual one—the well-known tendency of some men, especially those raised in the church, to see women either as Madonnas or as whores, a topic Roger writes about more than once in these pages. It is, of course, symbolic of what was for young Catholic men of our generation a much larger issue: the spiritual idealism, the church vs. the realities—or should I say the temptations?—of growing up on big city's *Mean Streets* (to borrow a phrase).

I'm not saying that that issue was the sole basis for the relationship that developed between Roger and me over the years. But it did establish an emotional contact point between us, a shared, sub-aesthetic understanding, that enabled him to see, and appreciate, things in my movies that were perhaps not so obvious to other reviewers. But I think it was in the realm of aesthetics that we bonded perhaps more closely. We were both kids who, I think, wanted to escape the noisy, contentious worlds of our families and friends, wanted to lose ourselves in fantasies that were, if not always more pleasing, then more all-consuming—for at least couple of hours (usually it was many more) every week. Most kids use the movies for that purpose—or at least they did a half century and more ago. But only a relatively small number of them develop the passion for them that we shared. We know movies in our bones. We can discuss them by the hour, often enough in shot-by-shot detail. We continue to go back to them again and again. We refer to them constantly in our work. And, naturally, in our conversations. They provide the central metaphors—hundreds of them—for our lives. This is not just a matter of being able to quote their most famous lines. It's a matter of being able to analyze closely a camera set-up or an edit—looking, sometimes perhaps absurdly, for their deeper meanings.

We are not intimate friends, Roger and I. But we are certainly long-standing ones. This is not as unusual as it may seem to some people. Filmmakers and film critics often establish such relationships. They are not based on self-interest; they are based on mutual interests, of the kind I've been describing. I can't imagine a critic or a director connecting in this way if they loathed each other's work. Or if there were fundamental disagreements about the nature of movies or about their most basic feelings about film.

That said, I must also say that the pieces I most enjoyed in this collection are the ones in which Roger registers his doubts about some of my movies. I'm thinking, for instance, of his writings about *The King of Comedy*. Or his politely phrased doubts about *Kundun*. Or his feelings that my attempts to make more mainstream movies like *The Color of Money* or *Cape Fear* are not my best work. It's the same with some of his enthusiasm. I'm still not as high on *Who's That Knocking* as he is. And his enthusiasm for *After Hours* and, perhaps, *Bringing Out the Dead* is something that puzzles me a little bit (his pieces on those films are critical minority reports). But that's not important. I think all a filmmaker dare ask of a critic is that he take the work seriously, wrestle with it earnestly, write about it—and his responses to it—soberly.

It is not important if a critic "likes" or "doesn't like" a movie. What is important is that he engages with it fully, brings to his responses the conviction, the passion, that the director brings to the film's making. Opinion is evanescent, but the work abides. Ideally, the kinds of first and second impressions in this volume simply begin a dialogue that will last for years — decades — to come. In the end, history is the only critic that counts, and it's important that the dialogue out of which its judgments arise begins with the kind of emotionally alert, historically informed, intellectually honest writing that Roger Ebert has collected here. I continue to feel in some ways unworthy of his attention, but honored that it has so often settled on me. I hope our long-standing dialog continues for a very long time.

Introduction

We were born five months apart in 1942, into worlds that could not have differed more — Martin Scorsese in Queens, me in downstate Illinois — but in important ways we had similar childhoods. We were children of working-class parents who were well aware of their ethnic origins. We attended Roman Catholic schools and churches that, in those pre–Vatican II days, would have been substantially similar. We memorized the Latin of the Mass; we were drilled on mortal sins, venial sins, sanctifying grace, the fires of hell; we memorized great swathes of the Baltimore Catechism. We were baffled by the concept of Forever, and asked how it was that God could have no beginning and no end. We were indoors children, not gifted at sports: "That boy always has his nose buried in a book."

We went to the movies all the time, in my case because television came unusually late to my hometown, in Scorsese's because to begin with his father took him, and then he went on his own, sometimes daily, watching anything and learning from it. He became fascinated by the details. I saw the story, he saw the films. He has spoken again and again of a single shot of Deborah Kerr in Powell and Pressburger's *Black Narcissus* that arrested his attention. Something had happened there, and he couldn't see what it was, or how it was done. Years later, he was to enlist Powell as a consultant, and discover the answer to his question. By then, he was already one of the greatest directors in film history.

I had been a film critic for seven months when I saw his first film, in 1967. It was titled *I Call First*, later changed to *Who's That Knocking at My Door*. I saw it in "the submarine"—the long, low, narrow, dark screening room knocked together out of pasteboard by the Chicago International Film Festival. I was twenty-five. The festival's founder, Michael Kutza, was under thirty. Everything was still at the beginning. This film had a quality that sent tingles up my arms. It felt made out of my dreams and guilts.

I had little in common with its loose-knit confederation of friends in Little Italy, but everything in common with J. R., its hero, played by Harvey Keitel. I, too, idealized women but shied away from their sexuality. In high school there were some girls I dated and some girls I furtively made out with, and they were not the same girls. I associated sex with mortal sin. I understood why J. R. could have nothing more to do with a young woman after he discovered she had been raped. She had been touched in a way that meant J. R. could not touch her, and he blamed her. I identified with the camaraderie of the friends J. R. ran with. Drinking had melted my solitary shyness and replaced it with shallow bravado. I identified with the movie's rock and roll, and indeed *I Call First* was the first movie I recall seeing with a sound track that was not a composed score, but cobbled together from 45 rpm records. The energy of the cutting grabbed me with such opening shots as when the street fight broke out and the hand-held camera followed it down the sidewalk. Everything about that movie stabbed me in the heart and soul. I had seen great films, I had in truth seen *greater* films, but never one that so touched me. Perhaps it was because of that experience that I *became* a film critic, instead of simply working as one.

I describe these feelings not because you are interested in me, but because I am interested in why I feel a lasting bond with this director. Since that first day, Scorsese has never disappointed me. He has never made an unworthy film. He has made a few films that, he confided, he "needed" to do to get other films made, but those films were well made, and if it is true, for example, that *After Hours* was done simply to keep him busy and distracted after the heartbreak of the first cancellation of *The Last Temptation of Christ*, it is also true that *After Hours* is one of his best films. He has fashioned the career of an exemplary man of the cinema, not only directing important films, but also using his clout to "present" or co-produce films by such directors as Antoine Fuqua, Wim Wenders, Kenneth Lonergan, Stephen Frears, Allison Anders, Spike Lee, and John McNaughton. He has founded the Film Foundation, dedicated to film preservation. He has produced and hosted long documentaries about American and Italian films. He has been a leading citizen of Movie City.

One of Scorsese's strengths is a technical mastery of the medium. Like Orson Welles long before him (who allegedly watched Ford's *Stagecoach* one hundred times before directing *Citizen Kane*), he learned his art not only in classrooms at New York University, but by the intense scrutiny of other directors' films. He talks often about the *Million-Dollar Movie* that would play every day for a week on a New York television station. He would watch it every day, all week. Once when I told him I had seen his personal print of Renoir's *The River* at the Virginia Film Festival, he told me he watches it at least three times a year. When Gene Siskel visited him during a low time in the 1970s, he took him into a screening room (in a basement, as I recall) and said he spent most of every day down in there, watching movies. He does not copy other directors, he does not do homage, but he absorbs and transmutes. Wikipedia observes that he often introduces his blonde heroines in idealizing slow-motion shots, in possible tribute to Hitchcock. I am as certain as I can be that his style reflects the feelings his protagonists have about those women. Jake LaMotta would have seen Vickie for the first time in slow motion even if Hitchcock had never made a film.

Scorsese has worked with the best cinematographers, recently Robert Richardson and Michael Ballhaus, but his look is always his own. In shots without obvious movement, he nevertheless likes a subtly moving camera, because he believes movement suggests voyeurism and a static camera indicates simply a gaze — but he is not afraid to gaze. The divinity of Christ or the Dalai Lama has a tendency to hold his camera in unmoving frames. Or notice the gradual acceleration of the

(3)

cutting pace in *GoodFellas*, as a leisurely criminal lifestyle turns paranoid. There are rarely shots that call attention to themselves merely for the sake of the shot; yes, *GoodFellas* has the famous unbroken take through the Copacabana, and *Raging Bull* the walk from the dressing room into the ring, but how many moviegoers are conscious of them? What Scorsese's camera says to me is not "look how I see this," but "look with me at this." He is urging the enterprise forward into the next moment of the narrative, not pausing to draw attention to the last. Even that shot in *Taxi Driver*, the sideways move away from the pay phone to look down a long, empty corridor, is not a stunt but a reflection of a subjective loneliness.

Of all directors of his generation and younger, he may make the best use of rock music in his films. His first film was scored with rock records, he was a supervising editor on *Woodstock*, he has done documentaries on The Band and Bob Dylan, and was working in late 2007 on a Rolling Stones concert tour. He uses period music for *New York, New York* or *The Aviator*, and he evokes a time period with Dean Martin (whom he once planned to make a film about), but you sense that he edits with rock in mind; it is worth remembering that he met his longest-serving collaborator, the great editor Thelma Schoonmaker, on *Who's That Knocking*, and worked on *Woodstock* with her. Michael Wadleigh, one of the cinematographers on *Knocking*, became the director of *Woodstock*. I remember sitting next to them on the floor of a New York loft and watching takes of that film while they were both vibrating like fans at a concert. Also on *Who's That Knocking* was his classmate Mardik Martin as a director's assistant, who went on to work on several screenplays with Scorsese. All kids starting together.

His protagonists are often awkward outsiders who try too hard or are not sure what to say. Travis Bickle; Rupert Pupkin; Max Cady in *Cape Fear*; Tommy DeVito in *GoodFellas*; Newland Archer in *The Age of Innocence*, who has no idea how to behave when he experiences real love; Vincent Lauria in *The Color of Money*; Frank Pierce in *Bringing Out the Dead*; Howard Hughes; even Jesus Christ, who is not the soul of tact. Scorsese is uninterested in conventional heroes. He often tells the story about sitting in his family's apartment in Little Italy and watching through the window as gangsters came and went at the social club across the street. Some of those memories are reflected in the opening scenes of *GoodFellas*. Scorsese's protagonists are not the guys with the shiny cars, although they are common enough in his movies. His identification is with the kid in the window.

He has been the embodiment of independence without making "Sundance films" or "indie films." Apart from the low-budget early films, he has always tended toward pictures as big as they need to be, or sometimes (as with *Gangs of New York*) bigger. It is the classic-studio period that engages his imagination. He can write screenplays, but hasn't often filmed his own solo work; after collaborating closely with his writers, he does his own writing with his camera. After outgrowing an early 1970s indie image of long hair, a beard, and scruffy jeans, he has become an expensively dressed man; like the Hollywood giants of the golden age, he exudes fashion and power. Still he is "Marty"— friendly, rapid-fire in speech, enthusiastic, funny, democratic, informal. I remember a night during an early New York Film Festival when he and I and Pauline Kael sprawled in a hotel room, drank, and talked movies until dawn. There was real enthusiasm. Years later, after his award at the Wexner Center in Columbus, he ended up in the library of a millionaire's mansion outside of town, with film students at his feet. Same kind of conversation. Same Marty.

(5)

I sense he has never made a film that does not speak to him on some fundamental level. Even when he expressed ambivalence about *The King of Comedy*, asking himself some days why he was even on the set, his finished film was fashioned into a Scorsese picture. If he had initial reluctance about the subject matter, he must have warmed to it as the De Niro performance grew, and he thinks it contains De Niro's finest work. The events and materials of *After Hours* might have made an entirely different kind of film in other hands, but he was quite willing to describe it as a reflection of his state of mind after everything went wrong with the first production of *The Last Temptation of Christ*. Even *Kundun*, the film I think owes least to his lifelong interests and inner compulsions, is a reflection of yearning for peace and certainty.

It is purely speculation, but I wonder if the Dalai Lama is the Scorsese protagonist he would most like to be.

He is a man of fierce energy, of inner fires burning high. He works hard, is endlessly curious, is intoxicated by great films, does not procure screenplays and film them, but uses screenwriters as collaborators to argue over ideas. Paul Schrader, who has worked with him so long, speaks of him as like a chess opponent who does not mind losing a piece to a good move. He likes the game. He doesn't bully writers, but engages with them. I wonder if he is too social and verbal to sit alone in a room and write a screenplay, as Schrader does by nature. I think for him writing, talking, and creating are associated processes.

This book is the record of an association with Scorsese that began when, as it happened, I wrote the first review he ever received. We met before he was famous and successful. Once he took me to the Feast of San Gennaro in Little Italy, and we ate in a neighborhood restaurant where he pointed out certain clients as of more than routine interest. He sent me drafts of two screenplays, titled *Jerusalem, Jerusalem* and *Season of the Witch*, intended to be the first and third films in the J. R. trilogy, "which will probably never be made but which fill out my obsessions with J. R. and his world." The *Witch* screenplay later became *Mean Streets*, which makes it clear that J. R. and Charlie were, in his mind, the same person.

In the *Jerusalem* treatment, the hero, Charlie, spends time at a religious retreat at a seminary, and is deeply impressed by a sermon telling the story of a young couple who were to be married in two weeks. One night, however, they could wait no longer, and had sex before marriage. Driving home, they were killed in a fiery crash, and went to hell. This story helps explain J. R.'s reluctance to sleep with The Girl (never named) in *Who's That Knocking*. During the sermon, J. R. envisions images from pornography, including a couple embracing on the altar. This juxtaposition of the divine and the profane also expresses itself in *Taxi Driver*, when Travis takes Betsy to a hardcore movie. Charlie in *Jerusalem* finds that warnings against sexuality bring it into his mind, and he "harbors" such thoughts. "Harboring impure thoughts" would have been one of the sins he was warned against in

Catholic school, if Scorsese's was anything like mine, and I have a feeling that it was.

I Call First, which began as a student film at NYU and was co-produced by his beloved mentor, Haig Manoogian, was released as *Who's That Knocking at My Door* a year after its Chicago premiere, when the distributor Joseph Brennan insisted on the title change and asked Scorsese to shoot the scene with J. R. and the prostitute, which supplied the poster art. Like all young directors, he could hardly see another film on his horizon. Then exploitation producer-director Roger Corman, who gave so many major directors (Francis Ford Coppola, James Cameron, Jonathan Demme, Ron Howard) their first or second films, hired him to do *Boxcar Bertha*, and Scorsese was on board. Not a Scorsese-type story, but make what you will of the crucifixion imagery.

(7)

We have never become close friends. It is best that way. We talk whenever he has a new film coming out, or at tributes, industry events, or film festivals. We have dinner. We sense things in common. But I do not take him for granted. I consider him the most gifted director of his generation, and have joked that I will never stop writing film reviews until he stops making films.

Gene Siskel would ask me, "When are you going to write your Scorsese book?" and I would agree that I had to. But I am not a long-form writer. I started as a full-time professional newspaperman (not an intern) at the age of fifteen, and have spent fifty years writing pieces of hundreds or thousands of words in length. That is my distance. After a fruitful collaboration with John Tryneski and Rodney Powell of the University of Chicago Press on the book *Awake in the Dark*, they observed that I had been writing about Scorsese from the first day, had interviewed him many times, and could compose a book of this nature.

The book includes my original reviews of the films, unaltered; the interviews I did with Scorsese at the time; "reconsiderations" of six films that I thought needed a second look (or, in the case of *The Last Temptation of Christ*, as you will see, really a first look); and longer, later pieces I wrote about *Mean Streets*, *Taxi Driver*, *Raging Bull*, *GoodFellas*, and *The Age of Innocence* for my series of "Great Movies" essays that has so far produced two books and is approaching a third. These are reconsiderations too, in their way. Labeled here as "Masterpieces," they are not his only five, and the Great Movies series will include him again in the future. There are also introductions to four periods that Scorsese's career seems to reflect.

Then there is the transcript of the conversation Scorsese and I had at the Wexner Center for the Arts at The Ohio State University, when he was honored with an award and a tribute. We spoke for perhaps two hours, maybe longer, but even so I was astonished to see that the transcript amounted to more than twenty thousand words, which came pouring out of Marty in the full flood of memory and enthusiasm. You will observe there, and in some of the interviews, that he is not guarded like members of subsequent film generations, cannot be limited to sound bites, will answer just about any question he is asked, including some he should really not answer. His longtime publicist, Marion Billings, is not the type of person who rehearses sound bites with her clients, but more of a supporter and a friend. His personality could not abide one of today's rigidly controlling publicists. The Billings philosophy: if Marty said it, that's what he said.

I only have one story left to tell. Siskel and I were asked to host a series of career tributes at the Toronto Film Festival. Our first choice was Scorsese, whom Gene admired no less than I did. On the afternoon of the tribute, we ran into Marty and his ebullient mother, Catherine, in the lobby of the hotel.

"What's the dress code tonight?" he asked.

"We are the presenters, and so of course we'll have to wear tuxedos," Gene said. "But you are the guest, and you can wear anything."

"Gee, maybe I'll just wear my jeans," he said.

"Martin!" Catherine said, her voice in italics. "You will wear your tuxedo!"

"Right, mom," he said. And he did.

(8)

Part 1 Beginning

Introduction

When Mardik Martin discusses the budget of Martin Scorsese's first feature, he doesn't mention dollars. "Pennies!" he says, in the short documentary *The Making of "Who's That Knocking at My Door,"* which is included on the DVD. Scorsese started the film as *Bring on the Dancing Girls* while still a student at New York University and then rejected much of his original footage, keeping only some shots of Harvey Keitel, and starting again. His professor, Haig Manoogian, noticed his determination to make films, and was so impressed by his early work that when *I Call First*, as it was originally titled, went into production he actually supported it with some of his own money, and funds he was able to raise. Still, "pennies." Yet it was shot on 35 mm, because for Scorsese that was the medium that counted. In some of the shots, Manoogian said, Keitel is three years younger, but nobody ever picked up on that.

For this and much of the information in this section I am indebted to *Martin Scorsese: The First Decade*, by Mary Pat Kelly, who met him after writing him a letter in the 1960s from St. Mary-of-the-Woods College in Indiana. (The "Kelly girls" were all beauties, and popular in Chicago; another sister, Mickey, became Bill Murray's first wife.) He responded with pages of advice, she recalled. Kelly became a nun, then left her order after ten years; her Catholicism connected with Scorsese's. Her book includes long interviews with Scorsese and Manoogian, who died in 1980.

Martin, a lifelong friend and collaborator, said he was impressed that even on *I Call First* Scorsese seemed to have an instinct for where to place the camera, how to frame a shot, and how to get exactly what he needed. His cinematographers were Richard Coll and Michael Wadleigh, whom he met at school, and his editor was Thelma Schoonmaker, universally known as "T." Wadleigh would go on to direct *Woodstock*, hiring both Scorsese and Schoonmaker. Scorsese would work with Schoonmaker for the rest of her career, during which she would win three Oscars and be nominated for three others.

The first film was all based, Scorsese told Kelly, on guys he grew up with, in some cases playing themselves in the film. It was intended as part of a trilogy; the first section, *Jerusalem, Jerusalem*, involved a retreat at a seminary and a playing out of images associated with the stations of the cross. It was rejected by all potential producers as too involved with religion. The third, titled *Season of the Witch*, became *Mean Streets*—again, based on childhood friends and observations. To the degree that the hero, J. R., later called Charlie, was autobiographical would have been because of his guilts and religious feelings, not his quasi-criminal actions.

I Call First was a long time being seen. It was rejected by many film festivals, Manoogian recalled, before being accepted by Venice—only to have the print languish in a loading area at the Rome airport so long it did not qualify for the festival. Michael Kutza of the new Chicago festival saw it in New York, invited it, and it had its world premiere on November 15, 1967, when I saw it and was so deeply impressed by it. A little less than a year later, having gained a nude scene and the title *Who's That Knocking at My Door*, it opened in New York to mixed reviews. (The title should correctly never end in a question mark; film-industry superstition teaches that question marks in titles are bad luck.)

After *Knocking* came the *Woodstock* experience, and then *Boxcar Bertha* (1972), with Roger Corman as producer. The Internet Movie Database has it that Scorsese showed the finished film to John Cassavetes, who hugged him and said, "Martin, you just spent a year of your life making shit!" That bad it wasn't; despite his poverty-row budget, Scorsese prepared thousands of storyboard drawings, and his visual confidence is always evident. But it was commissioned as an exploitation film, and Scorsese treated it as a learning experience, using much the same crew for *Mean Streets*. The scene involving the crucifixion of the David Carradine character was one of the elements that interested him in the screenplay.

Cassavetes had told him, "Make films about what you know." Manoogian advised him, "No more films about Italians." Scorsese went with the advice from Cassavetes, whose own *Shadows* (1959) had essentially founded the school of filmmaking that engendered *I Call First*. In *Mean Streets*, Scorsese told Kelly, "I put in all the stuff I left out of *Who's That Knocking*." It opened at the 1973 New York Film Festival, and earned its historic review by Pauline Kael, who announced the arrival of a great director.

(13)

According to Pauline Kael, "The clearest fact about Charlie is that whatever he does in his life, he's a sinner." Those not raised as Catholics might miss some of the film's specific references to the religion, although Charlie's obsession with holding his fingers above flames is a clear enough evocation of hellfire. Another shot, however, in which Charlie asks for a shot of whiskey and has the bartender pour it over his crossed fingers above the glass, is a literal reenactment of what the priest does when an altar boy pours water and wine over his fingers holding a chalice.

Although he has certainly had a hand in the writing of all of his films, the screenplay credit for *Mean Streets*, shared with Mardik Martin but based on a Scorsese original, would be the last time he took a writing credit until *GoodFellas*, seventeen years later. And that film also opened with a voiceover drawn directly from Scorsese's early memories. The earlier v.o. involved the church, then later the mob, and those were the two poles between which Charlie was torn. What is crucial, as I point out in my second review of *Mean Streets* in this book's "Masterpieces" section, is that for Charlie the crimes of gangsters (extortion, beating, killing) were insignificant compared to crimes involving sex. He felt more guilt about his lust for the girl Teresa than for taking a man's restaurant, his family's livelihood, away from him.

Mean Streets stands at a divide in Scorsese's life. It comes at about the end of his interaction with the street culture it celebrates, and at the beginning of his emergence as a successful, then honored, director. It was a film written before the flowering of his career, and released to stunning acclaim. ("An unequivocally first-class film," Vincent Canby wrote after its New York Film Festival premiere.) *Boxcar Bertha*, between, is insignificant in this progression except as a journeyman piece and a way to gain experience with a Hollywood crew.

A year later came *Alice Doesn't Live Here Anymore* (1974), with its three nominations, its Oscar for Ellen Burstyn, and the spin-off TV series *Alice*, and Scorsese, barely into his thirties, was solidly established as a successful and respected professional.

(14) The arrival of *Taxi Driver* in 1976 is hard to describe. It was, and is, such a passionate, challenging, raw, and powerful film that it created a space of its own. In screenwriter Paul Schrader, Scorsese found a lifelong soulmate, one whose own fundamentalist upbringing in the Dutch Reformed Church supplied him with religious obsessions to equal Scorsese's own. Schrader wrote the screenplay, he told me, in two weeks in a Los Angeles hotel room, and it became the first of his "man in a room" movies, beginning with a man in a room girding himself to face the world. Some of these he wrote for Scorsese (*Raging Bull*), others he directed himself (*American Gigolo*).

Their Travis Bickle remains one of the few movie characters most moviegoers know by name. De Niro, who had worked steadily since De Palma started using him in the 1960s, was nominated for best actor, and the film got three more nominations: best picture, supporting actress, and score. Jodie Foster was thirteen when she made it, and fourteen when, with cool confidence, she acted as the translator for the film's press conference after its showing at Cannes. I recall the tumult of that conference; the Europeans embraced the film, and the festival gave it the Golden Palm. The award came ten years after the premiere of *I Call First*.

There is a buried connection between Scorsese's first film and *Taxi Driver*. In *Who's That Knocking*, J. R. describes the plot of Ford's *The Searchers* in great detail to the girl he meets at the ferry terminal.

The plot of *Taxi Driver* is in broad outline the same story, of a hero rescuing a girl from "Sport," the nickname for Keitel's pimp character. The admiration for *The Searchers* is another link between Scorsese and Schrader, whose own *Hardcore* also owes a lot to the same plot.

Taxi Driver has held up well, Schrader told me on its twentieth anniversary. "It was massive serendipity. Particularly very early in your career, to have that weight lifted off of your shoulders—the question of, will I ever do anything worthwhile? You know you've done something worthwhile and now you can get down to working. People said it must be terrible, knowing I had to top it. I said, no, it's just the opposite. You're free from feeling that you're never going to accomplish anything."

Then came the mixed results of *New York, New York*, Scorsese's most ambitious film to date, embracing the studio style of the 1940s and 1950s that he loved. I discuss the film here in a "reconsideration" after my original review. A year later, he filmed *The Last Waltz*, abandoning the usual one- or two-camera style of most concert films, and using and improving on what he had learned and practiced during *Woodstock*, choreographing several cameras and working from detailed shot sheets so he knew where every camera should be at any point during a song.

Scorsese had gone from a classroom to the red carpet at Cannes. There was never again the slightest doubt of his stature. In the period between this success and the commencement of *Raging Bull*, however, he would pass through the greatest crisis of his life.

I Call First

NOVEMBER 17, 1967

Editor's note: Martin Scorsese's first feature, reviewed here for a festival showing under the title I Call First, *was released theatrically as* Who's That Knocking at My Door.

There has been a long wait for an American film like Martin Scorsese's *I Call First*, which made a stunning impact in its world premiere Wednesday night at the Chicago International Film Festival.

As a film, it has something to say to everyone. As a technical achievement, it brings together two opposing worlds of American cinema.

On the one hand, there have been traditional films like *Marty*, *A View from the Bridge*, *On the Waterfront*, and *David and Lisa*—all sincere attempts to function at the level where real lives are led and all suffering to some degree from their makers' romantic and idealistic ideas about such lives.

On the other hand, there have been experimental films from Jonas Mekas, Shirley Clarke, and other pioneers of the New York underground. In *The Connection*, *Shadows*, and *Guns of the Trees*, they used improvised dialog and scenes and hidden and hand-held cameras in an attempt to capture the freshness of a spontaneous experience.

Both groups have lacked the other's strong point. The films like *Marty* are technically well done and emotionally satisfying, but they lack the flavor of actual experience. Films like *Shadows* are authentic enough, but often poor in technical quality and lacking the control necessary to develop character and tell a story.

I Call First brings these two kinds of films together into a work that is absolutely genuine, artistically satisfying, and technically comparable to the best films being made anywhere. I have no reservations in describing it as a great moment in American movies.

Remarkably, writer-director Martin Scorsese is only twenty-five years old, and this is his first film. He tells a love story about two different kinds of people. His young man is from New York's Little Italy, has a strong Roman Catholic background, is intelligent but not very well educated and divides the women of the world into "nice girls" and "broads." The young woman is a college graduate, well read, more sophisticated, and has probably had an affair or two. She loves him enough to try to explain that she is a "nice girl" but not a virgin.

The divergent views of love and morality come into opposition, but they make a tremendous effort to understand and respect each other. In the end, they fail. Their story is told against a poetically evoked background of the young man's life with his friends, who were probably his high school and army buddies and will probably be his old age cronies. Two scenes—one in a bar, another at a party—are among the most evocative descriptions of American life I have ever seen.

I want to comment at length on the performances and details of the plot, but I will have to wait until the film begins its commercial run here. I hope that will be soon.

Who's That Knocking at My Door

MARCH 17, 1969

The possibilities in creating an independent feature film in this country are abundantly illustrated by *Who's That Knocking at My Door*, a first work by Martin Scorsese that has been knocking around for nearly two years now. I first saw it in November 1967, at the Chicago Film Festival, when it was titled *I Call First*. I found it a marvelous evocation of American city life, announcing the arrival of an important new director.

To be sure, Scorsese was occasionally too obvious, and the film has serious structural flaws, but nobody who loves movies believes a perfect one will ever be made. What we hope for instead are small gains on the fronts of hope, love, comedy, and tragedy. It is possible that with more experience and maturity Scorsese will direct more polished, finished films—but this work, completed when he was twenty-five, contains a frankness he may have diluted by then. The movies, in their compulsion to be contemporary, too often give us an unreal picture of "swinging youth." We get discotheques, anti-establishment clichés, New London fashions, and Christopher Jones being cooler at twenty-one than we hope to be by fifty. If we like these films, it is because we identify with them—not because they understand us. In *Who's That Knocking*, Scorsese deals with young manhood on a much more truthful level.

Here are no swingers making it with Yvette Mimieux, no graduates seduced by Anne Bancroft. Instead, we enter a world of young

Italian Americans in New York City who sit around and kill time and look at *Playboy* and cruise around in a buddy's car listening to the Top 40 and speculating aimlessly about where the action is, or might be, or ever was.

Occasionally on Saturday night they get together at somebody's apartment to drink beer, watch Charlie Chan in a stupefied daze, and listen to some guy who says he knows two girls whom he might be able to call up. In this world, still strongly under a repressive moral code, there are two kinds of girls: nice girls and broads. You try to make the broads and you place the nice girls on an inaccessible, idealized pedestal.

The hero of *Who's That Knocking* comes from this world but is not entirely of it. One day on the Staten Island ferry, he meets a nice girl, a blonde, who is reading a French magazine. She's taking the ride for fun—something the young man cannot comprehend. They get into a conversation about John Wayne, and reading French, and what their ambitions are. It is a marvelously acted scene, much of it shot in one take to retain continuity as the two people get over their embarrassment. The boy asks the girl for a date, and she accepts.

We gradually understand that they come from different backgrounds. She is a college student, she reads books, she lives in her own apartment, she doesn't even have a TV! He is very much still a part of the neighborhood gang. We see him at two parties (both directed by Scorsese with great improvisatory skill). We see him sitting at the end of a bar with his friends, throwing nuts and looking the other way. We see him still inhabiting this world even though he falls in love with the girl from outside. And then, eventually, when she tells him she isn't a virgin, he is unable to cope with this and he breaks it off.

Scorsese is gifted at handling subtle moments, but he has some trouble with the more obvious ones. The girl claims she was raped, and a scene (real? imagined?) illustrating her story is done with a melodramatic hand. A scene at the end of the film, when the boy visits a church and cuts his lip on a nail in a crucifix, is awkwardly contrived.

For another misplaced scene, however, Scorsese does not deserve full blame. In order to get distribution for his film, he was asked to shoot and insert some sort of nude scene to give the film sex exploita-tion angles (in fact, the ads are heavily, and misleadingly, sex-oriented). So he shot a fantasy scene from the boy's mind, showing him imagining encounters with prostitutes. The scene has no structural function in the film—but it is admittedly well directed and photographed.

This is essentially a director's film, but the performances are as good as we could possibly hope. Harvey Keitel as the boy, and Zina Bethune, former star of the TV series *The Nurses*, as the girl, find exactly the right tone together. And Lennard Kuras, who plays the hero's best buddy, is so good all you can say is, yes, guys like that are exactly like that.

Who's That Knocking at My Door

It is all there in the first film, almost all in the first twenty minutes: the themes and obsessions, the images and character types that would inspire Martin Scorsese for the whole of his career. A shot of his mother, kneading pasta. A statue of the Virgin Mary. Young men from the neighborhood, in an argument that explodes into a fight. Rock and roll on the sound track. A headlong, hand-held shot preceding the two fighters as one tries to escape down the sidewalk and the other chases him, hitting him with a pole. A high-angle view from across the street of the Eighth Ward Social Club. A poker game in progress. Sudden anger: a newcomer takes a player's cards, throws them down, says, "You lose 'cause you're playing with my money." The hero sits aside at a table by himself, remembering a blonde girl. We see him meeting her for the first time, in the terminal of the Staten Island ferry. He describes the plot of John Ford's *The Searchers*. Later, alone, they kiss passionately. She is ready to go further. He pulls away, and stands up: "I love you, but . . ." In a mirror, a reflection of the Virgin.

It is remarkable that a director would set out his agenda so clearly, almost instinctively, at the start of his career. Martin Scorsese's *I Call First*, retitled on release as *Who's That Knocking at My Door*, was a brilliant debut when I saw it in 1967, and forty years later it stands up as a powerful, evocative film. It has not aged because its underlying impulses are so strong and its visual style so effective. It tells the story of a young man named J. R. (Harvey Keitel) from Little Italy, who hangs out with fringe gangsters, falls in love with a woman known only as The Girl, idealizes her, discovers she has been raped, and recoils from her. In his mind she is forever tarnished and he cannot love her.

The film was shot in the neighborhood Scorsese was raised in. The characters are based on people he knew, smaller roles sometimes played by themselves. The J. R. character embodies Scorsese's own Catholic obsessions. The subculture of male camaraderie and violence would blossom into *Mean Streets* and later emerge in full bloom in *GoodFellas*. The curious camera, often subtly moving, would implicate us as voyeurs. The pop songs on the sound track, an innovation at the time, would evoke the period for us. Although the film was made on a rock-bottom budget, the old 45 rpm records were not used in place of a paid-for musical score, but as a conscious choice, one Scorsese would repeat many times.

It is significant that the young woman played by Zina Bethune is known only as The Girl. She is objectified as a symbol of the attributes J. R. projects on her: at first beautiful, pure, untouchable. Later, soiled beyond redemption. In a close-up profile shot, she bears an unmistakable resemblance to Vicki LaMotta, the idealized obsession of the hero of *Raging Bull*, a portrait of jealousy scarcely less wounding than *Othello*. Both women engender that irrational jealousy: Vicki because of an imagined affair with her brother-in-law, The Girl because J. R. instinctively considers it her fault that she was raped. How did she put herself in that position? She must have been asking for it. His eventual lame attempt at apology takes an odd form: "I forgive you." Forgive her for what? For being raped?

On their first date, he takes her to the movies: John Wayne in *Rio Bravo*. Walking out, he tells her, "That girl in that picture was a broad."

"What do you mean, a broad?"

"There are girls and then there are broads," he explains. "You don't marry a broad, you play around with them."

Later in the film, we see J. R. drinking in a kitchen with a group of his friends. They're all wearing suits and ties, in emulation perhaps of older gangsters. A gun is produced. They start drunken roughhousing, intercut with shots from *Rio Bravo*. Joey (Leonard Kuras), the dominant member of their crowd and the manager of the social club, grabs a friend around the neck and threatens him with the gun. The action becomes slow motion, as the mock gunplay becomes threatening. Dialog drops out, replaced by rock and roll. The guy in the hammerlock looks terrified, screams; the others, still laughing, duck behind a partition wall. The violence is right there below the skin.

At this point in *Who's That Knocking*, a sex scene appears that was not present in *I Call First*, but was required by the American distributor to make the film more saleable. J. R. is on a bed in an empty loft, and we see him having sex with a prostitute, and later spread-eagle on the bed in a crucifixion pose. I suppose the symbolism suggests that sex is one of Christ's scourges or punishments. This scene stands apart from the rest of the film, of course, but is well filmed on its own terms, with a restlessly moving camera.

(23)

Then there is a scene that at first seems equally apart from the main line of the film, as J. R. and his pals take a road trip to upstate New York, meet a guy in a bar, and the next day allow him to show them a "beautiful sight." This involves an arduous uphill trek through a thick woods, the trees bare of leaves, and then a still moment when J. R. sits on a high place and contemplates the natural vista. At this moment, and at no other time in the film, he seems at peace. It may be this moment that reflects impulses that Scorsese expressed in *Kundun*, the least readily explicable of his choices.

There is a scene explaining the original title, *I Call First*, filmed in the same location as the gunplay scene, in which two women are invited for a party that nearly turns into a gang rape. "I call first" refers to the rules of a childhood game, in which the first kid who says it gets to go first. The implied values about women as it is used in this scene are chilling.

While the gunplay scene was intercut with *Rio Bravo*, a later scene of J. R. getting drunk in a bar with his friends is intercut in his imagination with The Girl being raped. Later, at her apartment, he calls her a whore. And then there is the scene of J. R. going to confession, and a montage of art inside the church: saints displaying their self-mutilation, the wounds of Christ. The church footage is mirrored and expanded by Harvey Keitel scenes in *Mean Streets*.

Most first films are half-baked and confused. No doubt earlier versions of *I Call First* were; one was titled *Bring on the Dancing Girls*. But by the time the finished film resulted, it was a cohesive, affecting work, an evocation of the self-torture of a hero who cannot reconcile his lusts and his guilts. It is remarkable that Scorsese, in the first half of his twenties, was already so clear about the themes and characters that fascinated him. Revealing, too, that *The Searchers* was referenced, since it would provide Paul Schrader with the undertext of *Taxi Driver*. Both men, lifelong collaborators, were already drawn to the same narrative.

When I first saw *I Call First*, I must have seemed reckless in my praise: "An American masterpiece." Forty years later, those words still seem justified. Despite its low-budget roughness and a sometimes imperfect sound track, it stands by itself as a considerable film, even if Scorsese had never made another.

Woodstock

AN INTERVIEW WITH MARTIN SCORSESE & COMPANY

FEBRUARY 15, 1970

NEW YORK—They said making a movie about Woodstock was like . . . three days without sleep. The cameramen all wired together, with Wadleigh shouting instructions over the earphones. And Don Lenser crying during the Airplane's set, crying because he was right there on top of them, he practically had his camera shoved down Grace Slick's neck, he was practically in her mouth, and all that noise pounding through him, surrounded by banks of loudspeakers—big mothers!—and crying, you could hear him crying over the earphones, crying because he wasn't able to move because he had to hold the goddamn camera steady . . .

Wow . . . said softly. Wow. They were flying in vitamin B-12 shots on the helicopters to keep the crew going. Two of the cameramen got sprained knees. Yeah. Sprained knees. From squatting up there for like ten, twelve hours at a stretch. And finally crashing. Maybe crashing after twenty hours, and somebody else grabbing the camera. Crashing right there on the stage, surrounded by the music, waking up during the Grateful Dead. Waking up, thinking, this will finish. We will finish this. But then you'd go under again . . .

Yeah. I remember huddling under this blanket, and people falling over me in the dark. Waking up during the Dead, yeah. The sky all dark and the light so bad they were pushing the film up to one thousand ASA, trying to get something. Thinking, this has been forever. This has been all there ever has been . . .

After two days of this, you'd get into this . . . state. I remember during the Airplane's set, I'd been up like thirty-six hours, and they started this song, and they were into it, and they were away over there, up there somewhere, into their thing. And fifteen minutes later, still into it, and after half an hour, still, and you were floating, you were apart from whatever it was that was going on. And after, like, an hour you finally heard them coming back down into something else. And then you heard: you are the crown of creation . . . and you got it together again, remembering, hey, man, this is "Crown of Creation," this is the Airplane. Because you'd even forgotten who they were, man . . .

And this was in an Italian restaurant in New York, half a year later, and they were remembering. Martin Scorsese, the assistant director of *Woodstock*, sending his veal back to the kitchen because it was too rare, and remembering being at Woodstock. And Maggie Koven, eating lasagna: "I went to Woodstock as a schlep, and I came back as a schlep, but now I'm an assistant editor."

Scorsese figuring it out: "We had fourteen to eighteen cameras at Woodstock, counting wild cameras. And when those three days were over, we came back with fifty miles of film. One hundred and twenty hours of film. It took us more than two weeks just to look at the rushes."

Larry Johnson, the sound man, wincing: "I got two ear infections up there, man. One in each ear."

People sitting around the table mopping up spaghetti sauce with French bread, drinking red wine. Michael Wadleigh, the director of *Woodstock*, is a twenty-eight-year-old flash who, before he started this one, shot documentaries of the presidential campaigns: "I shot Nixon, Humphrey, McCarthy. I remember I had to split from the Nixon campaign to go over to the Paris riots. I shot some stuff there. When I got back, Nixon waved at me. 'Where you been, Mike?' he asked me. 'I just got back from the Paris riots,' I said. 'How were they?' he said. 'OK,' I said, 'I got beat up by the cops.'"

"What did Nixon say then?" Maggie wanted to know. Maggie, a lovely girl, long hair, big eyes, funny, humorous mouth.

"Oh, nothing," Wadleigh said. "He only nodded . . ."

And now everybody splits from the Italian restaurant and goes around the comer to this loft up on the fifth floor, served by a creeping freight elevator. A loft with a skylight and a lot of little rooms off the big one. "You know what picture was cut in this loft?" Scorsese says. "They made *Greetings* in this loft . . ."

The loft is a crazy, jumbled place, like a Hollywood studio planned by Alice. All these earnest young girls and serious guys bending over their Kellers. The Keller Editing Machine. The finest editing machine in the world, and the only one you can use to cut three-screen stuff with eight-track synch sound, with 35 mm and 16 mm film on the same machine at the same time.

"This particular Keller here," Wadleigh says, "is the machine Coppola cut *The Rain People* on. I think we have all of the Kellers in the country in this loft at this moment. We even brought one in from Canada."

(27)

A serious-faced Japanese kid with a white technician's smock is bending over his Keller like an acolyte at some strange technological dedication ceremony. He is trying to do something with the film they brought back on the Grateful Dead.

Shine on me . . . shine on me

"Stay back from the Keller," Wadleigh tells everybody. "If you puke, don't puke on the Keller."

Everybody laughs. "Wadleigh hates the Dead," Marty Scorsese explains.

"This is tougher than hell to cut," the acolyte says. He steps back from his Keller now, letting it hurry ahead without him. On all three screens you see the Dead: the side screens show them in each profile, and the center screen has them head on. On each of the side screens, you can see the camera on the other side of the stage shooting the film you can see on the opposite side screen. And all, as the man says, at the same time.

"Tougher than hell," the kid says. "What we have here is Pigpen singing, 'Let your love light shine, let your love light shine on me, shine on me, shine on me.' And singing that over and over. Singing the same goddamn thing for an hour. And you put it on the Keller, you're trying to synch three different pieces of film, and cut the hour down to maybe five minutes. And you're trying to do it with film that was shot when it was so dark you could hardly see Pigpen, who in any event is holding the mike right in front of his face. So how you going to synch this goddamn thing? You can't even see his mouth."

Commotion at the door. Bill Graham, proprietor of the Fillmore East and West, has arrived. Graham, the biggest honcho of rock-music promotions in the country. He's here to see rushes from the movie; rough cuts of acts he's interested in, or books, or manages. All the acts in the movie will be paid; they'll split up about $300,000, which will be about a third of the total costs. Graham is here to see how *Woodstock* is shaping up, and how his boys look on the silver screen.

Everybody goes into the projection room. It's lined with thick sheets of soundproofing, and there is a big screen covering the opposite wall, and three big speakers lined up underneath it. On this end of the room, there are three projectors lined up and synchronized, so that even from the rushes you can see how the movie will look with the split-screen technique. The soundproofing in the doorway is cut out in the shape of Mike Wadleigh with his hat on, something you figure out when Wadleigh walks through it and fits. People sit on sofas and on the floor. The lights go out and the first rushes are of Richie Havens.

The camera is right on Havens. In a shot from another angle, you can see a cameraman on his knees directly in front of Havens, his camera pointed right into his mouth. He's inches away. Havens doesn't have any upper teeth. Who gives a damn? He's singing. When the lights go on again, Graham unwinds and says softly: "He's powerful as a bitch."

"So what do you think about the film?" Bob Maurice asks. Maurice, long hair, beard, soft, thoughtful voice, is the guy who floated the $120,000 loan to finance the movie.

"You got something here," Graham says. "How long is your rough cut so far?"

"We've got about seven hours of stuff we like," Maurice says. "That includes about 60 percent music, and about 40 percent documentary aspects: the kids, the cops, the mud, the lifestyle things."

"Seven hours?" Graham says. "You gonna sell it in two parts like *War and Peace*? Or what?"

"No, we're gonna cut it down," Wadleigh says. He's standing in front of the projection room, quietly proud, because he can see the Havens's footage really turned people on. He can see Graham was impressed. Hell, everybody was.

It's strong. It's the next generation of music documentaries, after *Festival* and *Monterey Pop*. Wadleigh explains that they had coverage. They had two, three, maybe six cameras at different places on the stage and in the audience at any given moment. All the cameras were simultaneously shooting complete sets. So, with synched sound, they can cut back and forth from one camera to another, or use split screen to show different parts of the same group at the same moment in a number. It's like being inside the engine when the car is running.

(29)

"Each group you'd handle differently," Wadleigh explains, while they're rethreading the projectors. "Canned Heat we did in one un-broken ten-minute take, with the camera just wandering around the group. And then holding on Bear, Bob Hite, bobbing up and down. It was fun to figure out who was gonna take it next. For The Who, on the other hand, we used multiple cameras and did a montage with six screens. We could do that because we had such extensive coverage."

Graham nods, impressed. "I dunno," he says in a speculative voice. "I'm thinking about closing the Fillmore this summer. This summer every jerk in the world is gonna have his own rock festival. Every two-bit promoter in the world is gonna try to get in on it. We might even close the Fillmore to live music this summer and open *Woodstock* there. We could put in the screen; we have great sound equipment. Whaddya think?"

"Not a good idea," Maurice, the producer, says. "It's better to have a small theater with five to six hundred seats. You'll have a longer run if people have to stand in line and be turned away. That way word-of-mouth gets out, you have a hit. It's horrible to say so, but it's true."

"I still like the idea of opening the movie in the Fillmore," Graham says. "Rock should have its own Grauman's Chinese. We could have cement impressions of Dylan's elbows, Morrison's schnook . . ."

The lights go down again.

"Now comes the socially redeeming message," Bob Maurice says. "Arlo Guthrie."

Arlo is shown arriving in a helicopter, getting out, walking up the long, long gangway, and looking out at the maybe four hundred thousand people who stretch away to the horizons of Woodstock Nation.

"Isn't that far out?" Arlo says. "Too much. Dig it, man . . ."

"What's this? What's this?" Graham says in the dark projection room. "Who writes this guy's dialog? Sounds like he memorized the Hip Dictionary."

"Far out," Arlo, on the screen, says again softly.

The screening lasts until midnight. Wadleigh runs through The Who, Santana, Jimi Hendrix. Hendrix is incredible. The camera is two inches from his fingers. He's stretching the strings, punishing them, winging out on an improvisation of "The Star Spangled Banner" where you hear rockets bursting in air . . .

Afterwards, Bob Maurice the businessman talking now. "I'm not sure you can do a story about this movie unless you talk to me," he said. "The way this movie was conceived is the way a lot of movies are going to be made from here on out. The Hollywood studios are no longer plugged into the market, and they're scared. There has to be an alternative source of films. Like us. They have to come to us. Believe me, Warner Brothers wouldn't put up with us for one second if they could make this film themselves."

Warner Brothers, Maurice explains, made a deal with them after Woodstock was over. They take over the film and distribute it, for a percentage. It will be released next month, assuming Wadleigh finishes the editing in time.

"No one else could have made a film about Woodstock," Maurice says. "No one else could have physically gotten there. And they wouldn't have been willing to gamble enough money. But we knew. We used our own money, initially, because we knew after Woodstock was over somebody would want to buy it. And we did a daring thing. We extended ourselves for $120,000 credit." He grins. "Which of course we didn't have."

Maurice says his job is to maintain "a defense network" around the movie, negotiating with the Warner people without letting them interfere with the making of the film. "They wanted an exploitation quickie, to come out as soon as possible," he says. "We said no. We believe people will dig *Woodstock* as a film, not because of the exploitation angles."

He waves his arm in an arc to indicate the loft.

"All the people you see here," he says, "were in the shooting crew. The people who shot the movie are involved in finishing it. This is our film. Sonja was there. Jean, over there, was an assistant cameraman. All the chicks were up there; none of these chicks are just . . . secretaries. Sure, the office has an atmosphere one could mistake for disorganization. It's run informally, personally. But we get things done.

"The people from Warners were up here, and they were amazed. Sure, we have long hair, we speak the language. But we're so far ahead of Hollywood in technical competence too, man. We don't make movies because we have union jobs and tenure. We do it because we love it.

"We brought the first Kellers into this country, for example. A film like this would be impossible without them. Warner Brothers itself has equipment left over from the '30s. Like, we have eight-track stereo equipment here. There's not a single eight-track on the entire Warners' lot."

Boxcar Bertha

JULY 19, 1972

Boxcar Bertha is a weirdly interesting movie and not really the sleazy exploitation film the ads promise. It finds its inspiration in the exploits of Boxcar Bertha Thompson, an outlaw folk hero who operated in Arkansas during the Depression. I am not sure whether she was called "Boxcar" because of the way she was built or because of where she liked to spend her evenings, but I can report that Barbara Hershey, who plays her in the movie, is built like the proverbial structure of brick. For that we can be grateful.

The movie is set in a murky Southern territory of sweat and violence, and gives us Bertha as a forthright young girl who gets involved in violence almost by accident. She falls in love with a certain Big Bill Shelley (David Carradine), who seems loosely modeled on the anarchist organizer Big Bill Haywood. The two of them meet other friends: Rake Brown, a slick young gambler with a yellow streak, and Von Morton, a sturdy black who wields harmonica and shotgun.

And then their gang is complete and their first murder just sort of happens when Bertha shoots a gambler who is about to shoot Rake. The movie's progression from young love to the most-wanted list reminds us of *Bonnie and Clyde*, and I suppose it was meant to. But there's a lot more going on than a remake or rip-off.

I have the notion that Roger Corman, American-International's most successful producer of exploitation films, sent his actors and crew south with the hope of getting a nice, simple, sexy, violent movie for the summer trade. What he got is something else, and something better. Director Martin Scorsese has gone for mood and atmosphere more than for action, and his violence is always blunt and unpleasant—never liberating and exhilarating, as the New Violence is supposed to be. We get the feeling we're inhabiting the dark night of a soul.

The character of Bertha is developing along unexpected lines, too. She is promiscuous with her body but not with her mind, and when Big Bill is sent to prison, she remains in love with him but goes to work in a whorehouse anyway. The way Scorsese choreographs this scene is interesting: The madam brings Bertha into the parlor. Bertha looks. Turns around to leave. Then turns around again, matter-of-factly deciding to stay. You have to adapt to survive.

There are some good visuals in the movie: a shot of convicts running between piles of lumber, a shot of the gang running down a seeming cattle chute, and the curiously circular use of the railway. Bertha and her gang are forever hopping freights, and once they even think they've made it to Memphis, but all of their train rides take them back to where they were before, as if Godot were waiting at the end of the line.

Scorsese remains one of the bright young hopes of American movies. His brilliant first film won the 1968 Chicago Film Festival as *I Call First* and later played as *Who's That Knocking at My Door*. He was an assistant editor and director of *Woodstock*, and now, many frustrated projects later, here is his first conventional feature. He is good with actors, good with his camera, and determined to take the grade-zilch exploitation film and bend it to his own vision. Within the limits of the film's possibilities, he has succeeded.

Mean Streets

OCTOBER 2, 1973

Martin Scorsese's *Mean Streets* isn't so much a gangster movie as a perceptive, sympathetic, finally tragic story about how it is to grow up in a gangster environment. Its characters (like Scorsese himself) have grown up in New York's Little Italy, and they understand everything about that small slice of human society except how to survive in it.

The two most important characters, Charlie and Johnny Boy, move through the Mafia environment almost because it's expected of them. Charlie is a Catholic with pathological guilt complexes, but because the mob is the family business, he never quite forces himself to make the connection between right and wrong and what he does. Not that he's very good at being a Mafioso: he's twenty-seven, but he still lives at home; he's a collector for his uncle's protection racket, but the collections don't bring in much. If he has any luck at all, he will be able to take over a bankrupt restaurant.

He is, at least fitfully, a realist. Johnny Boy, on the other hand, is a violent, uncontrolled product of romanticized notions of criminal street life. Little Italy is all around him, and yet he seems to have formed his style and borrowed half his vocabulary from the movies. He contains great and ugly passions, and can find no way to release them except in sudden violent bursts. Charlie is in love with Johnny Boy's sister, and he also feels a dogged sense of responsibility for Johnny Boy: he goes up on a roof one night when Johnny is shooting out streetlights and talks him down. At least Johnny releases his angers in overt ways.

Charlie suppresses everything, and sometimes in desperation passes his hand through a flame and wonders about the fires of hell. He takes his Catholicism literally.

Scorsese places these characters in a perfectly realized world of boredom and small joys, sudden assaults, the possibility of death, and the certainty of mediocrity. He shot some exteriors in Little Italy, where he was born and where he seems to know every nuance of architecture and personality (though most of the movie was shot in Los Angeles), and his story emerges from the daily lives of the characters. They hang out. They go to the movies. They eat, they drink, they get in sudden fights that end as quickly as a summer storm. Scorsese photographs them with fiercely driven visual style.

We never have the sense of a scene being set up and then played out; his characters hurry to their dooms while the camera tries to keep pace. There's an improvisational feel even in scenes that we know, because of their structure, couldn't have been improvised.

Scorsese got the same feel in his first feature, *Who's That Knocking at My Door* (1967). *Mean Streets* is a sequel, and Scorsese gives us the same leading actor (Harvey Keitel) to assure the continuity. In the earlier film, he was still on the edge of life, of sex, of violence. Now he has been plunged in, and he isn't equal to the experience. He's not tough enough to be a Mafia collector (and not strong enough to resist). Johnny Boy is played by Robert De Niro and it's a marvelous performance, filled with urgency and restless desperation.

The movie's scenes of violence are especially effective because of the way Scorsese stages them. We don't get spectacular effects and skillfully choreographed struggles. Instead, there's something realistically clumsy about the fights in this movie. A scene in a pool hall, in particular, is just right in the way it shows its characters fighting and yet mindful of their suits (possibly the only suits they have). The whole movie feels like life in New York; there are scenes in a sleazy nightclub, on fire escapes, and in bars, and they all feel as if Scorsese has been there.

(35)

Alice Doesn't Live Here Anymore

DECEMBER 1, 1974

Martin Scorsese's *Alice Doesn't Live Here Anymore* opens with a parody of the Hollywood dream world little girls were expected to carry around in their intellectual baggage a generation ago. The screen is awash with a fake sunset, and a sweet little thing comes strolling along home past sets that seem rescued from *The Wizard of Oz*. But her dreams and dialog are decidedly not made of sugar, spice, or anything nice: this little girl is going to do things her way.

That was her defiant childhood notion, anyway. But by the time she's thirty-five, Alice Hyatt has more or less fallen into society's rhythms. She's married to an incommunicative truck driver, she has a precocious twelve-year-old son, she kills time chatting with the neighbors. And then her husband is unexpectedly killed in a traffic accident and she's left widowed and—almost worse than that—independent. After all those years of having someone there, can she cope by herself?

She can, she says. When she was a little girl, she idolized Alice Faye and determined to be a singer when she grew up. Well, she's thirty-five, and that's grown-up. She has a garage sale, sells the house, and sets off on an odyssey through the Southwest with her son and her dreams. What happens to her along the way provides one of the most perceptive, funny, occasionally painful portraits of an American woman I've seen.

The movie has been both attacked and defended on feminist

grounds, but I think it belongs somewhere outside ideology, maybe in the area of contemporary myth and romance. There are scenes in which we take Alice and her journey perfectly seriously, there are scenes of harrowing reality, and then there are other scenes (including some hilarious passages in a restaurant where she waits on tables) where Scorsese edges into slight, cheerful exaggeration. There are times, indeed, when the movie seems less about Alice than it does about the speculations and daydreams of a lot of women about her age, who identify with the liberation of other women, but are unsure on the subject of themselves.

A movie like this depends as much on performances as on direction, and there's a fine performance by Ellen Burstyn (who won an Oscar for this role) as Alice. She looks more real this time than she did as Cybill Shepherd's available mother in *The Last Picture Show* or as Linda Blair's tormented mother in *The Exorcist*. It's the kind of role she can relax in, be honest with, allow to develop naturally (although those are often the hardest roles of all). She's determined to find work as a singer, to "resume" a career that was mostly dreams to begin with, and she's pretty enough (although not good enough) to almost pull it off. She meets some generally good people along the way, and they help her when they can. But she also meets some creeps, especially a deceptively nice guy named Ben (played by Harvey Keitel, the autobiographical hero of Scorsese's two films set in Little Italy). The singing jobs don't materialize much, and it's while she's waitressing that she runs into a divorced young farmer (Kris Kristofferson).

They fall warily in love, and there's an interesting relationship between Kristofferson and Alfred Lutter, who does a very good job of playing a certain kind of twelve-year-old kid. Most women in Alice's position probably wouldn't run into a convenient, understanding, and eligible young farmer, but then a lot of the things in the film don't work as pure logic. There's a little myth to them, while Scorsese sneaks up on his main theme.

The movie's filled with brilliantly done individual scenes. Alice, for example, has a run-in with a fellow waitress with an inspired vocabulary (Diane Ladd, an Oscar nominee for this role). They fall into

(37)

a friendship and have a frank and honest conversation one day while sunbathing. The scene works perfectly. There's also the specific way her first employer backs into offering her a singing job, and the way Alice takes leave from her old neighbors, and the way her son persists in explaining a joke that could only be understood by a twelve-year-old. These are great moments in a film that gives us Alice Hyatt: female, thirty-five, undefeated.

Taxi Driver

FEBRUARY 27, 1976

Taxi Driver shouldn't be taken as a New York film; it's not about a city but about the weathers of a man's soul, and out of all New York he selects just those elements that feed and reinforce his obsessions. The man is Travis Bickle, ex-marine, veteran of Vietnam, composer of dutiful anniversary notes to his parents, taxi driver, killer. The movie rarely strays very far from the personal, highly subjective way in which he sees the city and lets it wound him.

It's a place, first of all, populated with women he cannot have: unobtainable blonde women who might find him attractive for a moment, who might join him for a cup of coffee, but who eventually will have to shake their heads and sigh, "Oh, Travis!" because they find him . . . well, he's going crazy, but the word they use is "strange."

And then, even more cruelly, the city seems filled with men who can have these women—men ranging from cloddish political hacks to street-corner pimps who, nevertheless, have in common the mysterious ability to approach a woman without getting everything wrong.

Travis could in theory look for fares anywhere in the city, but he's constantly drawn back to 42nd Street, to Times Square and the whores, street freaks, and porno houses. It's here that an ugly kind of sex comes closest to the surface—the sex of buying, selling, and using people. Travis isn't into that, he hates it, but Times Square feeds his anger. His sexual frustration is channeled into a hatred for the creeps he obsessively observes. He tries to break the cycle—or maybe he just sets himself up to fail again.

He sees a beautiful blonde working in the storefront office of a presidential candidate. She goes out with him a couple of times, but the second time he takes her to a hardcore film and she walks out in disgust and won't have any more to do with him. All the same, he calls her for another date, and it's here that we get close to the heart of the movie. The director, Martin Scorsese, gives us a shot of Travis on a pay telephone—and then, as the girl is turning him down, the camera slowly dollies to the right and looks down a long, empty hallway. Pauline Kael's review called this shot—which calls attention to itself—a lapse during which Scorsese was maybe borrowing from Antonioni. Scorsese calls this shot the most important one in the film.

Why? Because, he says, it's as if we can't bear to watch Travis feel the pain of being rejected. This is interesting, because later, when Travis goes on a killing rampage, the camera goes so far as to adopt slow motion so we can see the horror in greater detail.

That Scorsese finds the rejection more painful than the murders is fascinating, because it helps to explain Travis Bickle, and perhaps it goes some way toward explaining one kind of urban violence. Travis has been shut out so systematically, so often, from a piece of the action that eventually he has to hit back somehow.

Taxi Driver is a brilliant nightmare and like all nightmares it doesn't tell us half of what we want to know. We're not told where Travis comes from, what his specific problems are, whether his ugly scar came from Vietnam—because this isn't a case study, but a portrait of some days in his life. There's a moment at a political rally when Travis, in dark glasses, smiles in a strange way that reminds us of those photos of Bremer just before he shot Wallace. The moment tells us nothing, and everything: We don't know the specifics of Travis's complaint, but in a chilling way we know what we need to know of him. The film's a masterpiece of suggestive characterization; Scorsese's style selects details that evoke emotions, and that's the effect he wants. The performances are odd and compelling: he goes for moments from his actors, rather than slowly developed characters. It's as if the required emotions were written in the margins of their scripts: give me anger, fear, dread.

Robert De Niro, as Travis Bickle, is as good as Brando at suggesting emotions even while veiling them from us (and in many of his close-ups, Scorsese uses almost subliminal slow motion to draw out the revelations). Cybill Shepherd, as the blonde goddess, is correctly cast, for once, as a glacier slowly receding toward humanity. And there's Jodie Foster, chillingly cast as a twelve-year-old prostitute whom Travis wants to "save." Harvey Keitel, a veteran of all of Scorsese's films (he was the violent maniac in *Alice Doesn't Live Here Anymore*), is the pimp who controls her, and he's got the right kind of toughness that's all bluff.

These people are seen almost in flashes, as if darkness threatens to close over them altogether. *Taxi Driver* is a hell, from the opening shot of a cab emerging from stygian clouds of steam to the climactic killing scene in which the camera finally looks straight down. Scorsese wanted to look away from Travis's rejection; we almost want to look away from his life. But he's there, all right, and he's suffering.

(41)

An Interview with Martin Scorsese and Paul Schrader

MARCH 3, 1976

I met Martin Scorsese for the first time in 1969, when he was an editor on *Woodstock*. He was one of the most intense people I'd ever known—a compact, nervous kid out of New York's Little Italy who'd made one feature film and had dreams of becoming a big-time director one day. It would take him five years.

The first feature was *Who's That Knocking at My Door*, the major discovery of the 1967 Chicago Film Festival. It was the semi-autobiographical story of an Italian American youth coming of age; it won praise and prizes for Scorsese, but didn't do any business, and he supported himself with editing, teaching, and odd jobs. The night I met him, we went to Little Italy and drank Bardolino wine and he talked about projects he was being offered.

He finally took one of them—a Roger Corman exploitation picture called *Boxcar Bertha*—because he needed to direct again. "Corman thinks it's an exploitation picture," Scorsese told me, "but I think it'll be something else." He was right; his talent made the film, which starred Barbara Hershey and David Carradine, better than it had to be.

The movie got him more work. In 1973, on a small budget but with total artistic freedom, he made *Mean Streets*, a sequel to *Who's That Knocking*. It was a ferocious, painful, deeply felt masterpiece. In 1974 he made his big critical and box-office success, *Alice Doesn't Live Here Anymore*, for which Ellen Burstyn won an Oscar. Scorsese was established, was "bankable."

His new film, which opens here Friday at the McClurg Court, Lincoln Village, and five suburban theaters, is *Taxi Driver* with Robert De Niro—a violent and frightening return to the New York of *Mean Streets*. It looks like another hit.

Scorsese and I met for lunch during his visit last week to Chicago and were joined by Paul Schrader, who wrote the screenplay for *Taxi Driver*. They were a study in opposites: Schrader, a midwestern Protestant in pullover sweater and tie, and Scorsese, a New York Italian American, in jeans and a beard. But they'd been working together on this screenplay since 1972.

SCORSESE: Because there's a lot of violence to this picture, some of the New York reviews are calling it an exploitation film. Jesus! I went flat broke making this film. My films haven't made a lot of money. Right now, I'm living off my next film.

SCHRADER: If it's an exploitation film, I wish we had a dollar for every time we were told it would never be a success at all. This screenplay was turned down by everybody.

SCORSESE: We showed it to some New York media educators, and I thought we'd get lynched. And we showed it to some student editors ... there was one wise guy there I recognized from a screening we had of *Alice*. He asks whether, after all my success, I'm about ready to fall on my ass. I've hardly gotten started!

SCHRADER: We get almost no valid reactions immediately after the screenings. The immediate response is usually very visceral and angry. But if this film weren't controversial, there'd be something wrong with the country.

EBERT: What you give us in this guy, De Niro, who comes from nowhere—we get hardly any background—and drives a cab in New York and eventually we realize he's seething inside, he's got all this violence bottled up ...

SCORSESE: And he goes back again and again to where the violence is. One of the reviewers, I think it was Andrew Sarris, said how many times can you use 42nd Street as a metaphor for hell? But that's the thing about hell—it goes on and on. And he couldn't get out

(43)

of it. But you're right that we don't tell you where he comes from, or what his story is. Obviously, he comes from somewhere and he picked up these problems along the way.

SCHRADER: I wrote it that way after thinking about the way they handled *In Cold Blood*. They tell you all about Perry Smith's background, how he developed his problems, and immediately it becomes less interesting because his problems aren't your problems, but his symptoms are your symptoms.

EBERT: Pauline Kael has said that Scorsese, Robert Altman, and Francis Ford Coppola are the three most interesting directors in the country right now—and that it might be due to their Catholicism, that after Watergate, the nation feels a sort of guilt and needs to make a form of reparation, and that Catholics understand guilt in a way that others don't, that they were brought up on it.

SCORSESE: Guilt. There's nothing you can tell me about guilt.

SCHRADER: I've got a lot of Protestant guilt.

SCORSESE: You can't make movies any more in which the whole country seems to make sense. After Vietnam, after Watergate, it's not just a temporary thing; it's a permanent thing the country's going through. All the things we held sacred—the whole Time-Life empire . . . whoosh! Well, *Time*'s still left.

EBERT: In a lot of your movies, there's this ambivalent attitude toward women. The men are fascinated by women, but they don't quite know how to relate to them . . .

SCORSESE: The goddess-whore complex. You're raised to worship women, but you don't know how to approach them on a human level, on a sexual level. That's the thing with Travis, the De Niro character—the taxi driver. The girl he falls for, the Cybill Shepherd character—it's really important that she's blonde, a blue-eyed goddess.

SCHRADER: He goes from a goddess to a child goddess. The twelve-and-a-half-year-old prostitute he's trying to rescue—she's unapproachable, too, for him.

SCORSESE: She has the candles burning in her bedroom, she's like a saint to him. He can't imagine these pimps treating her the way they do. Before he goes to avenge her, it's almost like he cleanses himself, like in *The Virgin Spring* when Max von Sydow scourges himself with the branches before he goes out to avenge his daughter's death.

SCHRADER: We actually had that shot in the movie, and we took it out. Travis whips himself with a towel before he goes out with his guns. We took it out because it looked a little forced and unnatural.

SCORSESE: But the Catholic thing? I suppose there are a lot of Catholic references in the film, even if they're only my own personal reference. Like the moment when he burns the flowers before he goes out to kill. And when he's buying the guns and the dealer lays them out one at a time on the velvet, like arranging the altar during Mass.

Schrader left for another interview, and Scorsese and I continued our conversation in his hotel room, which was furnished with two reminders of home: a large box of cookies from Cafe Roma in Little Italy ("My mother sent them, she knew I'd be homesick") and a stack of the latest issues of film magazines. Scorsese got married recently to a freelance writer named Julia Cameron, from Libertyville, and he was planning to have dinner with his new in-laws that night. He thought he'd bring along the cookies.

EBERT: You talked about living off your next film.

SCORSESE: It'll be called *New York, New York*. It takes place in the 1940s and 1950s, it's about the big bands. Liza Minnelli plays a singer and De Niro will be her husband. It's not a musical; it's a film with music. I got that definition from Billy Wilder, who said you can't call it a musical unless the people sing in situations where you don't expect them to. It'll be about their marriage breaking up, about their problems in relating to one another . . .

EBERT: Will it take a feminist position? A lot of people embraced *Alice Doesn't Live Here Anymore* as feminist.

SCORSESE: Well, it'll be about the problems of a career marriage. I don't know if it's feminist. Actually, not *Alice*, but *Taxi Driver*— this is my feminist film. Who says a feminist movie has to be about women? Alice was never intended as a feminist tract. At the end, she's making the same mistakes. The first shot of her in Kris Krist-offerson's house shows her washing the dishes. A big close-up.

EBERT: And *Taxi Driver*, where the hero can't relate to women at all, is . . .

SCORSESE: Feminist. Because it takes macho to its logical conclusion: the better man is the man who can kill you. This one shows that kind of thinking, shows the kinds of problems some men have, bouncing back and forth between the goddesses and whores. The whole movie is based, visually, on one shot where the guy is being turned down on the telephone by the girl, and the camera actually pans away from him. It's too painful to see that rejection.

EBERT: The film is dedicated to Bernard Hermann, the great movie composer. He died just after he finished the score.

SCORSESE: God, that was terrible. Immediately after. He was so happy, he was back in Hollywood, he had a full orchestra, people were getting down on their knees to him. He was do-ing some jazz passages, and he insisted on finishing that day. I told him we should do it next week, because he looked tired. "No," he said, "let's do it now." That was on December 23. The next morning, the day of Christmas Eve, he was found dead.

That Sunday, Julia and I flew to Chicago to get married . . .

EBERT: I wanted to ask about the violent scenes, the scenes where Travis freaks out and starts shooting.

SCORSESE: We shot those in slow motion. In forty-eight frames to the second, which is twice the ordinary twenty-four frames—and, of course, if you shoot it twice as fast and project it at the regular speed, it comes out half as fast . . .

EBERT: Which is what everyone gets backwards about slow motion.

SCORSESE: Right. And in the scenes of the killing, the slow motion and De Niro's arms . . . we wanted him to look almost like a mon-ster, a robot, King Kong coming to save Fay Wray. Another thing: all of the close-ups of De Niro where he isn't talking were shot forty-eight frames to the second—to draw out and exaggerate his reactions. What an actor, to look so great up against a technique like that! I shot all those shots myself, to see for myself what kind of reaction we were getting.

EBERT: The whole movie's very stylized, expressionistic . . . you fragment scenes into very striking details, you control your colors to get a certain feel, there's the garish lighting . . .

SCORSESE: And then I read that I'm a realist, a naturalist! Somebody compared the picture to *Shoeshine*! Really! I'm not interested in a realistic look—not at all, not ever. Every film should look the way I feel.

EBERT: I read that De Niro really drove a cab to prepare for this role.

SCORSESE: Yeah. I drove with him several nights. He got a strange feeling when he was hacking. He was totally anonymous. People would say anything, do anything in the backseat—it was like he didn't exist. Finally a guy gets in, a former actor, who recognizes his name on the license. "Jesus," he says, "last year you won the Oscar and now you're driving a cab again." De Niro said he was only doing research.

"Yeah, Bobby," says the actor. "I know. I been there, too."

After *Mean Streets* was released, I wrote a review saying that Scorsese had a chance to become the American Fellini in ten years or so. The next time we met after the review appeared, Marty looked serious and concerned: "Do you really think it's going to take ten years?"

New York, New York

JULY 5, 1977

Martin Scorsese's *New York, New York* never pulls itself together into a coherent whole, but if we forgive the movie its confusions we're left with a good time. In other words: abandon your expectations of an orderly plot, and you'll end up humming the title song. The movie's a vast, rambling, nostalgic expedition back into the big band era, and a celebration of the considerable talents of Liza Minnelli and Robert De Niro.

She plays a sweet kid with a big voice who starts as a band vocalist and ends up as a movie star. He plays an immature, aggressive, very talented saxophone player whose social life centers around the saloon fights. A generation before punk rock, here's punk swing. They get married for reasons the movie never makes quite clear (oh, they're in love, all right, but he's so weird it's a miracle she'll have him). And then their marriage starts to disintegrate for reasons well hallowed in showbiz biographies: her success, his insecurity, his drinking, their child.

De Niro comes off as certifiably loony from the start, and some of the movie's best scenes are counterpoint between his clowning and her rather touching acceptance of it. Maybe because he's really shy underneath, he likes to overact in social situations. He's egotistical, self-centered, inconsiderate, and all sorts of other things she should leave him because of, and there are times when the Minnelli character is so heroically patient that it's gotta be love. The movie doesn't really explore the nuances of their personalities, though; the characters are seen mostly by their surfaces, and they inhabit a cheerfully phony Hollywood back-lot New York. Scorsese, who knows how to shoot New York in California so it looks real (see *Mean Streets*), is going for a frankly movie feel with his sets and decors, and especially with his colors, which tend toward lurid rotogravure.

The look is right for the movie's musical scenes, and there are a lot of them: we start with a loving re-creation of V-J Day, with Tommy Dorsey's orchestra playing all the obligatory standards and De Niro trying with desperate zeal to pick up Minnelli. And then maybe half of the movie from then on will be music, mostly very good music (the movie's new songs deserve comparison with the old standards), and wonderfully performed. That Liza Minnelli has not been making an annual musical for the last decade is our loss; she's hauntingly good and so much more, well, human than Barbra Streisand.

It's a good thing the movie inhabits a familiar genre, though, because the fact that we've seen dozens of other musical biographies helps us fill in the gaps in this one. And there are a lot of them; the movie originally came in at something like four hours, and the cuts necessary to get it down to a more commercial length are responsible for a lot of confusion. The confusions, as I've suggested, can be forgiven because the movie has so many good things in it. And in the video version, to make amends, they've put back two musical numbers that weren't seen in the theater.

But the ending is still puzzling. We've seen De Niro, totally unable to deal with the fact that he's become a father, tearfully (and amusingly) end their marriage right there in the maternity ward. Six years pass, there are Liza's great final production numbers, and then they have a backstage reunion after her night of triumph. Great, we're thinking, we've been here before, we relish the obligatory romantic reunion scene in the dressing room. But, no, he leaves. Then he calls her from a pay phone: he can't stand the people she's with, but would she like to sneak out, meet by the stage door, eat some Chinese food, and talk about themselves? Sure, she would. He waits outside the door. She approaches it from inside, pauses, sees no one there, and goes back to her dressing room. End of movie (with a nicely evocative night

(49)

street scene). But did she change her mind and decide not to go out and meet him, or did she expect him to be waiting inside the door— and assume the cocky SOB had stood her up again? This particular confusion is hard to forgive.

So the movie's flawed. It's not Scorsese's best work, or De Niro's (there are scenes in which his personality quirks and bizarre behavior make him seem uncannily like his Travis Bickle in Scorsese's *Taxi Driver*). Liza Minnelli's musical numbers are wondrous, as I've said, but the movie doesn't provide her with a character as fully understood as *Cabaret* did. So I guess we go to *New York, New York* to enjoy the good parts, and spend just a moment regretting the absence of a whole.

New York, New York

A RECONSIDERATION

I don't know for sure what romantic chemistry is, but I know for sure what it isn't. It isn't whatever inexplicable energy exists between Francine Evans and Jimmy Doyle, who are meant to be in love in *New York, New York*. Instead of lovers in union, the film gives us separate pathologies that travel together for a time, and that is the critical miscalculation of Scorsese's 1977 film. At no moment could I believe they were intended to be together, and much of the time, neither could they.

A musical film has other things on its mind than the dramatic soundness of its plot. It wants to think about songs, choreography, sets, smiles, costumes, settings — anything except fundamental questions about the central relationship. I'm not thinking of the usual cooked-up crisis that has to be resolved in the third act, as when Gene Kelly escorts Jean Hagen instead of Debbie Reynolds to the *Singin' in the Rain* premiere; I'm thinking of grating emotional dysfunction. At the center of *New York, New York*, Jimmy (Robert De Niro) is unfeeling, jealous, insecure, cold, and possessive. And Francine (Liza Minnelli) is a sweet kid, loving and loyal, able to endure Jimmy to the point of masochism. Why is she so patient and forgiving? Why does she stand by her man, when he doesn't stand by her? Why does he want to remain linked with a woman he evidently finds so flawed and untrustworthy?

The impossible relationship poisons the entire film, I think. Yet *New York, New York* has its pleasures, particularly for the movie-literate who will observe the many ways that Scorsese is trying to emulate a traditional big-studio musical. We know from everything he's told us that he has no desire to function outside the system with Jarmusch, Cassavetes, or Lynch. He wants to have been directing in the 1940s and 1950s. We see that in his long videos, *A Personal Journey with Martin Scorsese through American Movies* (1995) and *My Voyage to Italy* (1999), where he is ecstatic even about the typefaces in titles. We sense it in his romantic alliances with the daughters of Vincente Minnelli and Roberto Rossellini and Ingrid Bergman. We see it very early in *New York, New York*, where he has an astonishing crane shot above thousands of extras celebrating on the streets on V-J Day; it's a shot as extensive, I think, as the famous "street of dying men" shot in *Gone with the Wind*, and done with real extras, not digital fabrications.

(52)

Attend to Scorsese's on-camera introduction to the DVD of *New York, New York*, and you can hear him praising the big-studio look, which above all means Metro-Goldwyn-Mayer. He says he wanted to go for a period look (and by period I think he is referring not to the time of his action but to the years when such films were being made). And then he wants to put an improvisational acting style on top of it. We sense that attempt in the long opening scene at a victory dance, where countless extras jitterbug below the benevolent eye of bandleader Tommy Dorsey, and Jimmy tries tirelessly to pick up Francine. The huge set and costumed extras would usually back up a crisp dialog duel, but De Niro here seems vaguely like his Travis Bickle in *Taxi Driver*, released the year before. His riffs on a repeated phrase, his manner of looking away as if seeking guidance and then quickly turning back again, his self-evident lies ("My father and mother and brother and sister are right over there"), his attempts at grandiosity (did he really serve in uniform? I doubt it)—all of those elements run counter to the usual requirements of such a scene. I'm not complaining, just observing.

You can appreciate the homage to the Arthur Freed era at MGM even in the opening titles, not simply in the huge *New York, New York* graphics looming up from behind a cut-out skyline but even in certain credits. Sydney Guilaroff, credited as the hair stylist, worked on 394 pictures, including dozens of great musicals. Makeup was by Michael Westmore of the famous Westmore family. The production design is by the legendary Boris Levin, the costumes by Theadora van Runkle. Am I wrong to suspect Scorsese was tickled to have their names in the credits? Scorsese even slips in a nod to his hero, the director Michael Powell, when Jimmy checks into a hotel under an assumed name: "Mr. M. Powell."

Scorsese observes that many of his sets look deliberately artificial. They certainly do, such as a scene in a train station where an obviously one-dimensional fabricated train pulls away, its windows filled with the immobile outlines of passengers. There was a joke that in the early days of Technicolor, the company required its representatives to be present on sets to be sure lots of colors were used. They wouldn't have been needed for this picture, where Scorsese and Levin go for bold colors. Consider a nightclub bathed in red, the color of passion, and how Jimmy stalks away into a bar in the background that is bathed in green, the color of jealousy. Consider too an astonishing green hotel room, with lighting or offstage sources of purple and blue, deep shadows, and the *Mona Lisa* on the wall. Not where a lot of traveling musicians would have stayed. A car pulls away from in front of a motel room toward an obvious backdrop. A dark doorway in a club is framed by walls of light. The long crane shot at the start ends at a high angle with a red neon arrow pointing down at Jimmy. The camera chooses a vertiginous high angle to look down at Jimmy under a spotlight. Francine's solo at the end of *New York, New York* begins in a nightclub and ends in a spotlight on her face.

That famous song itself is a crucial element in the movie, giving it a unity the story lacks, but I'm secretly in sympathy with Jimmy when he questions some of Francine's lyrics. Yes, Liza Minnelli and Frank Sinatra have made it a standard, but a chamber of commerce committee couldn't have made it more banal.

And on the DVD, we can see even more of Scorsese's homage to classic Hollywood. The film, released at 153 minutes, was cut by the studio to 136, and then Scorsese added deleted scenes to bring it up to 163 on the DVD. One of those scenes is the "Happy Endings" number.

At MGM, in movies like *An American in Paris* and *Singin' in the Rain*, the studio departed from the main line of stories to present elaborate musical ballet numbers; in *Singin'*, Cyd Charisse materialized as a leggy brunette to tempt Gene Kelly; in *American*, there was a sequence called by the movie's credits "The American in Paris Ballet."

Scorsese resurrects the old tradition, focusing on Francine in a series of elaborately staged numbers leading up to Minnelli's "New York, New York." One can sense, in a way, why some of this material was cut; it works as itself, but not in the flow of the movie.

Looking at the film again after a period of years, I can see clearly that two impulses are at work in the director's mind. He wants to make an MGM musical, and he has (perhaps) inflexible ideas about the Jimmy and Francine characters that do not translate well into the performances by De Niro and Minnelli. Minnelli would be perfectly at home in a traditional musical. De Niro cannot see himself as her husband in life or in fiction, and cannot bring himself to act as if he can. So Minnelli faithfully plays a woman in love with a man only she can see—the man the movie requires, but does not provide. And the production itself suggests that if Scorsese had worked within the Arthur Freed Unit during the Golden Age at MGM, Freed would have had many long, sad conferences with him about the screenplay.

The Last Waltz

APRIL 19, 2002 (RELEASED 1978)

I wonder if the sadness comes across on the CD. The music probably sounds happy. But the performers, seen on screen, seem curiously morose, exhausted, played out. Recently, I was at a memorial concert for the late tenor sax man Spike Robinson, and the musicians—jazz and big band veterans—were cheerful, filled with joy, happy to be there. Most of the musicians in *The Last Waltz* are, on average, twenty-five years younger than Spike's friends, but they drag themselves onstage like exhausted veterans of wrong wars.

The rock documentary was filmed by Martin Scorsese at a farewell concert given on Thanksgiving Day 1976 by The Band, which had been performing since 1960, in recent years as the backup band for Bob Dylan. Now the film is back in a twenty-fifth anniversary restoration. "Sixteen years on the road is long enough," says Robbie Robertson, the group's leader. "Twenty years is unthinkable." There is a weight and gravity in his words that suggests he seriously doubts if he could survive four more years.

Drugs are possibly involved. Memoirs recalling the filming report that cocaine was everywhere backstage. The overall tenor of the documentary suggests survivors at the ends of their ropes. They dress in dark, cheerless clothes, hide behind beards, hats, and shades, pound out rote performances of old hits, don't seem to smile much at their music or each other. There is the whole pointless road-warrior mystique, of hard-living men whose daily duty it is to play music and get wasted. They look tired of it.

Not all of them. The women (Joni Mitchell, Emmylou Harris) seem immune, although what Mitchell's song is about I have no clue, and Harris is filmed in another time and place. Visitors like the Staple Singers are open-faced and happy. Eric Clapton is in the right place and time. Muddy Waters is on sublime autopilot. Lawrence Ferlinghetti reads a bad poem, badly, but seems pleased to be reading it. Neil Diamond seems puzzled to find himself in this company, grateful to be invited.

But then look at the faces of Neil Young or Van Morrison. Study Robertson, whose face is kind and whose smile comes easily, but who does not project a feeling of celebration for the past or anticipation of the future. These are not musicians at the top of their art, but laborers on the last day of the job. Look in their eyes. Read their body language.

The Last Waltz has inexplicably been called the greatest rock documentary of all time. Certainly that would be *Woodstock*, which heralds the beginning of the era which The Band gathered to bury. Among 1970s contemporaries of The Band, one senses joy in the various Rolling Stones documentaries, in Chuck Berry's *Hail! Hail! Rock 'n' Roll*, and in concert films by the Temptations or Rod Stewart. Not here.

In *The Last Waltz*, we have musicians who seem to have bad memories. Who are hanging on. Scorsese's direction is mostly limited to close-ups and medium shots of performances; he ignores the audience. The movie was made at the end of a difficult period in his own life, and at a particularly hard time (the filming coincided with his work on *New York, New York*). This is not a record of serene men, filled with nostalgia, happy to be among friends.

At the end, Bob Dylan himself comes on. One senses little connection between Dylan and The Band. One also wonders what he was thinking as he chose that oversized white cowboy hat, a hat so absurd that during his entire performance I could scarcely think of anything else. It is the haberdashery equivalent of an uplifted middle finger.

The music probably sounds fine on a CD. Certainly it is well rehearsed. But the overall sense of the film is of good riddance to a bad time. Even references to groupies inspire creases of pain on the faces of the rememberers: the sex must have been as bad as anything else. Watching this film, the viewer with mercy will be content to allow the musicians to embrace closure, and will not demand an encore. Yet I give it three stars? Yes, because the film is such a revealing document of a time.

Part 2 Achieving

Introduction

At some point in the later 1970s, Scorsese, like so many of his contemporaries, began using cocaine. The drug had become almost commonplace in Hollywood, and I remember James Toback observing the number of movies and scenes that featured cocaine, and saying: "They love it so much, they can't keep it off of the screen." As an interviewer or critic I have avoided gossip about my subjects, and I would not mention this detail about Scorsese were it not fairly widely known, and had he not told me about it after he was securely clean and sober. In 1978, toward the end of his period of usage, he overdosed, and it resulted in a trip to the emergency room and a hospital stay.

"In AA," I said, "they say you have to find bottom, your own personal bottom, before you can get sober."

"I almost died," he told me. "I would consider that my personal bottom."

De Niro had been trying to convince him to make the movie *Raging Bull* for a few years, but he'd always refused. Now he had entered a period when he believed he would never make another film. He endured such periods from time to time as a younger man, although in recent years he has been spared them.

"I was in the hospital one day," he said, "and De Niro came in, and threw Jake LaMotta's autobiography on the bed, and said, 'Now, do you wanna shoot it?'"

Mardik Martin was enlisted to write the screenplay, Paul Schrader took over for restructuring and rewrites, and Scorsese and De Niro did the final draft. Scorsese was at the peak of his outrage over the deterioration of modern color film, and determined to work in black and white: "Also, of course, the audience wouldn't have been able to stand the sight of that much blood." He wanted to shoot lean and mean, almost as a cleansing exercise, and in De Niro he found a collaborator who was ready to absorb any punishment during the filming.

The character of Jake LaMotta has often been compared with Othello. Both seize upon tiny scraps of imagined evidence to generate a jealous rage. I believe one of Scorsese's inspirations going into the film was George Cukor's 1947 Broadway film noir, *A Double Life*, with Ronald Colman as an actor playing Othello who has the character take over his life. An important scene in both films is similar. In *A Double Life*, Colman takes the woman he is dating (Shelley Winters) to a party in a large apartment. Happening to look into another room, he sees her laughing within a circle of admiring men. His face darkens with jealousy. There is a similar scene in *Raging Bull*, involving Jake seeing Vicki in another room. We know that Scorsese has seen uncounted movies and seems to retain them all, but how can we be sure he saw this film? Because he "presented" it in the VHS edition, and taped an introduction for it, commenting on the way that Colman's face reflects in real life what is happening in his career and imagination.

I was able to go through the film with the shot-by-shot approach with Thelma Schoonmaker at the University of Virginia, and some scenes brought up memories. "We were all packed into an incredibly crowded little living room," she recalled, "for the scene of Jake getting jealous and accusing his brother of having designs on Vicki. It was so hard to get right. That was one of the days Marty said this was going to be his last film."

One other story: there is a famous continuous shot that begins in Jake's dressing room, accompanies him down a stadium corridor and into the arena, and pulls back to show him entering the ring. "Marty shot it five times," Schoonmaker said, "but the ring announcer never took his cue. Finally Marty said, 'Print it! Nobody will notice.' He was right. If you look, the announcer's lips are not moving, but everyone is looking at the boxer."

If you want to discuss a film in detail, ask the editor, who knows its cells and sinews. She discussed the way Scorsese used variable ring sizes to manipulate our perception of LaMotta, how slow motion was employed (as it had been in *Taxi Driver*) to objectify women, how the ropes around the ring represented in a sense the lines on a musical score, how animal roars were incorporated into crowd noises during the fight scenes, how a camera inside the ring played the role of a boxer surrogate.

Raging Bull, the film he thought would end his career, became the most indelible film Scorsese would ever make, and was voted by four groups the best film of the decade. It won Oscars for De Niro and Schoonmaker, and got six other nominations, losing out for best picture to *Ordinary People*. If the Academy did not immediately know it was the year's best film, neither did I, placing it second on my "best ten" list after *The Black Stallion*. Today, as fine a film as *The Black Stallion* was, that decision seems inexplicable.

The King of Comedy was another film De Niro wanted Scorsese to make, and he was correct that he would be perfect as Rupert Pupkin but perhaps wrong about the film; I discuss it in a reconsideration. Then came *After Hours*, another film many critics found problematical, also the subject of a reconsideration here. It's interesting that *Raging Bull* and *After Hours*, in my view two of his best films, followed *New York, New York* and *King of Comedy*, two films Scorsese has expressed dissatisfaction with.

Then came, at last, a film that in one way or another Scorsese had been planning ever since the days of the *Jerusalem, Jerusalem* screenplay. His *The Last Temptation of Christ* would now be based on a novel by Nikos Kazantzakis, but it reflected all the thoughts and feelings he had about Christ's dual identity as god and man. How better to express Freud's Madonna-whore complex than with a film containing the original Madonna, and the prostitute that Christ accepted as a worthy human being? The screenplay again was by Schrader, who seemed to synch with Scorsese whenever religion and guilt were involved.

(63)

Not everyone remembers now that Scorsese's life was threatened during the film's shooting and release period. I tell some of the story in my reconsideration after the review. It was a film that this director had to make, and its conflict between the spiritual and the carnal is his most direct expression of his recurring theme. Looking at it again recently, I wondered if the character of Judas (Harvey Keitel) was Scorsese's alter ego in the film, and I explain why in the reconsideration.

The decade that began with one of the greatest of all films ended with Scorsese winning a tacit three-way competition with his colleagues Francis Ford Coppola and Woody Allen. Each directed a third of the *New York Stories* trilogy, and it was universally concluded that Scorsese's was the best—indeed, some critics believed, the only successful one. It was Scorsese's first opportunity to work with Nick Nolte, who would return two years later in *Cape Fear*.

Raging Bull

DECEMBER 19, 1980

Martin Scorsese's *Raging Bull* is a movie about brute force, anger, and grief. It is also, like several of Scorsese's other movies, about a man's inability to understand a woman except in terms of the only two roles he knows how to assign her: virgin or whore. There is no room inside the mind of the prizefighter in this movie for the notion that a woman might be a friend, a lover, or a partner. She is only, to begin with, an inaccessible sexual fantasy. And then, after he has possessed her, she becomes tarnished by sex. Insecure in his own manhood, the man becomes obsessed by jealousy—and releases his jealousy in violence.

It is a vicious circle. Freud called it the Madonna-whore complex. Groucho Marx put it somewhat differently: "I wouldn't belong to any club that would have me as a member." It amounts to a man having such low self-esteem that he (a) cannot respect a woman who would sleep with him, and (b) is convinced that, given the choice, she would rather be sleeping with someone else. I'm making a point of the way *Raging Bull* equates sexuality and violence because one of the criticisms of this movie is that we never really get to know the central character. I don't agree with that. I think Scorsese and Robert De Niro do a fearless job of showing us the precise feelings of their central character, the former boxing champion Jake LaMotta.

It is true that the character never tells us what he's feeling, that he is not introspective, that his dialog is mostly limited to expressions of desire, fear, hatred, and jealousy. But these very limitations—these stone walls separating the character from the world of ordinary feel-ings—tell us all we need to know, especially when they're reflected back at him by the other people in his life. Especially his brother and his wife, Vickie.

Raging Bull is based, we are told, on the life of LaMotta, who came out of the slums of the Bronx to become middleweight champion in the 1940s, who made and squandered millions of dollars, who became a pathetic stand-up comedian, and finally spent time in a prison for corrupting the morals of an underage girl. Is this the real LaMotta? We cannot know for sure, though LaMotta was closely involved with the production. What's perhaps more to the point is that Scorsese and his principal collaborators, actor Robert De Niro and screenwriter Paul Schrader, were attracted to this material. All three seem fascinated by the lives of tortured, violent, guilt-ridden characters; their previous three-way collaboration was the movie *Taxi Driver*.

Scorsese's very first film, *Who's That Knocking at My Door* (1968), starred Harvey Keitel as a kid from Little Italy who fell in love with a girl but could not handle the facts of her previous sexual experience. In its sequel, *Mean Streets* (1973), the same hang-up was explored, as it was in *Taxi Driver*, where the De Niro character's Madonna-whore complex tortured him in sick relationships with an inaccessible, icy blonde, and with a young prostitute. Now the filmmakers have re-turned to the same ground, in a film deliberately intended to strip away everything but the raw surges of guilt, jealousy, and rage coursing through LaMotta's extremely limited imagination.

Raging Bull remains close to its three basic elements: a man, a woman, and prizefighting. LaMotta is portrayed as a punk kid, stub-born, strong, and narrow. He gets involved in boxing, and he is good at it. He gets married, but his wife seems almost an afterthought. Then one day he sees a girl at a municipal swimming pool and is transfixed by her. The girl is named Vickie, and she is played by Cathy Moriarty as an intriguing mixture of unstudied teenager, self-reliant survivor, and somewhat calculated slut.

LaMotta wins and marries her. Then he becomes consumed by the conviction she is cheating on him. Scorsese finds a way to visually suggest his jealousy: from LaMotta's point of view, Vickie sometimes floats in slow motion toward another man. The technique fixes the moment in our minds; we share LaMotta's exaggeration of an innocent event. And we share, too, the LaMotta character's limited and tragic hang-ups. This man we see is not, I think, supposed to be any more subtle than he seems. He does not have additional "qualities" to share with us. He is an engine driven by his own rage. The equation between his prizefighting and his sexuality is inescapable, and we see the trap he's in: LaMotta is the victim of base needs and instincts that, in his case, are not accompanied by the insights and maturity necessary for him to cope with them. The raging bull. The poor sap.

The King of Comedy

MAY 15, 1983

Martin Scorsese's *The King of Comedy* is one of the most arid, painful, wounded movies I've ever seen. It's hard to believe Scorsese made it; instead of the big-city life, the violence and sexuality of his movies like *Taxi Driver* and *Mean Streets*, what we have here is an agonizing portrait of lonely, angry people with their emotions all tightly bottled up. This is a movie that seems ready to explode—but somehow it never does.

That lack of release disturbed me the fist time I saw *The King of Comedy*, back in January. I kept straining forward, waiting for the movie to let loose and it kept frustrating me. Maybe that was the idea. This is a movie about rejection, with a hero who never admits that he has been rejected and so there is neither comic nor tragic release—just the postponement of pain.

I walked out of that first screening filled with dislike for the movie. Dislike, but not disinterest. Memories of *The King of Comedy* kept gnawing at me, and when people asked me what I thought about it, I said I wasn't sure. Then I went to see the movie a second time, and it seemed to work better for me—maybe because I was able to walk in without any expectations. I knew it wasn't an entertainment, I knew it didn't allow itself any emotional payoffs, I knew the ending was cynical and unsatisfactory, and so, with those discoveries no longer to be made, I was free to simply watch what was on the screen.

What I saw the second time, better than the first, were the

performances by Robert De Niro, Jerry Lewis, Diahnne Abbott, and Sandra Bernhard, who play the movie's most important characters. They must have been difficult performances to deliver, because nobody listens in this film; everybody's just waiting for the other person to stop talking so they can start. And everybody's so emotionally isolated in this movie that they don't even seem able to guess what they're missing.

The movie stars Robert De Niro as Rupert Pupkin, a nerdish man in his thirties who fantasizes himself as a television star. He practices down in his basement, holding condescending conversations with life-size cardboard cutouts of Liza Minnelli and Jerry Lewis. His dream is to get a standup comedy slot on the late-night talk show hosted by Lewis (whose name in the movie is Jerry Langford). The movie opens with Rupert's first meeting with Jerry; he barges into Jerry's limousine and is immediately on an obnoxious first-name basis. Jerry vaguely promises to check out Rupert's comedy routine, and the rest of the movie is devoted to Rupert's single-minded pursuit of fame. He arrives at Jerry's office, is politely brushed off, returns, is rejected again, arrives at Jerry's country home with a "date" in tow, is ejected again, and finally decides to kidnap Jerry.

This sounds like an entertaining story, I suppose, but Scorsese doesn't direct a single scene for a payoff. The whole movie is an exercise in cinema interruptus; even a big scene in a bar, where Rupert triumphantly turns on the TV set to reveal himself on television, is deliberately edited to leave out the payoff shots—reaction shots of the amazed clientele. Scorsese doesn't want laughs in this movie, and he also doesn't want release. The whole movie is about the inability of the characters to get any kind of a positive response to their bids for recognition.

The King of Comedy is not, you may already have guessed, a fun movie. It is also not a bad movie. It is frustrating to watch, unpleasant to remember, and, in its own way, quite effective. It represents an enormous departure for Scorsese, whose movies teemed with life until he filmed this emotional desert, and whose camera used to prowl restlessly until he nailed it down this time. Scorsese and De Niro are the most creative, productive director/actor team in the movies right now, and the fact that they feel the freedom to make such an odd, stimulating, unsatisfying movie is good news, I guess. But *The King of Comedy* is the kind of film that makes you want to go and see a Scorsese movie.

Scorsese

NEW YORK—Walking back to my hotel after dinner with Martin Scorsese, I asked myself how much longer he would go on driving himself up the wall with his obsession of finding happiness with a woman. For all of his adult life, Scorsese has been searching for love and serenity with a woman, and he has never found those comforts for very long.

Out of his pain, however, he has directed some of the best films ever made about loneliness and frustration. Pausing for a stoplight, looking up at the Manhattan canyons where lonely people sleep on shelves all the way to the stars, I reflected that Scorsese's hurt has at least inspired great films. If he stays miserable, I thought, he might make some more masterpieces like *Taxi Driver*. On the other hand, he might simply go off the deep end into bitterness and despair.

We had just talked for three hours about *The King of Comedy*, Scorsese's problematical new film—a movie the studio was ready to give up on, until some good reviews started coming in. For Scorsese, the making of the film coincided with a painful period of his life, a time when he fell in love with Ingrid Bergman's daughter, Isabella Rossellini, was married, and was divorced. Although it is easy to see *The King of Comedy* as the most barren and unemotional of all Scorsese's films, that is not the way he sees it. Maybe that's because each scene is connected in his memory with a hurt in his life.

"The amount of rejection in this film is horrifying," Scorsese said.

"There are scenes I almost can't look at. There's a scene where De Niro is told, 'I hate you!' and he nods and responds, 'Oh, I see, right, you don't want to see me again!' I made the movie during a very painful period in my life. I was going through the Poor Me routine. And I'm still very lonely. Another relationship has broken up."

Since Isabella?

"Since. I'm spending a lot of time by myself now. I go home and watch movies on video and stay up all night and sleep all day. If I didn't have to work I'd sleep all the time. I've never had such a long period when I've been alone."

Just the way he said that, quietly, without emphasis, much more softly than he usually speaks, places it in a special category. Perhaps it gives an additional dimension to *The King of Comedy*, a movie about a man so desperately isolated that even his goals do not include a relationship with another human being.

The character, Rupert Pupkin, played by Robert De Niro, has constructed a set for a talk show in his basement, and he sits down there night after night, holding chatty, condescending conversations with life-size cardboard cut-outs of Liza Minnelli and Jerry Lewis. Rupert Pupkin doesn't feel cut off from life—he feels cut off from talk shows. His life consists of waiting. He waits outside stage doors, outside office buildings, in waiting rooms, and on telephones. He wants to be on television. He wants to be on first-name terms with Liza and Jerry and Tony and Joyce and the other members of America's amorphous extended family of television "personalities," who all seem to know each other so very well.

Rupert does not know how to have a conventional conversation, but he knows the form for talk shows; he has studied talk-show host Jerry Langford (Jerry Lewis) so carefully that he even knows how he dresses, and what his credo for beginning comics is: "Don't tell them it's the punch line, just tell them the punch line."

Scorsese says that both Rupert Pupkin and Jerry Langford remind him of himself. Pupkin is young Marty Scorsese, camped out in agents' offices, scrounging loans to finish his student film, hustling jobs as an editor in between directing assignments. Langford is Martin Scorsese at forty, famous, honored, admired, besieged by young would-be film-makers asking him for a break.

"Last night," Scorsese said, "I went to the 10 PM show of *King of Comedy*. On the screen, the scene is playing where Rupert pushes into Jerry's limousine and says he's gotta talk to him. He's out of breath. 'Take it easy, kid,' Jerry tells him. Meanwhile, in the back row of the theater, a kid grabs me by the arm and he's saying he's got to talk to me. He's out of breath I tell him to take it easy. It's the exact same scene that's on the screen!"

Time. What that story is about is time. There was a time when Marty Scorsese was an intense, asthmatic, talented kid from New York University who wanted to make movies. He had a lot of self-confidence. Now time has passed and Scorsese has achieved all the things he dreamed of. There are those who believe he is the greatest of American directors, the most personal, the most obsessed. But if he once thought that success would bring him happiness, he now thinks again. Since famous film directors are supposed to be able to have whatever they want, the fact that Scorsese is famous and yet still unhappy must seem to him a terrible irony.

Scorsese at forty is bearded, slight, and often cheerful, despite the burden of his unhappiness. He comes to dinner dressed like a successful undertaker, wearing an expensive dark-blue suit and a double-breasted navy-blue topcoat. Perhaps he looks like the well-dressed Mafioso who ran New York's Little Italy when he was growing up there. He was in Israel recently to scout locations for a project called *The Last Temptation of Christ*, and when they took him out in the desert in a helicopter, he wore the blue suit and the blue topcoat and the expensive black shoes. Most directors wear desert jackets to dinner. Scorsese wears a suit to the desert.

"The studio was ready to give up on *King of Comedy*," he said. "They sneak-previewed it. The response was not great. Good, but not great. I told them this was not the kind of movie where preview audiences meant anything. If you are not prepared in your mind to see this movie, it can be a very strange experience. The way to sell this movie is, basically, on the track records of De Niro and myself, and on the story line.

The studio was ready to put the movie on the shelf. It was dead and buried. Then some of the good reviews started coming in, and they reversed themselves. Now it looks like it might do all right."

One of the reasons the studio was afraid of the movie (Scorsese did not add) was that the subject matter is extremely touchy. In the movie, Rupert Pupkin kidnaps Jerry Langford and holds him for ransom. The ransom demand is a ten-minute slot for a standup comedy routine on the talk show. Since it is well known that Scorsese's *Taxi Driver* (about an alienated assassin) was seen by John Hinckley before he shot Reagan, *The King of Comedy* seemed in some circles almost like an invitation to trouble for someone like Johnny Carson.

Such fears were not alleviated by Paul Zimmerman, the onetime *Newsweek* film critic who wrote the movie, and who brashly told a New York press conference, "It is not the job of art to serve as a security system for celebrities."

For Scorsese, though, the movie does not precisely seem to be about kidnapping a celebrity. That is simply the plot line, in a screenplay that Zimmerman wrote twelve years ago and that Scorsese originally turned down six years ago. "It seemed like a one-joke movie at the time," he said. "But then I began to see that it wasn't about kidnapping, it was about rejection. It required a new visual style for me. I'm known for my moving camera. I'm usually all over the place.

"This film has very little camera movement, and when the camera moves, it means something. Look at the scene where the receptionist tells Pupkin that Jerry won't be back until Monday, and Pupkin says he'll wait. Look how the camera moves. It moves to show how solidly planted Rupert is. It's a nice move."

But it comes, I said, out of your sense of loneliness and rejection?

"Yes."

Simple as that?

"Simple as that."

Scorsese's first movie, *Who's That Knocking at My Door*, was about an Italian American kid from New York who fell in love with a blonde on the Staten Island ferry, and wanted to marry her before he discovered that she was not a virgin. Angry and confused, he rejected her, and at the end of the movie they were both alone and we had the feeling that he would stay that way. Freud wrote about the Madonna-whore complex, the hang-up of men who have only two categories for women: first they idealize them, and then, when they discover that their perfect woman is only human after all, they rigidly reject them.

Without getting into your personal psychology, I said to Scorsese, are you still replaying the same scenario?

"I'm still stuck at the *Who's That Knocking* stage," he said "Except it's not so much that I reject, as that something goes wrong. Maybe I'm impossible to be with."

The same pattern, of idealization and rejection, turns up in Scorsese's other movies, including *Mean Streets*, *Taxi Driver*, and *Raging Bull* (where Robert De Niro, as Jake LaMotta, marries a sixteen-year-old sexpot and then is driven mad with jealousy when other men look at her). I could only guess at the forms that Scorsese's own obsessions take, and I did not want to really press the subject, although he seemed willing to talk about it.

What eventually happened, toward the end of our dinner, was that I discovered by accident how deeply he was hurt. I mentioned a new film named *Exposed*, by James Toback, starring Nastassja Kinski. I said I thought Kinski possessed whatever rare magic Marilyn Monroe had; that whatever Kinski appears in, good or bad, she commands the screen.

"I can't bear to see Kinski in anything," Scorsese said. "She reminds me too much of Isabella. It tears me apart. I can't even go to see a film by the Taviani brothers, because Isabella and I had a little courtship on the set of one of their films. I can't ever go back to the island of Salina, where Visconti's *The Leopard* was shot, because we were there. In fact, I can hardly even watch a film by Visconti without growing depressed."

By memories of Isabella?

"By memories of a period when I thought I was happy, I'll put it that way. A period when I really thought I had the answers."

OK, then, I said. I've got a new movie that can't possibly depress you or bring up any old associations. It's called, *Say Amen, Somebody*, and it's this wonderful documentary about gospel music.

"Can't see it." Scorsese was grinning, but he was serious.

Why not?

"It's distributed by United Artists Classics." He sighed.

You mean you can't see a film that is distributed by a company that is connected to a woman you once loved?

He smiled. "I'd see the United Artists logo and it would ruin the movie for me."

Maybe you could come in after the logo had left the screen? "I'd know."

With some directors, you fear that they will lose their early fire and obsession, and, in middle age, turn to directing safe and cheerful commercial projects. With Martin Scorsese, I don't think we have that to worry about.

The King of Comedy

A RECONSIDERATION

What is my problem with *The King of Comedy*? I have seen the movie, what? Ten times? Fifteen? I left my first viewing, I wrote, filled with "dislike, but not disinterest." I dreaded going to dinner with Scorsese later that night, and remember reluctantly telling him, "I'm not sure I liked it." I was very sure, but I couldn't say why. He took that well enough, and began talking about his identification with the constant rejection that Rupert Pupkin experiences; that interview is in this book. I was surprised, and not for the first time, about how open and frank he was. Unlike most important people in the film industry, he gives you the feeling that, if you ask, he will answer anything.

Time and again I've returned to *The King of Comedy*, for classes, festivals, or shot-by-shots, and I always begin by thinking that I was mistaken, that I missed the point, that this time the movie is working for me. And by the end I always come around to an emptiness. Yet despite everything the movie stays with me. Rupert Pupkin is one of the most specific and vivid characters in the cinema, and he is framed by the extraordinary performances of Jerry Lewis and Sandra Bernhard, and the pitch-perfect casting of supporting roles — including even an actor named Chuck Low, who sits behind Rupert at a Chinese restaurant, mocks him, and tries to pick up his date.

There were other, personal reasons why Scorsese was unhappy making the film, but they do not make it a bad film (or a good one). His health, never robust, was at a low ebb. It is now more or less known that he had a problem with cocaine that reached its peak during *New York, New York*. Not long after finishing that film, he told me, he was hospitalized, and had concluded his career was over. Then De Niro walked into his hospital room, threw the *Raging Bull* project on his bed, and said, "You know, we could make this picture." Scorsese thought maybe that saved his life. That, and stopping the drug use, of course.

The self-destructive jealousy of Jake LaMotta, he said, spoke to something inside Scorsese, who married Julia Cameron in 1975, divorced her during *New York, New York* (1977), was said to be involved with Minnelli for a time, and was married to Isabella Rossellini from 1979 to 1983, including the period when he was making *Raging Bull*. While finishing *The King of Comedy* (1983), he met Barbara De Fina, the postproduction supervisor, and married her in 1985, divorcing in 1991. Since 1999, he has been married, happily, I believe, to the writer Helen Morris. I am reluctant to speculate about that period of acceptance and loss. I dislike gossip, and am wary of pop psychology, but it seems likely Scorsese might have been receptive when De Niro came to him with another project, the screenplay for *The King of Comedy*, by onetime *Newsweek* film critic Paul D. Zimmerman. "The amount of rejection in this film is horrifying," Scorsese told me that night after I saw the film. "There are scenes I almost can't look at."

Other factors were at work during the filming. He was ill during much of the shooting: "Physically I didn't feel ready," he says in *Scorsese on Scorsese*. "I shouldn't have done it and it soon became clear that I wasn't up to it. By the second week of shooting I was begging them not to let me go on. I was coughing on the floor and sounding like a character from *The Magic Mountain*. Finally it got so bad that some days I wouldn't get there until 2:30 in the afternoon."

There were days, he told me during an Ohio State interview, when he didn't know why he was on the set. "The reason you're there is because the actors are there, the camera's there, you gotta shoot, you know. Well, it's gotta be more than that for me. And it was there but I was kinda rehabilitating in a way and I found that, again, you just can't go off and do films for your friends. You have to try to stick to stuff you wanna do."

Perhaps because of this underlying feeling, perhaps because of exhaustion and illness, Scorsese used a moving camera less in *The King of Comedy* than any of his other features. The movie is largely in static long and medium shots, with few close-ups. It benefits from that approach by keeping De Niro and Bernhard often in full frame, so we can appreciate their body language: De Niro awkward, nervous, compulsively adjusting his tie and lapels while Bernhard ranges through shots like a hunting beast. Lewis is the island of calm, making the talk-show host Jerry Langford a detached, contemptuous man, never showing fear.

What is frightening about the Pupkin character is that he is so single-minded. He wants fame. He wants to be Jerry Langford. He has never heard of Andy Warhol, but he demands his fifteen minutes of fame. He cannot be rejected, because he cannot hear rejection, with his mind always racing ahead to fantasies of acceptance. Bernhard as his fellow celebrity-stalker, Masha, on the other hand, doesn't want to be Langford but to have him, and when she slinks across the dinner table toward him like a cat in heat, we feel a ferocious need. There is no sexual component at all in Pupkin's character. He approaches the tall, gravely sensuous Rita (Diahnne Abbott, De Niro's wife from 1976 to 1988) for two reasons: to impress someone he was too shy to speak to in grade school, and to have arm candy to impress Jerry. "What is it that you *want*, Rupert?" Rita asks him, after he begs off her invitation to come upstairs for coffee.

We see the interiors of four homes in the film: Masha's expensive-looking apartment, Langford's sterile apartment in the city, and his country home that Rita compares to a funeral parlor. Of Rupert's home we see only the basement, with cardboard cut-outs to make a TV studio. We hear his mother's offstage voice screaming downstairs to "Turn it down! People are trying to sleep!" He replies "Mom!" in a whiny little boy voice. At the end of a basement corridor is a toilet. Different domestic styles, all bespeaking loneliness.

In *Taxi Driver*, *New York, New York*, and again in *The King of Comedy*,

Scorsese sets a conversation for two over a table in a coffee shop or restaurant. It is possible that when Rupert takes Rita to dinner in the Chinese restaurant, some viewers do not even notice the man seated alone at a table behind him in the right background. The man at the table makes it no secret that he is eavesdropping and that he finds Rupert's conversation laughable. He looks boldly at Rita, even mocks Rupert's hand gestures, leaves to stand by a pay phone in obvious readiness to pick her up. In the Zimmerman screenplay, he does pick her up, which would be one more rejection that Rupert would somehow be oblivious to. That might have been a rejection too many however. Watch very closely how subtle Rita is in making split-second eye contact with the man, making him no promises, giving Rupert no hints.

The actress Diahnne Abbott was in few important roles: in this film, *New York, New York,* and films by Cassavetes, Alan Rudolph, and Richard Pryor, and then bit work in later TV and movies. Married to De Niro for twelve years, she had the contacts. Maybe she didn't want the work. I think she has a sensuous self-awareness, an amusement, a calm sexuality. She plays Rupert exactly the right way: not deceived for a moment, but going along for the ride.

Still I avoid the question: what is my problem with this movie? Disliking it, and saying so, I nevertheless gave it three stars in my 1983 review. I would explain that by saying star ratings are meaningless and this movie is not to be dismissed. But I cannot give myself to it. It has no emotional point of entry. All of the characters are closed doors. Everyone gets what he deserves, except Rupert, who in the coda gets much more than he deserves. But are the final shots intended to be real, or another of Rupert's daydreams? Do they have an occult relationship with the puzzling ending of *Taxi Driver*, where Travis Bickle also becomes a folk hero?

Scorsese and De Niro worked together four times in seven years, and after this film not again for the next seven years. It isn't that they fought, or came to dislike each other. I don't know how accurate the quote is, but IMDb writes: "Scorsese said that he and Robert De Niro may have not worked together again for seven years because making *The King of Comedy* was so emotionally grueling." More grueling than

Raging Bull? Perhaps more painful. With *Raging Bull* they must have sensed at some level they were doing the film of a lifetime. Now they were making a film that they were not so sure about, perhaps not so in love with. There is something odd about it, something wounding, but I would see it again right now, gladly. If it has greatness, perhaps it is in its mystery.

After Hours

OCTOBER 11, 1985

Martin Scorsese's *After Hours* is a comedy, according to the strict definition of that word: it ends happily, and there are indications along
the way that we're not supposed to take it seriously. It is, however, the
tensest comedy I can remember, building its nightmare situation step
by insidious step until our laughter is hollow, or defensive. This is the
work of a master filmmaker who controls his effects so skillfully that
I was drained by this film — so emotionally depleted that there was a
moment, two-thirds of the way through, when I wondered if maybe I
should leave the theater and gather my thoughts and come back later
for the rest of the "comedy."

The movie tells the story of a night in the life of Paul Hackett
(Griffin Dunne), a Midtown Manhattan word-processing specialist
who hates his job and his lonely private life. One night in a restaurant
he strikes up a conversation with a winsome young woman (Rosanna
Arquette). They seem to share some of the same interests. He gets her
telephone number. He calls her, she suggests he come downtown to
her apartment in SoHo, and that is the beginning of his Kafkaesque
adventure.

The streets of SoHo are dark and deserted. Clouds of steam escape from the pavement, as they did in Scorsese's *Taxi Driver*, suggesting that Hades lurks just below the field of vision. The young
woman is staying for a few days in the apartment of a friend (Linda
Fiorentino), who makes bizarre sculptures, has kinky sexual tastes,

and talks in a strange, veiled way about being burned. In Arquette's bedroom, Dunne makes the usual small talk of a first date, and she gushes that she's sure they will have a great time, but then everything begins to fall apart.

At first, we think perhaps Dunne is the victim of random bad luck, as he is confronted with nightmares both tragic and trivial: ominous strangers, escalating subway fares, a shocking suicide, sadomasochistic sexual practices, a punk nightclub where he almost has his head shaved, a street mob that thinks he is a thief. Only later, much later, on this seemingly endless night do we find how everything is connected — and even then, it doesn't make any logical sense. For Paul Hackett, as for the Job of the Old Testament, the plague of bad luck seems generated by some unexplained divine wrath.

And yet Scorsese has not simply made a horror movie, or some kind of allegory of doom. Each of his characters is drawn sharply, given quirky dialog, allowed to be offbeat and funny. Teri Garr has a scene as a waitress who has tried to make sense of New York for so long that it has driven her around the bend. Fiorentino has a dry, sardonic angle on things. Arquette speaks wonderingly of a lover who was so obsessed by *The Wizard Oz* that he always called her Dorothy in bed. John Heard is a bartender who has seen everything walk in through the doors of his all-night saloon, and has lost the capacity for astonishment.

After Hours is another chapter in Scorsese's continuing examination of Manhattan as a state of mind; if he hadn't already used the title *New York, New York*, he could have used it this time. The movie earns its place on the list with his great films: *Mean Streets*, *Taxi Driver*, and *Raging Bull*.

For New Yorkers, parts of the film will no doubt play as a documentary. In what other city is everyday life such an unremitting challenge? Take, for example, the mob that forms after it believes that Dunne is a thief. Would neighbors form a posse in many other cities? I imagine not; in most cities, theft is still a sort of individual thing, and does not happen so habitually that whole neighborhoods weary of being ripped off. Audiences from other parts of the country are likely to

(83)

think some of Scorsese's scenes are fantasy, while New Yorkers may see them as merely exaggerations of reality.

After Hours is a brilliant film, one of the year's best. It is also a most curious film. It comes after Scorsese's *The King of Comedy*, a film I thought was fascinating but unsuccessful, and continues Scorsese's attempt to combine comedy and satire with unrelenting pressure and a sense of all-pervading paranoia. This time he succeeds. The result is a film that is so original, so particular, that we are uncertain from moment to moment exactly how to respond to it. The style of the film creates in us the same feeling that the events in the film create in the hero. Interesting.

After Hours

After Hours approaches the notion of pure filmmaking, in that it is a nearly flawless example of—itself. It lacks, as nearly as I can determine, a lesson or message, and is content to show the hero facing a series of interlocking challenges to his safety and sanity. It is *The Perils of Pauline* told boldly and well. Critics have called it "Kafkaesque" almost as a reflex, but that is a descriptive term, not an explanatory one. Is the film a cautionary tale about life in the city? To what purpose? New York may offer a variety of strange people awake after midnight, but they seldom find themselves intertwined in a bizarre series of coincidences, all focused on the same individual. You're not paranoid if people really are plotting against you, but strangers do not plot against you to make you paranoid. The film has been described as dream logic, but it might as well be called screwball logic; apart from the nightmarish and bizarre nature of his experiences, what happens to Paul Hackett is like what happens to Buster Keaton: just one damned thing after another.

The project was not personally developed by Scorsese, who was involved at the time in struggles over *The Last Temptation of Christ*. Paramount's abrupt cancellation of that film four weeks before the start of production (the sets had been built, the costumes prepared) sent Scorsese into deep frustration. "My idea then was to pull back, and not to become hysterical and try to kill people," he told his friend Mary Pat Kelly. "So the trick then was to try to do *something*." After rejecting piles of scripts, he received one from producers Amy Robinson and Griffin Dunne, who thought it could be made for $4 million. It had been written by Joseph Minion, then a graduate student at Columbia, and Scorsese was later to recall that Minion's teacher, the Yugoslavian director Dusan Makavejev, gave it an *A*. He decided to make it: "I thought it would be interesting to see if I could go back and do something in a very fast way. *All style.* An exercise completely in style. And to show they hadn't killed my spirit."

It was the first film of his long collaboration with the German cinematographer Michael Ballhaus, who had worked much with Fassbinder and knew all about low budgets, fast shooting schedules, and passionate directors. It was shot entirely at night, sometimes with on-the-spot improvisation of camera movements, as in the famous shot where Paul Hackett (Dunne), the hero, rings the SoHo bell of Kiki Bridges (Linda Fiorentino) and she throws down her keys and Scorsese uses a POV shot of the keys dropping toward Paul. In pre-digital days, that really had to happen. They tried fastening the camera to a board and dropping it toward Paul with ropes to stop it at the last moment (Dunne was risking his life), but after that approach produced out-of-focus footage, Ballhaus came up with a terrifyingly fast crane move. Other shots, Scorsese said, were in the spirit of Hitchcock, fetishizing close-ups of objects like light switches, keys, locks, and especially faces. If the close-up is a device to underline the importance of a moment to a character, Scorsese used that knowledge to exploit unmotivated close-ups; Paul thought something critical had happened, but much of the time it had not. In an unconscious way, an audience raised on classic film grammar would share his expectation and disappointment. Pure filmmaking.

Another device was to offhandedly suggest alarming possibilities about characters, as when Kiki hints that she has burns and Paul finds a graphic medical textbook about burn victims in the bedroom of Marcy (Rosanna Arquette), the girl he has gone to meet at Kiki's apartment. Were Kiki's burns accidental, or deliberate? The question is open because Kiki is into sadomasochism. Trying to find a shared conversational topic, Paul tells Marcy the story of the time he was a little boy in the hospital, and was left for a time in the burn unit, but blindfolded and warned not to remove the blindfold. He did, and what he saw horrified him. Strange, that entering the lives of two women obsessed with burns, he would have his own burn story, but coincidence and synchronicity are the engines of the plot.

After Hours has some relationship to the films of the 1990s and 2000s that came to be called hypertext movies, in which disparate elements of the plot are found to be associated in an occult way. In Scorsese's film such elements as a suicide, a method of sculpture, a plaster-of-paris bagel, a $20 bill, and a string of burglaries all reveal connections that only exist because Paul's adventures link them. This generates the film's sinister undertone, as in a scene where he tries to explain all the things that have befallen him, and fails, perhaps because they sound too absurd even to him. One thing many viewers of the film have reported is the high (some say almost unbearable) level of suspense in *After Hours*, which is technically a comedy but plays like a Satanic version of the classic Hitchcock plot formula, The Innocent Man Wrongly Accused.

With different filmmakers and other actors, the film might have played more safely, like *Adventures in Babysitting*. But there is an intensity and drive in Scorsese's direction that gives it desperation; it really seems to matter that this devastated hero struggle on and survive. Scorsese has suggested that Paul's implacable run of bad luck reflected his own frustration during the *Last Temptation of Christ* experience. Executives kept reassuring him that all went well, backers said they had the money, Paramount greenlighted it, agents promised him it was a "go," everything was in place, and then time after time an unexpected development would threaten everything. In *After Hours*, each new person Paul meets promises that they will take care of him, make him happy, lend him money, give him a place to stay, let him use the phone, trust him with their keys, drive him home—and every offer of mercy turns into an unanticipated danger. The film could be read as an emotional autobiography of that period in Scorsese's life.

The director said he began filming without an ending. The Internet Movie Database claims, "One idea that made it to the storyboard stage had Paul crawling into June's womb to hide from the angry mob, with June [Verna Bloom, the lonely woman in the bar] giving 'birth' to him on the West Side Highway." An ending Scorsese actually filmed had Paul still trapped inside the sculpture as the truck driven by the burglars (Cheech and Chong) roared away. Scorsese said he showed that version to his father, who was angry: "You can't let him die!" That was the same message he had been hearing for weeks from Michael Powell, the great British director who had come on board as a consultant and was soon to marry Scorsese's editor, Thelma Schoonmaker. Powell kept repeating that Paul not only had to live at the end, but to end up back at his office. And so he does, although after Paul returns to the office, close examination of the very final credit footage shows that he has disappeared from his desk.

After Hours is not routinely included in lists of Scorsese's masterpieces. Its appearance on DVD was long delayed. On IMDb's ranking of his films by user vote (a notoriously unreliable but sometimes interesting reflection of popular opinion), it ranks sixteenth. But I recall how I felt after the first time I saw it: wrung out. Yes, no matter that it was a satire, a black comedy, an exercise in style, it worked that first time above all as a story that may have flown in the face of common sense, but that I became invested in. I've seen it many times since, I know how it ends, and despite my suspicion of "happy endings," I agree that Paul could not have been left to die. I no longer feel the suspense, of course, because I know what will happen. But I feel the same admiration. "An exercise completely in style," Scorsese said. But he could not quite hold it to that. He had made a great film because, perhaps, at that time in his life, with the collapse of *The Last Temptation*, he was ready to, he needed to, and he could.

The Color of Money

OCTOBER 17, 1986

If this movie had been directed by someone else, I might have thought differently about it because I might not have expected so much. But *The Color of Money* is directed by Martin Scorsese, the most exciting American director now working, and it is not an exciting film. It doesn't have the electricity, the wound-up tension, of his best work, and as a result I was too aware of the story marching by.

Scorsese may have thought of this film as a deliberately mainstream work, a conventional film with big names and a popular subject matter; perhaps he did it for that reason. But I believe he has the stubborn soul of an artist, and cannot put his heart where his heart will not go. And his heart, I believe, inclines toward creating new and completely personal stories about characters who have come to life in his imagination—not in finishing someone else's story, begun twenty-five years ago.

The Color of Money is not a sequel, exactly, but it didn't start with someone's fresh inspiration. It continues the story of "Fast Eddie" Felson, the character played by Paul Newman in Robert Rossen's *The Hustler* (1961). Now twenty-five years have passed. Eddie still plays pool, but not for money and not with the high-stakes, dangerous kinds of players who drove him from the game. He is a liquor salesman, a successful one, judging by the long, white Cadillac he takes so much pride in. One night, he sees a kid playing pool, and the kid is so good that Eddie's memories are stirred.

This kid is not simply good, however. He is also, Eddie observes, a "flake," and that gives him an idea: with Eddie as his coach, this kid could be steered into the world of big-money pool, where his flakiness would throw off the other players. They wouldn't be inclined to think he was for real. The challenge, obviously, is to train the kid so he can turn his flakiness on and off at will—so he can put the making of money above every other consideration, every other lure and temptation, in the pool hall.

The kid is named Vincent (Tom Cruise), and Eddie approaches him through Vincent's girlfriend, Carmen (Mary Elizabeth Mastrantonio). She is a few years older than Vince and a lot tougher. She likes the excitement of being around Vince and around pool hustling, but Eddie sees she's getting bored. He figures he can make a deal with the girl; together, they'll control Vince and steer him in the direction of money.

A lot of the early scenes setting up this situation are very well handled, especially the moments when Eddie uses Carmen to make Vince jealous and undermine his self-confidence. But of course these scenes work well, because they are the part of the story that is closest to Scorsese's own sensibility. In all of his best movies, we can see this same ambiguity about the role of women, who are viewed as objects of comfort and fear, creatures that his heroes desire and despise themselves for desiring. Think of the heroes of *Mean Streets*, *Taxi Driver*, and *Raging Bull* and their relationships with women, and you sense where the energy is coming from that makes Vincent love Carmen, and distrust her.

The movie seems less at home with the Newman character, perhaps because this character is largely complete when the movie begins. "Fast Eddie" Felson knows who he is, what he thinks, what his values are.

There will be some moments of crisis in the story, as when he allows himself, to his shame, to be hustled at pool. But he is not going to change much during the story, and maybe he's not even free to change much, since his experiences are largely dictated by the requirements of the plot.

Here we come to the big weakness of *The Color of Money*: it exists in a couple of timeworn genres, and its story is generated out of standard Hollywood situations. First we have the basic story of the old pro and the talented youngster. Then we have the story of the kid who wants to knock the master off the throne. Many of the scenes in this movie are almost formula, despite the energy of Scorsese's direction and the good performances. They come in the same places we would expect them to come in a movie by anybody else, and they contain the same events.

Eventually, everything points to the ending of the film, which we know will have to be a showdown between Eddie and Vince, between Newman and Cruise. The fact that the movie does not provide that payoff scene is a disappointment. Perhaps Scorsese thought the movie was "really" about the personalities of his two heroes, and that it was unnecessary to show who would win in a showdown. Perhaps, but then why plot the whole story with genre formulas, and only bail out at the end? If you bring a gun onstage in the first act, somebody will have been shot by the third.

The side stories are where the movie really lives. There is a warm, bittersweet relationship between Newman and his longtime girlfriend, a bartender wonderfully played by Helen Shaver. And the greatest energy in the story is generated between Cruise and Mastrantonio—who, with her hard edge and her inbred cynicism, keeps the kid from ever feeling really sure of her. (Mastrantonio, an Oak Park and River Forest High graduate, will be in town this weekend for a reunion.) It's a shame that even the tension of their relationship is allowed to evaporate in the closing scenes, where Cruise and the girl stand side by side and seem to speak from the same mind, as if she were a standard movie girlfriend and not a real original.

Watching Newman is always interesting in this movie. He has been a true star for many years, but sometimes that star quality has been thrown away. Scorsese has always been the kind of director who lets his camera stay on an actor's face, who looks deeply into them and tries to find the shadings that reveal their originality. In many of Newman's close-ups in this movie, he shows an enormous power, a concentration and focus of his essence as an actor.

Newman, of course, had veto power over who would make this movie (because how could they make it without him?), and his instincts were sound in choosing Scorsese. Maybe the problems started with the story, when Newman or somebody decided that there had to be a young man in the picture; the introduction of the Cruise character opens the door for all of the preordained teacher-pupil clichés, when perhaps they should have just stayed with Newman and let him be at the center of the story.

Then Newman's character would have been free (as the Robert De Niro characters have been free in other Scorsese films) to follow his passions, hungers, fears, and desires wherever they led him—instead of simply following the story down a well-traveled path.

The Last Temptation of Christ

AUGUST 28, 1988

Christianity teaches that Jesus was both God and man. That he could be both at once is the central mystery of the Christian faith, and the subject of *The Last Temptation of Christ*. To be fully man, Jesus would have had to possess all of the weakness of man, to be prey to all of the temptations—for as man, he would have possessed God's most troublesome gift, free will. As the son of God, he would of course have inspired the most desperate wiles of Satan, and this is a film about how he experienced temptation and conquered it.

That, in itself, makes *The Last Temptation of Christ* sound like a serious and devout film, which it is. The astonishing controversy that has raged around this film is primarily the work of fundamentalists who have their own view of Christ and are offended by a film that they feel questions his divinity. But in the father's house are many mansions, and there is more than one way to consider the story of Christ—why else are there four Gospels? Among those who do not already have rigid views on the subject, this film is likely to inspire more serious thought on the nature of Jesus than any other ever made.

That is the irony about the attempts to suppress this film; it is a sincere, thoughtful investigation of the subject, made as a collaboration between the two American filmmakers who have been personally most attracted to serious films about sin, guilt, and redemption. Martin Scorsese, the director, has made more than half of his films about battles in the souls of his characters between grace and sin.

Paul Schrader, the screenwriter, has written Scorsese's best films (*Taxi Driver*, *Raging Bull*) and directed his own films about men torn between their beliefs and their passions (*Hardcore*, with George C. Scott as a fundamentalist whose daughter plunges into the carnal underworld, and *Mishima*, about the Japanese writer who killed himself as a demonstration of his fanatic belief in tradition).

Scorsese and Schrader have not made a film that panders to the audience—as almost all Hollywood religious epics traditionally have. They have paid Christ the compliment of taking him and his message seriously, and they have made a film that does not turn him into a garish, emasculated image from a religious postcard. Here he is flesh and blood, struggling, questioning, asking himself and his father which is the right way, and finally, after great suffering, earning the right to say, on the cross, "It is accomplished." The critics of this film, many of whom have not seen it, have raised a sensational hue and cry about the final passages, in which Christ on the cross, in great pain, begins to hallucinate and imagines what his life would have been like if he had been free to live as an ordinary man. In his reverie, he marries Mary Magdalene, has children, grows old. But it is clear in the film that this hallucination is sent to him by Satan, at the time of his greatest weakness, to tempt him. And in the hallucination itself, in the film's most absorbing scene, an elderly Jesus is reproached by his aging apostles for having abandoned his mission. Through this imaginary conversation, Jesus finds the strength to shake off his temptation and return to consciousness to accept his suffering, death, and resurrection.

During the hallucination, there is a very brief moment when he is seen making love with Magdalene. This scene is shot with such restraint and tact that it does not qualify in any way as a "sex scene," but instead is simply an illustration of marriage and the creation of children. Those offended by the film object to the very notion that Jesus could have, or even imagine having, sexual intercourse. But of course Christianity teaches that the union of man and wife is one of the fundamental reasons God created human beings, and to imagine that the son of God, as a man, could not encompass such thoughts within his intelligence is itself a kind of insult. Was he less than the rest of us? Was he not fully man? There is biblical precedent for such temptations. We read of the forty days and nights during which Satan tempted Christ in the desert with visions of the joys that could be his if he renounced his father. In the film, which is clearly introduced as a fiction and not as an account based on the Bible, Satan tries yet once again at the moment of Christ's greatest weakness. I do not understand why this is offensive, especially since it is not presented in a sensational way.

I see that this entire review has been preoccupied with replying to the attacks of the film's critics, with discussing the issues, rather than with reviewing *The Last Temptation of Christ* as a motion picture. Perhaps that is an interesting proof of the film's worth. Here is a film that engaged me on the subject of Christ's dual nature, that caused me to think about the mystery of a being who could be both God and man. I cannot think of another film on a religious subject that has challenged me more fully. The film has offended those whose ideas about God and man it does not reflect. But then, so did Jesus.

Scorsese's *Last Temptation*

JULY 24, 1988

Why is it that censors always seem to attack the serious works of art, and ignore the trivial ones? Why is it that religious controversies have swirled around two films in recent years — Martin Scorsese's *The Last Temptation of Christ* and Jean-Luc Godard's *Hail, Mary* — while uncounted hundreds of other films have opened and closed unremarked, despite the fact that they reject the teachings of any known religious tradition?

I believe it is because self-appointed censors fear only those films that might make people think. They aren't concerned about escapist entertainment, even when, as in the case of the *Friday the 13th* films, they contain a moral view that is pagan at best and Satanist at worst. But let a film dare to consider the implications of the teaching that Jesus was born both God and man, and they start circulating their petitions and organizing their picket lines.

I have not seen Scorsese's new film, but that does not put me at a disadvantage, because those who would ban it have not seen it, either. They have read a ten-year-old version of the screenplay, have been offended by scenes that Scorsese has said are not in his film, and have mounted a national campaign to prevent Universal Pictures from even releasing the movie.

According to those who have seen *The Last Temptation of Christ*, the scenes likely to cause controversy occur while Jesus is on the cross, and has a hallucination imagining that he might have married

Mary Magdalene and led the normal life of a man. He rejects this temptation. But some religious groups are upset that a movie could even suggest that Christ could have such thoughts. One California broadcaster recently suggested that the film is so sacrilegious that it might inspire divine wrath.

I doubt it. In the most simple of Christian terms, God created man as a fallible being, and he choose to make his son both God and man. Christ would not have been man if he had not possessed the potential to experience the full range of human weaknesses, and he would not have been God if he had not been able to overcome them. To show the process by which he overcame temptation seems to me like an act of devotion, not blasphemy. But those who would suppress *The Last Temptation of Christ* are uncomfortable with this reasoning. They reject the notion that a film should depict a tempted Christ, even one who overcomes temptation.

If I were a theologian, I might be tempted myself—tempted to suggest that these censors are themselves committing heresy, by attempting to fashion an image of Christ that denies his manhood. But I am not a theologian, I am a journalist, and I suspect that at least some of the would-be censors have succumbed to the universal temptation to do other people's thinking for them.

In *Hail, Mary*, Christ was seen as a modern-day gas-station attendant, and some people found that blasphemous, although it was an honest job and more common today than carpentry. Recently the Bravo cable channel cancelled a scheduled showing of the film, in reaction to a handful of protests. In *The Last Temptation of Christ*, Jesus is seen as a man who is capable of knowing human desires and feelings, and struggling with them. Jean-Luc Godard, who made *Hail, Mary*, is a man of unannounced religious beliefs, if any. Martin Scorsese has been known for some time as a filmmaker more interested in issues of good and evil than any of his contemporaries. He is also, I believe, the greatest living American film director, and in his seriousness one of the few who deserves comparison with the great Swedish moralist Ingmar Bergman.

If you will go back and look at his work (something I doubt the censors will find time to do), you will find that *The Last Temptation of Christ* echoes a theme that is present in all of his films, even his first one, *Who's That Knocking at My Door* (1967). In that film, a guilt-ridden young Italian Catholic from New York falls in love with a young woman, but is unable to have anything more to do with her after he discovers she had once been raped. He is unable to reconcile his image of her purity with the fact that she exists in a sinful world, and has been an innocent victim of it. The same self-torture is undergone by the boxer in Scorsese's *Raging Bull*, who is driven mad with jealousy over his young wife. He is attracted to her sexuality, yet repelled that she possesses it. The same theme turns up throughout Scorsese's career, and is obviously important to him.

(98)

In a sense, the would-be censors of *The Last Temptation of Christ* suffer from the same complex as the heroes of those Scorsese films. Just as the Robert De Niro character cannot accept the fact that his "ideal" wife is a human woman with normal ideas and feelings, so they cannot accept a Christ who is fully a man as well as fully divine.

This ambiguity towards sexuality can lead to the kinds of moral contradictions that apparently existed in the cases of Jimmy Swaggert and Jim Bakker. But both of those men have now asked for forgiveness, indicating that God can forgive any sin. If that is so, then God can certainly understand a Christ who does not sin, even though he experiences and overcomes temptation.

So what is the controversy really about? I return to my opening speculation: movies like *The Last Temptation of Christ* encourage people to think for themselves about the subject, and censors are obviously not people who are comfortable with that notion. How do I know that? Because who else would seek to prevent the actual public exhibition of a film? What other kind of mentality would be so arrogant as to assume that it knew best what we should choose to see for ourselves?

I mentioned earlier that the censors always seem to attack serious works, not trivial ones. Yet trivial films are seen by the largest audiences, and have the greatest influence. Today's typical Hollywood horror-thriller films all share the following assumptions:

1. There is no benevolent God, and evil is stronger than good.

2. Physical death is not permanent—not for the Jasons or the Freddies, who are indestructable.

3. Hope and prayer are futile, because death awaits all of the characters on the screen, except for a few survivors who will be spared so they can die in the sequel.

4. Human life is meaningless, so the scripts need never deal with the implications of death. Once a character is dead, he or she is forgotten as the plot marches on.

I have seen dozens of movies in recent years that reflect those assumptions, which I believe to be profoundly nihilistic. Films with those values are the weekly fodder of American teenagers going to the movies or renting videos. Are they likely to be corrupted by a film in which Christ is depicted as a moral being who must make choices, and who resists temptation and makes the right ones? Not likely. In fact, they are not likely to even see it, not when a movie is playing right down the street that embraces doom.

Do I advocate censoring the nihilistic horror films? Not at all. I am quaint enough to trust that, in the long run, people will find their own values and make up their own minds. The only thing that can prevent that process is thought control, in which self-appointed moralists assume the right to decide what we can see and, by implication, what we should think. There is, I believe, a temptation the censors should honestly ask themselves if they have yielded to. It is the temptation to commit the sin of pride.

The Last Temptation of Christ

A RECONSIDERATION

Reading my 1988 review of *The Last Temptation of Christ*, I find it is more concerned with theology than cinema. It is hardly a movie review at all. It must have driven Scorsese crazy to read many similar reviews, in which critics appointed themselves arbiters of the manhood or godliness of Jesus Christ, and scarcely mentioned the direction, the writing, the acting, the images, or Peter Gabriel's harsh, mournful music. Or perhaps Scorsese understood. It is useful to remember the temper of the time. The film was the target of a firestorm of wrath from the Christian right, who accused Scorsese of blasphemy and worse. It had earlier been pulled from the MGM production schedule after the United Artists theater chain flat-out refused to book it. After Universal reactivated the project, at a much smaller budget, Scorsese was targeted by death threats and the jeremiads of TV evangelists.

On vacation in London, I was invited to preview the film at a private screening for my eyes only on Wardour Street. This was not a perk. It was a security measure. I was begged not to tell anyone the title of the movie I had seen, or even to mention that a print was in England. Stopping in New York on the way home, I was directed to a pay phone on Madison Avenue, called the number I was given, and followed instructions to the townhouse where Scorsese was living. I was greeted at the door by a security guard. Upstairs in his living room, Scorsese and I had coffee in front of a big bookcase filled mostly with classics. "I've joined the Folio Society," he said. "I'm doing a lot of reading these days. I don't go out much."

Under the circumstances, perhaps it was inevitable that my review involved a defense of the film against charges of heresy. That both Scorsese and I had attended Catholic schools, and fell easily into the language of religion classes, only encouraged me. We have spoken often about Catholicism, which in pre–Vatican II days was a seductive labyrinth of logic, ritual, vision, and guilt. Pauline Kael felt the most creative American directors of the 1970s (she listed Scorsese, Altman, and Coppola) benefited from being raised within that traditional Roman Catholic imagery. Scorsese's frequent writing partner Paul Schrader grew up in a no less intense Calvinist environment. To Scorsese's image in *Mean Streets* of Charlie holding his hand over a candle flame and imagining the fires of hell, we can add Schrader's mother stabbing him with a pin and telling him hell was a million times worse and it never ended.

But all of that theological debate was twenty years ago, and now my focus should be on the film itself, as it should always have been. Watching it again, I realized it was Scorsese's first film shot largely outdoors since *Boxcar Bertha* (1972). He is a filmmaker of the city, of bars, clubs, bedrooms, kitchens, night clubs, boxing rings, pool halls, and taxis. On location in Morocco, he found desert vistas to challenge *Lawrence of Arabia*, and vast, hostile expanses of hard soil, distant mountains, and struggling vegetation. The sun there is merciless. What image more starkly evokes hell than the one where Christ stands in the middle of a pockmarked landscape and damaged men crawl up out of holes and caves? This is an Old Testament land, not hospitable to the message of love and forgiveness.

The character of Christ himself is radically different from most previous film portraits, although it has some kinship with the Christ in Pasolini's *The Gospel according to St. Matthew* (1964). He is a weary, self-doubting man, not always willing to carry the souls of man on his shoulders. There are many times when he seems not to know or believe he is the son of God, and when he does, he uses that knowledge as a reason to rebuke his mother and the memory of Joseph. He berates and hectors his followers, and confides mostly in Judas, who is radically recast in this story as a good man who is only following instructions. The film follows the bold revisionism of Nikos Kazantzakis, whose novel was placed on the church's index of forbidden books.

The fact is, the film is indeed technically blasphemous. I have been persuaded of this by a thoughtful essay by the critic Steven D. Greydanus of the *National Catholic Register,* a mainstream writer who simply and concisely explains why. But I have no desire to return to theology. I mention this only to suggest that a film can be blasphemous, or anything else that the director desires, and we should only hope that it be as good as the filmmaker can make it, and convincing in its interior purpose. Certainly useful things can be said about Jesus Christ by presenting him in a non-orthodox way. There is a long tradition of such revisionism, notably in D. H. Lawrence's novel *The Man Who Died*, where Jesus returns from the dead, travels into Egypt, and has a sexual relationship with a priestess. And there is the foolishness of *The Da Vinci Code*. The story by Kazantzakis, Scorsese, and Schrader grapples with the central mystery of Jesus, that he was both God and man, and uses the freedom of fiction to explore the implications of such a paradox.

In the title role, Willem Dafoe creates a man who is the embodiment of dutiful masochism. Whether he is right or wrong about his divinity, he is prepared to pay the price, and that kind of faith is more courageous than certainty would be. Even in the last half of the film, when he begins performing miracles, he seems almost an onlooker at his own accomplishments, taking little joy in them. A key shot, I think, is when Michael Ballhaus's camera pushes past Jesus into the sepulcher of the dead Lazarus. It is black inside, contrasted with the blinding sun, and then blacker and blacker until the whole screen is filled with blackness, and held for a few seconds. I take this as an emblem of Jesus's experience of his miracles, during which he is reaching into an unknowable and frightening void.

Judas is the film's other vivid character, played by Harvey Keitel as, in a sense, Christ's manager. He does strategy, issues ultimatums, is the closest friend of Jesus. If the story commits sacrilege in suggesting

Judas was doing his duty by betraying Christ, at least in explaining that action it frees him for his greater degree of intimacy. Jesus does not seem to have close relationships with any of the other disciples, who he seems to believe will follow along of their own accord. He is closer, I suppose, with Mary Magdalene, but their conversations seem guarded or cryptic, she more open than he. Scorsese makes no attempt to suggest Christ's charisma, assuming it as a given.

What all of these decisions do is focus attention on Christ's inner struggle more than his worldly role. I think that's the intent. This is not the story of Jesus as a leader of men but as a follower of his own inner voices. More than one character says he is mad. So he would be, apart from the assumption that he is right about the voices. Everything leads up to the incendiary climactic scenes when the kind little angel takes him down from the cross, kisses his wounds, and leads him to the world of ordinary men, who marry, have children, grow old. Surely a man of Christ's intelligence should recognize this as a wile of Satan. That he does not, that he indulges and continues within the hallucination, or dream, or whatever it is, shows his willingness to do so. This is known (forgive me more theology) as harboring a sinful thought. Christ succumbs to the temptation more readily than he should, although apparently it is his subconscious that summons the disciples to his deathbed, and has them demonstrate what he really already knows: that the angel is Satan.

I am left after the film with the conviction that, Kazantzakis and Schrader aside, it is as much about Scorsese as about Christ. In his films he performs miracles, but for years could be heard to despair that each film would be his last. The Catholic Church was for him like a heavenly father to whom he had a duty, although he did not always fulfill it. These speculations about him may be wild and unfounded, ideas I am taking to him rather than finding in him, but particularly during his earlier years I believe the church played a larger role in his inner life than was generally realized. Talking with me about one of his divorces, he told me, "I am living in sin, and I will go to hell because of it." I asked him if he really, truly believed that. "Yes," he said, "I do."

What makes *The Last Temptation of Christ* one of his great films is not that it is true about Jesus but that it is true about Scorsese. Like count-less others, he has found aspects of the Christ story that speak to him; he found them in the original novel, which is why he felt compelled to film it, and he focused on those passages that, in a book, he would have underlined. This is the Jesus of his two most autobiographical characters, Charlie in *Mean Streets* and J. R. in *Who's That Knocking at My Door*. Both of those characters were played by Keitel. Interesting that he choose Keitel, this time, to play Judas. Perhaps Judas is Scorsese's autobiographical character in *The Last Temptation of Christ*. Certainly not the Messiah, but the mortal man walking beside him, worrying about him, lecturing him, wanting him to be better, threatening him, confiding in him, prepared to betray him if he must. Christ is the film, and Judas is the director.

New York Stories: "Life Lessons"

MARCH 3, 1989

New York Stories is an anthology—a gathering of short films by Martin Scorsese, Francis Ford Coppola, and Woody Allen, all three taking New York City as the backdrop, although the Scorsese and Allen films could have been set in many big cities. Anthologies were popular in the 1940s (*Trio*; *Quartet*) and in the 1960s (*Boccacio 70*; *Yesterday, Today and Tomorrow*) but have fallen on hard times recently, perhaps because, in an age of megaproductions, the movie industry is not interested in short stories.

Of the three films, the only really successful one is "Life Lessons," the Scorsese story of a middle-age painter and his young, discontented girlfriend . . .

Although Scorsese's film begins before the director is identified, there's not a moment's doubt whose work it is. His restless nature is obvious from the first shots. Nestor Almendros's camera moves almost unceasingly throughout the film, and most of the cuts are on movement, so that we rarely get the feeling that there is anything still and contented in the soul of his hero.

This is a man named Lionel Dobie (Nick Nolte), a large, shaggy painter who works in a loft, weaving back and forth in front of his canvas like a boxer, painting to very loud rock and roll. He uses a garbage can lid as a palette, and there is a voluptuous scene in which the camera follows his brush back and forth from paint to canvas.

Dobie lives with a twenty-two-year-old woman (Rosanna Arquette), whose bedroom is perched on a balcony below the ceiling. She wants to leave him, and in the long reaches of the night he looks up sometimes at her bedroom window like a middle-age Romeo who has lost his Juliet.

Dobie is verbally clever but emotionally uncertain. In his attempts to keep the woman, he flatters her, makes promises of reform, explains that he can help her career, says he needs her. She has some canvasses of her own around the studio—anemic, unfocused, skeletal figures on muddy backgrounds—and she wants to know if she will ever be any good. But the one compromise Dobie cannot bring himself to make is to lie about the quality of a painting.

The film moves easily in the New York art world of dealers and openings, seeing and being seen. The girl has a crush on a young "performance artist," and Dobie takes her to his show, which consists of bad stand-up comedy and flashing searchlights in an abandoned subway station. Dobie's gesture is intended to show he understands her, but in fact he has contempt for the performer ("you sing, you dance, you act—what's performance art?"). And the girl, uncertain what she wants but certain that she must escape his smothering possessiveness, drifts away.

"Life Lessons" seems the longest of these short films, because it has the greatest density, the most to say. It is not about love. It is about how the girl is first attracted by Dobie's power, then grows restless because there is no role in it for her, except as cheerleader and sex trophy. It is about how Dobie really does have deep loneliness and need, but that it does not require this woman to satisfy them; he is so needy, any woman will do. The movie never steps wrong until the final scene, which Scorsese continues for just a few lines too many.

Dobie sees another young woman at a party. She admires him. His eyes light up. The scene could have ended there; everything else is where we came in.

[Remainder of review omitted.]

Martin Scorsese and His "New York" Story

MARCH 5, 1989

"Before I was introduced to Catholicism," Martin Scorsese was explaining, "I wanted to be a painter. Painting was my first great love."

Before? But weren't you raised as a Catholic?

"Well, my parents are Catholics, but Italians are pagans. I took up Catholicism on my own. They were actually a little disappointed when I was going to be a priest. But before that, it was painting. I had asthma, I couldn't run around or anything, so I would paint watercolors. I was always fascinated by the richness of the color, the texture. That's what got me. And when I saw *Lust for Life*, all the close-ups of the paintings by Van Gogh, my God . . ."

You could imagine Scorsese sitting in a movie theater and looking at *Lust for Life* and vibrating with excitement, because he was vibrating now, remembering it. We were sitting in front of a glass wall that opened onto a panorama of New York, seventy-five floors below, spread out like a postcard, but in his mind, Scorsese was seeing paint on canvas.

"I don't think I could have ever been a painter, because I'm so allergic. Even on this picture, the paint pots were uncovered for the two weeks we were shooting in that loft, and I had a terrible time."

But he stuck it out, and made a film that expresses the passion of a painter in action, actually at work, better than any other film I've seen. He did it in under forty minutes, too, in "Life Lessons," his segment of the new movie *New York Stories*, a trilogy of short films by Woody Allen, Francis Coppola, and himself. (It opened Friday in many cities.)

The Scorsese contribution is generally agreed to be the best of the three segments, starring Nick Nolte as an artist who is professionally successful but emotionally needy, and Rosanna Arquette as the latest in what we suspect has been a long series of beautiful young "assistants" who have come to share the room up on the balcony in his loft, and study his lessons in life.

The most dramatic sequence in the movie has Nolte in a frenzy of creation, his oils squeezed out in big rich gobs of color on the garbage-can lid he uses as a palette. Dancing back and forth in front of his canvas, Nolte paints at a frenzied pace while Bob Dylan's "Like a Rolling Stone" booms from a ghetto blaster and the paint goes on in great, thick, sensuous, tactile globs and sweeps and exclamations. He paints so fast, we can't tell if he's mixing the colors on the palette or on the canvas, and the camera darts back and forth, inches from the painter's hand, following the progress of the work with panting intensity.

"I wanted to be really physical," Scorsese said. "I wanted the paint all over him, over his glasses, his hands, his shoes, his $16,000 watch."

If you watch "Life Lessons" while observing the camera work as carefully as the story, you'll find the same passion in Scorsese's visuals that he finds in the painting style of his hero. Nestor Almendros's camera rarely pauses throughout the movie. He and Scorsese cut from one movement to another, restlessly but with smooth precision, the joy of the artist expressed by the steady hand of the craftsman. There is a scene where Nolte has slammed a door to trap Arquette in a restroom, during a fight they're having at an art opening. Some would-be patrons come to talk to Nolte, and the camera starts the next shot close on the door as Arquette bursts from it, then pulls back to include Nolte and then pans left and pulls out to bring the whole scene together, having moved from a one-shot to a two-shot to the complete picture in a way that tells a little story of its own: her anger, his embarrassment, their comprehension.

"I always wonder about moving the camera the way I like to move it," Scorsese was saying. "And in this picture, I use the iris shot a lot. (Iris shots, an old-fashioned optical effect much beloved by D. W. Griffith, begin or end with a small circle on the screen around a crucial detail.) It's not invisible filmmaking. You see the hand of the director. One of the funniest moments, to me, is when he's in the girl's bedroom, obsessed by her, and we use an iris to close in on just her foot. He is in love with every part of her body. And she goes, 'You're nuts!' and pulls her foot away at the same time we zoom out and pull the iris out, and it cuts to her, almost as if she knew her foot was in his iris."

Scorsese laughed. Zoe, his poodle, became alarmed and jumped out of his lap and began running in circles, barking. Then she jumped back in his lap for reassurance.

"It drives her crazy, living on the seventy-fifth floor," he said. "She barks at the street and it has absolutely no effect."

In addition to the view, the room was furnished with a large sectional sofa, a 16 mm movie projector, a projection TV equipped with tape and LaserVision, and a big pull-down screen on the wall. This is the man who composed one of the fight sequences in *Raging Bull* by breaking down Hitchcock's shower scene in *Psycho*, shot by shot, and then rebuilding it in a boxing ring.

"I wonder. I always wonder," he said. "Maybe if you live long enough and you see these movies years later, it's going to seem self-conscious, moving the camera that way. But it's fun. And it gives an edge to the picture. When he looks up at that room, and the camera comes in low, and then we see his face, and he looks up, and then he goes up into that room, it's kind of interesting to me. It gives an edge of danger that's inherent in every relationship. Especially two people in a room together."

Do you plan every shot in a movie before you start shooting?

"Oh, yeah. I draw the shots. Every one of them. On *The Last Temptation of Christ*, the first time around at Paramount in 1983, I got two-thirds of the way through the script, and that's when the picture was canceled. So for a few years I had all the drawings in a drawer, and when the picture was started again, I finished the last third and revamped the first part. And with a picture on a low budget, like that one, what the drawings tell me is, there are at least three angles I have to get to make this scene work, and then there are four more that if we have the time, it will be a blessing. I was really, really paring away. Where it was really crucial was in the crucifixion scene. We had to get seventy setups in three days. And we figured, OK, the sun comes up at 7:00, we can start shooting at 7:10, the sun goes down at 4:30, we can shoot until 5:00 if we pump enough artificial light in for some close-ups."

Scorsese's fellow professionals admired his work on *Last Temptation* enough to nominate him in the best director category for this year's Academy Awards, but when I mentioned that, he said a nomination really should have gone to his production and set-design people, for recreating the biblical world in less than seven weeks.

"Why I got the nomination, I think, is that a lot of the people who vote in the director's category were thinking, what if I have to make a picture I'm going to get flak about . . ."

Scorsese has by now weathered last summer's storm over *Last Temptation*, which has been thoroughly upstaged by the controversy over *The Satanic Verses*, and he will start shooting his next feature, *Wiseguy*, on April 1. Based on the book by Nicholas Pileggi, it's an insider look at what he calls a "Mafia tragedy."

"It's a nostalgia piece from the early 1960s when I grew up," he said. "Where I grew up, the people around me, a lot of them were connected that way. To me, they were cousins, or they were friends, they were friends of my father. I would eat at their house, they were like family, it was just life. There was no moral judgment, because we weren't aware of a great deal of what they actually did when they left the block—when they went around the corner, or up on the roof, or to Brooklyn. When a gangster has to kill another gangster, it's a tragedy, because these people are like family.

"What people don't understand is that a gangster's job is not to go around killing people. A gangster's job is to make money. That's the main thing. Everyone makes a lot of money. Someone gets out of line, and it ruins making the money for everybody, and he's got to go. It's simple. It just happens to be their line of work. I can't make a picture where they're bad guys. They can't be bad guys to me."

Mean Streets (1973), the first film that won wide attention for both Scorsese and Robert De Niro, his favorite actor, was a story about young punk gangsters trying to get a foot on the first rung of the Mafia ladder. It was inspired, Scorsese has always said, by the people he knew and observed when he was a sickly kid growing up in the 1950s and 1960s in New York's Little Italy. He still talks about that time and place with a wonderment, mixed with humor. "The thing is," he said, "it was all geographical. The Neapolitans, when they came over, somehow they wound up on Mulberry Street. So Mulberry Street became Little Naples. The same thing happened with Elizabeth Street and the Sicilians. But Naples is one city, and Sicily is a lot of little towns, and very often my mother would say, 'Oh, yeah, he married so-and-so, but she was a different nationality.' A different village, she's talking about.

"They all had their own saints. We preferred our own little saints. Saint Gennaro was very rich, he had a big feast day, they blocked off lots of streets, but the Sicilian saints were very poor. St. Ciro's feast only took up half a block. That was it. St. Rocca was another one, on Mott Street. Half a block. All the old Italian women would walk with wax effigies of the parts of their bodies they had diseases on. They'd walk in procession, holding breasts, holding a leg."

Who made the wax effigies?

"Some people in Brooklyn. It's a lost trade."

The thing about the Mafia, he said, was that it was also a kind of local government. The new arrivals from Italy did not trust the police there, and so they had no reason to trust the Irish police in New York. They took their problems to the don.

"That's where you get the mythology of Don Corleone. Even Lucky Luciano, you mention his name today, the old timers hold him in the greatest reverence. He's the man who was responsible for the Night of the Sicilian Vespers, in the early 1930s, in which on one night, all the old Moustache Petes were killed. This was a slaughter. But it was business. It wasn't personal. If you had personal dealings with Luciano, he was great. Some of those old guys, they're still alive. I remember when we were all kids, our mothers would send us out to get haircuts, and we would have to wait all day on the bench in the barber shop. Just when it was our turn, another one of the guys would walk in and ask, 'You got anybody waiting?' And the barber would always say, 'Only the kids. Take a chair.'"

Part 3 **Establishing**

Introduction

GoodFellas, one of Scorsese's very best films, is the flowering of *Who's That Knocking at My Door* and *Mean Streets*, showing essentially similar characters now growing to maturity and power. The sound track once again establishes the period and mood with pop songs—with more expensive music rights, of course, than he could afford for *Knocking*. It was based on a book by Nicholas Pileggi and a screenplay by Pileggi and Scorsese, and illustrated once again Scorsese's ability to find stories personal to him in work by others.

It begins with voiceover narration echoing the story I and everyone he knew had heard from Scorsese, about the asthmatic kid sitting in the window, watching the gangsters coming and going from the social club across the street. They became a powerful population in his imagination, with their expensive cars and clothes and women, moving through areas of the city where everyone knew exactly who they were and never said so. Scorsese said that one of his earliest influences was Mel Brooks; if Brooks taught him "It's fun to be the king," *GoodFellas* opens by declaring "It's fun to be a gangster."

That narration recalls: "Even before I first wandered into the cabstand for an after-school job, I knew I wanted to be a part of them. It was there that I knew that I belonged. To me, it meant being somebody in a neighborhood that was full of nobodies. They weren't like anybody else. I mean, they did whatever they wanted. They double-parked in front of a hydrant and nobody ever gave them a ticket. In the summer when they played cards all night, nobody ever called the cops."

In a sense, the film is Scorsese's autobiography in an alternate universe, one in which he did not have the same parents or the same talents but had the same hungers and was seduced by the lifestyles of the most powerful and glamorous men in Little Italy. It is all wonderment and fun, the selling of stolen goods, the camaraderie of the organization, until it turns to drugs and turns bad. One senses it is the most accurate portrayal of daily life in the Mafia, not romanticized and elevated to ritual as in *The Godfather*, but seen at ground level. The most revealing scene may be the one where the guys with the body in the trunk of their car visit the house of Tommy (Joe Pesci) at midnight, to borrow a knife and a shovel from his mother. Why? Because they hit a deer? Only a Mafia mother (played by Catherine Scorsese) would believe that, and insist on feeding them before they went out again.

I discuss the film at greater length in an essay after the review, and again in part 6. Its very structure mirrors its content, with the easygoing, everything-flowing rhythms of the opening scenes quickening to a tempo of paranoia toward the end. It stands with *Raging Bull* and *Taxi Driver* at the summit of his work.

Cape Fear is a more problematic film, although Scorsese finds room in his remake of J. Lee Thompson's 1962 thriller to explore some of his obsessions. It had a $35 million budget, Steven Spielberg as executive producer, and Spielberg's confederates Kathleen Kennedy and Frank Marshall as co-producers, as well as, on the Scorsese side, his then-wife Barbara De Fina and himself as producers. It was made by Spielberg's Amblin Entertainment, and Spielberg himself had been set to direct, before recruiting Scorsese, who was not eager to join on. But it would be Scorsese's largest budget, and Spielberg suggested it might open his doors to more generous Hollywood financing.

Now indulge me in this fantasy. If we imagine the young Marty Scorsese with his nose pressed against a window, watching the Good-Fellas coming and going in their omnipotence, can we imagine the real Scorsese, always hustling for funds, denied the Oscar for best director, his nose pressed against a window, watching the coming and going of a Hollywood giant like Spielberg? There is nothing in Scorsese's portfolio to suggest he enjoyed living hand-to-mouth with independent productions, and everything to show his admiration for the studio golden age.

Cape Fear is a good film, but it is not really a Scorsese film. There is nothing in his life to draw him toward a story set in southern Florida, with the drawling redneck Max Cady (De Niro) and the family man lawyer (Nick Nolte). The most Scorsesian character may be Nolte's daughter, played by Juliette Lewis, who is drawn to Cady precisely because of his danger. Lewis was eighteen when she made the film and Cathy Moriarty was nineteen when she made *Raging Bull*; from both actresses, Scorsese drew performances that transcended all their previous work.

Scorsese is a fan of film noir, but J. Lee Thompson was perhaps not first on his list of admired directors, nor was the original *Cape Fear* a transcendent masterpiece. (Robert Mitchum, who played the original Max Cady, appeared in a smaller role for Scorsese and was said to fear comparison with De Niro's Cady, but he never had to decide, because he never saw either film.)

Scorsese's next film, *The Age of Innocence*, about New York high society circa 1870, was based on the novel by Henry James's friend and contemporary Edith Wharton, and seems at first to look even less like Scorsese's kind of material. But not at all. He was given the novel by his friend Jay Cocks, the former film critic for *Time*, who would eventually write the screenplay. Scorsese told me: "In 1980, Jay gave me *The Age of Innocence* and said, 'When you do your costume piece, when you do your romance, this is you.' Not meaning, of course, that I'm Archer or Ellen, whatever. It was the spirit of it—the spirit of the exquisite romantic pain. The idea that the mere touching of a woman's hand would suffice. The idea that seeing her across the room would keep him alive for another year. That's something I guess that is part of me. He knew me, by that time, fairly well."

Perhaps Cocks also noticed, right there in plain view, the fundamental Madonna-whore theme: the hero, Newland Archer, torn between

(117)

the flawless high-society heroine and the divorced, therefore scandalous, woman recently returned from Europe. What is remarkable about the film is the subtlety with which Scorsese portrays a society where the smallest gesture, the slightest intonation, can be violence in coded terms. The film illuminates one like *GoodFellas* in showing that in a different milieu, in different accents, in a different ethnic group, the same subtlety of intonations and gestures is observed; notice the rituals and rules by which the Joe Pesci character first offends, then is punished.

An interview with Scorsese and a longer essay about the film come later in this book. The elegant *Age of Innocence* seems as much an oddity as *Kundun* in Scorsese's filmography, but proceeds directly from his obsessions, while the tough-guy crime film *Cape Fear* does not.

Casino, a film about the Mafia's enterprises in Las Vegas, was not as well-received as *GoodFellas*, but I believe it is much better than it has sometimes been given credit for. It's another biopic, based on another book by Nicholas Pileggi, another screenplay by Pileggi and Scorsese, inspired by a real life. Frank "Lefty" Rosenthal was the mob's brilliant number cruncher in Vegas, the man who worked out the odds. He is called "Ace" Rothstein in the movie, but there is a real Rosenthal, and I have seen him dining alone at lunch, as he often does, at Joe's Stone Crab in Miami Beach.

The underlying pattern is again of an outsider made an insider, glorying in his power and wealth, his effortless influence, then brought to ruin by his jealousy about a woman. These themes circle so needfully through the work of Scorsese that they function almost as proof of the auteur theory. His stories came from many places, but they are all shaped into personal statements.

Both *Casino* and *GoodFellas* fascinate us with their insider details. Pileggi is a good reporter, and observes casino security men disabling a card-counter with a stun gun, carrying him away on a stretcher as a "heart attack victim," then offering him appalling punishment in a back room. Or notice too the addressing of such details as: if you have stolen from a casino real, physical cash, coins and dollars, how do you get it off the premises?

In 1995, the same year *Casino* was released, Scorsese released his four-hour documentary *A Personal Journey with Martin Scorsese through American Movies*. One cannot imagine another American director at full flood pausing to make such an ambitious work pro bono. In Europe, a Bertrand Tavernier, perhaps. No scholar could have taken the "personal journey" more knowledgably, and in it we can see his love for the very nature of film. I know of no other director so important, with work so personal and original, who has a greater depth of knowledge about the cinema.

GoodFellas

SEPTEMBER 21, 1990

There really are guys like this. I've seen them across restaurants and I've met them on movie sets, where they carefully explain that they are retired and are acting as technical consultants. They make their living as criminals, and often the service they provide is that they will not hurt you if you pay them. These days there is a certain guarded nostalgia for their brand of organized crime, because at least the mob would make a deal with you for your life, and not just kill you casually, out of impatience or a need for drugs.

Martin Scorsese's *GoodFellas* is a movie based on the true story of a midlevel professional criminal named Henry Hill, whose only ambition, from childhood on, was to be a member of the outfit. We see him with his face at the window, looking across the street at the neighborhood Mafiosi, who drove the big cars and got the good-looking women and never had to worry about the cops when they decided to hold a party late at night. One day the kid goes across the street and volunteers to help out, and before long he's selling stolen cigarettes at a factory gate and not long after that the doorman at the Copacabana knows his name.

For many years, it was not a bad life. The rewards were great. The only thing you could complain about was the work. There is a strange, confused evening in Hill's life when some kidding around in a bar leads to a murder, and the guy who gets killed is a "made man"—a man you do not touch lightly, because he has the mob behind him—and the body needs to be hidden quickly, and then later it needs to be moved, messily. This kind of work is bothersome. It fills the soul with guilt and the heart with dread, and before long Henry Hill is walking around as if there's a lead weight in his stomach.

But the movie takes its time to get to that point, and I have never seen a crime movie that seems so sure of its subject matter. There must have been a lot of retired technical consultants hanging around. Henry Hill, who is now an anonymous refugee within the federal government's witness protection program, told this life story to the journalist Nicholas Pileggi, who put it into the best seller *Wiseguy*, and now Pileggi and Scorsese have written the screenplay, which also benefits from Scorsese's firsthand observations of the Mafia while he was a kid with his face in the window, watching the guys across the street.

Scorsese is in love with the details of his story, including the Mafia don who never, ever talked on the telephone, and held all of his business meetings in the open air. Or the way some guys with a body in the car trunk will stop by to borrow a carving knife from one of their mothers, who will feed them pasta and believe them when they explain that they got blood on their suits when their car hit a deer. Everything in this movie reverberates with familiarity; the actors even inhabit the scenes as if nobody had to explain anything to them.

GoodFellas is an epic on the scale of *The Godfather*, and it uses its expansive running time to develop a real feeling for the way a lifetime develops almost by chance at first, and then sets its fateful course. Because we see mostly through the eyes of Henry Hill (Ray Liotta), characters swim in and out of focus; the character of Jimmy Conway (Robert De Niro), for example, is shadowy in the earlier passages of the film, and then takes on a central importance. And then there's Tommy DeVito (Joe Pesci), always on the outside looking in, glorying in his fleeting moments of power, laughing too loudly, slapping backs with too much familiarity, pursued by the demon of a raging anger that can flash out of control in a second. His final scene in this movie is one of the greatest moments of sudden realization I have ever seen; the development, the buildup, and the payoff are handled by Scorsese with the skill of a great tragedian.

GoodFellas isn't a myth-making movie, like *The Godfather*. It's about ordinary people who get trapped inside the hermetic world of the mob, whose values get worn away because they never meet anyone to disagree with them. One of the most interesting characters in the movie is Henry Hill's wife, Karen (Lorraine Bracco), who is Jewish and comes from outside his world. He's an outsider himself—he's half Irish, half Italian, and so will never truly be allowed on the inside—but she's so far outside that at first she doesn't even realize what she's in for. She doesn't even seem to know what Henry does for a living, and when she finds out, she doesn't want to deal with it. She is the co-narrator of the film, as if it were a documentary, and she talks about how she never goes anywhere or does anything except in the company of other mob wives. Finally she gets to the point where she's proud of her husband for being willing to go out and steal to support his family, instead of just sitting around like a lot of guys.

The parabola of *GoodFellas* is from the era of "good crimes," like stealing cigarettes and booze and running prostitution and making book, to bad crimes involving dope. The godfather in the movie (Paul Sorvino) warns Henry Hill about getting involved with dope, but it's not because he disapproves of narcotics (like Brando's Don Corleone), it's because he seems to sense that dope will spell trouble for the mob, will unleash street anarchy and bring in an undisciplined element. What eventually happens is that Hill makes a lot of money with cocaine but gets hooked on it as well, and eventually spirals down into the exhausted paranoia that proves to be his undoing.

Throbbing beneath the surface of *GoodFellas*, providing the magnet that pulls the plot along, are the great emotions in Hill's makeup: a lust for recognition, and a fear of powerlessness and guilt. He loves it when the head waiters know his name, but he doesn't really have the stuff to be a great villain—he isn't brave or heartless enough—and so when he does bad things, he feels bad afterwards. He begins to hate himself. And yet he cannot hate the things he covets. He wants the prizes, but he doesn't want to pay for the tickets.

And it is there, on the crux of that paradox, that the movie becomes Scorsese's metaphor for so many modern lives. He doesn't parallel the mob with corporations, or turn it into some kind of grotesque underworld version of yuppie culture. Nothing is that simple. He simply uses organized crime as an arena for a story about a man who likes material things so much that he sells his own soul to buy them— compromises his principles, betrays his friends, abandons his family, and finally even loses contact with himself. And the horror of the film is that, at the end, the man's principal regret is that he doesn't have any more soul to sell.

Why *GoodFellas* was the Best Film of 1990

FROM THE 1992 EDITION OF ROGER EBERT'S *MOVIE HOME COMPANION*

For two days after I saw Martin Scorsese's new film, *GoodFellas*, the mood of the characters lingered within me, refusing to leave. It was a mood of guilt and regret, of quick stupid decisions leading to wasted lifetimes, of loyalty turned into betrayal. Yet at the same time there was an element of furtive nostalgia, for bad times that shouldn't be missed, but were.

Most films, even great ones, evaporate like mist once you've returned to the real world; they leave memories behind, but their reality fades fairly quickly. Not this film, which shows America's finest filmmaker at the peak of his form. No finer film has ever been made about organized crime—not even *The Godfather*, although the two works are not really comparable.

GoodFellas is a memoir of life in the Mafia, narrated in the first person by Henry Hill (Ray Liotta), an Irish Italian kid whose only ambition, from his earliest teens, was to be a "wiseguy," a Mafioso. There is also narration by Karen, the Jewish girl (Lorraine Bracco) who married him, and who discovered that her entire social life was suddenly inside the Mafia; mob wives never went anywhere or talked to anyone who was not part of that world, and eventually, she says, the values of the Mafia came to seem like normal values. She was even proud of her husband for not lying around the house all day, for having the energy and daring to go out and steal for a living.

There is a real Henry Hill, who disappeared into the anonymity of the federal government's witness protection program, and who over a period of four years told everything he knew about the mob to the reporter Nicholas Pileggi, whose *Wiseguy* was a best-seller. The screenplay by Pileggi and Scorsese distills those memories into a fiction that sometimes plays like a documentary, that contains so much information and feeling about the Mafia that finally it creates the same claustrophobic feeling Hill's wife talks about: the feeling that the mob world is the real world.

Scorsese is the right director—the only director—for this material. He knows it inside out. The great formative experience of his life was growing up in New York's Little Italy as an outsider who observed everything—an asthmatic kid who couldn't play sports, whose health was too bad to allow him to lead a normal childhood, who was often overlooked but never missed a thing.

There is a passage early in the film in which young Henry Hill looks out the window of his family's apartment and observes with awe and envy the swagger of the low-level wiseguys in the social club across the street, impressed by the fact that they got girls, drove hot cars, had money, that the cops never gave them tickets, that even when their loud parties lasted all night, nobody ever called the police. That was the life he wanted to lead, the film's narrator tells us. The memory may come from Hill and may be in Pileggi's book, but the memory is also Scorsese's, and in the twenty-three years I have known him, we have never had a conversation that did not touch at some point on that central image in his vision of himself—of the kid in the window, watching the neighborhood gangsters.

Like *The Godfather*, Scorsese's *GoodFellas* is a long movie, with the space and leisure to expand and explore its themes. It isn't about any particular plot; it's about what it felt like to be in the Mafia—the good times and the bad times. At first they were mostly good times, and there is an astonishing camera movement in which the POV follows Henry and Karen on one of their first dates, to the Copacabana night club. There are people waiting on line at the door, but Henry takes her in through the service entrance, past the security guards and the off-duty waiters, down a corridor, through the kitchen, through the service area, and out into the front of the club, where a table is literally lifted into the air and placed in front of all the others so that the young couple can be in the first row for the floor show. This is power.

Karen doesn't know yet exactly what Henry does. She finds out. The method of the movie is a slow expansion through levels of the Mafia, with characters introduced casually and some of them not really developed until later in the story. We meet the don Paul Cicero (Paul Sorvino), and Jimmy "the Gent" Conway (Robert De Niro), a man who steals for the sheer love of stealing, and Tommy DeVito (Joe Pesci), a likeable guy except that his fearsome temper can explode in a second, with fatal consequences. We follow them through thirty years, at first through years of unchallenged power, then through years of decline (but they have their own kitchen in prison, and boxes of thick steaks and crates of wine), and then into betrayal and decay.

At some point the whole wonderful romance of the Mafia goes sour for Henry Hill, and that moment is when he and Jimmy and Tommy have to bury a man whom Tommy kicked almost to death in a fit of pointless rage. First they have to finish killing him (they stop at Tommy's mother's house to borrow a knife, and she feeds them dinner), then they bury him, then later they have to dig him up again. The worst part is, their victim was a "made" guy, a Mafioso who is supposed to be immune. So they are in deep, deep trouble, and this is not how Henry Hill thought it was going to be when he started out on his life's journey.

From the first shot of his first feature, *Who's That Knocking at My Door* (1967), Scorsese has loved to use popular music as a counterpoint to the dramatic moments in his films. He doesn't simply compile a sound track of golden oldies; he finds the precise sound to underline every moment, and in *GoodFellas* the popular music helps to explain the transition from early days when Henry sells stolen cigarettes to guys at a factory gate, through to the frenetic later days when he's selling cocaine in disobedience to Paul Cicero's orders, and using so much of it himself that life has become a paranoid labyrinth.

In all of his work, which has included arguably the best film of the 1970s (*Taxi Driver*) and of the 1980s (*Raging Bull*), Scorsese has never done a more compelling job of getting inside someone's head as he does in one of the concluding passages of *GoodFellas*, in which he follows one day in the life of Henry Hill, as he tries to do a cocaine deal, cook dinner for his family, placate his mistress, and deal with the suspicion that he's being followed.

This is the sequence that imprinted me so deeply with the mood of the film. It's not a straightforward narrative passage, and it has little to do with plot; it's about the feeling of walls closing in, and the guilty feeling that the walls are deserved. The counterpoint is a sense of duty, of compulsion; the drug deal must be made, but the kid brother must also be picked up, and the sauce must be stirred, and meanwhile Henry's life is careening wildly out of control.

Actors have a way of doing their best work—the work that lets us see them clearly—in a Scorsese film. Robert De Niro emerged as the best actor of his generation in *Taxi Driver*. Joe Pesci, playing De Niro's brother in *Raging Bull*, created a performance of comparable complexity. Both De Niro and Pesci are here in *GoodFellas*, essentially playing major and very challenging supporting roles to Ray Liotta and Lorraine Bracco, who establish themselves here as clearly two of our best new movie actors. Liotta was Melanie Griffith's late-arriving, disturbingly dangerous husband in *Something Wild*, and here he creates the emotional center for a movie that is not about the experience of being a Mafioso, but about the *feeling*. Bracco was the cop's wife from out in the suburbs in *Someone to Watch Over Me*, a film in which her scenes were so effective that it was with a real sense of loss that we returned to the main story. The sense of their marriage is at the heart of this film, especially in a shot where he clings to her, exhausted. They have made their lifetime commitment, and it was to the wrong life.

Many of Scorsese's best films have been poems about guilt. Think of *Mean Streets*, with the Harvey Keitel character tortured by his sexual longings, or *After Hours*, with the Griffin Dunne character involved in an accidental death and finally hunted down in the streets by a misinformed mob, or think of *The Last Temptation of Christ*, in which even Christ is permitted to doubt.

GoodFellas is about guilt more than anything else. But it is not a

(127)

straightforward morality play, in which good is established and guilt is the appropriate reaction toward evil. No, the hero of this film feels guilty for not upholding the Mafia code—guilty of the sin of betrayal. And his punishment is banishment, into the witness protection program, where nobody has a name and the headwaiter certainly doesn't know it.

What finally got to me after seeing this film—what makes it a great film—is that I understood Henry Hill's feelings. Just as his wife Karen grew so completely absorbed by the Mafia inner life that its values became her own, so did the film weave a seductive spell. It is almost possible to think, sometimes, of the characters as really being good fellows. Their camaraderie is so strong, their loyalty so unquestioned. But the laugher is strained and forced at times, and sometimes it's an effort to enjoy the party, and eventually the whole mythology comes crashing down, and then the guilt—the real guilt, the guilt a Catholic like Scorsese understands intimately—is not that they did sinful things, but that they want to do them again.

Cape Fear

NOVEMBER 13, 1991

The way he sees the character of Sam Bowden is the key to why Martin Scorsese wanted to remake the 1962 thriller *Cape Fear*. Bowden, played by Nick Nolte, is a defense attorney who is threatened by a man from his past—a rapist who has finished a fourteen-year prison sentence and wants revenge for what he believes (correctly) was a lousy defense.

In the original film, Sam Bowden was a good man trying to defend his family from a madman. In the Scorsese version, Bowden is flawed and guilty, and indeed everyone in this film is weak in one way or another, and there are no heroes. That's the Scorsese touch.

The movie, filmed near Fort Lauderdale, shows Nolte at the head of a troubled family. He and his wife (Jessica Lange) have been through counseling because of his infidelities, and now he seems to be in the opening stages of a new affair. They live in a rambling house on a lot of land, but there isn't space enough for their daughter (Juliette Lewis), who hates it when they fight and locks herself in her bedroom to brood and watch MTV. This is a family with a lot of problems even before Max Cady arrives on the scene.

Cady is played by Robert De Niro, in a role filled by Robert Mitchum in 1962. Covered with tattoos spelling out dire biblical warnings, Cady is an iron-pumping redneck who learned to read in prison ("I started with Dick, Jane, and Spot and went on to law books"). He drives into town in a Mustang convertible and offers to teach Bowden something about the law.

And soon, everywhere Bowden looks, he sees the ominous, threatening presence of Max Cady: outside a restaurant, in a movie theater, on the wall bordering his property.

But Cady is clever and stays just this side of the law; he doesn't actually trespass, and he doesn't do physical harm to Bowden.

It's almost a game with Cady to taunt Bowden to the breaking point.

Bowden goes to the cops, to a lawyer, to a private investigator, and as he seeks help we begin to realize that no one in this universe is untainted. Among the corrupt are Mitchum, as a cop who hints that the lawyer should take the law into his own hands, and Gregory Peck, as a lawyer who represents Bowden.

What we are looking at here is a film noir version of the classic Scorsese hero, who in film after film is a man tortured by guilt and the weakness of the flesh, seeking forgiveness and redemption.

And with this new version of Max Cady, Scorsese gives us not simply a bad man, but an evil one—whose whole purpose is to show Sam Bowden he's a criminal, too.

A stratum of evil underlies the whole film and is dramatized in the character of Danielle, the Bowdens' daughter, who is going on sixteen and is attracted to the menace and implied sexuality of Max Cady. It's as if she likes anybody who can bug her parents. In a tense, disturbing scene, Cady poses as a drama teacher, and Danielle goes along even after she knows who he really is—allowing herself to be verbally seduced because evil and danger are attractive to her.

Nolte's character is more complex. He is not a bad man, but not a very good one, and he finally agrees with his private eye (Joe Don Baker) that maybe three guys should be hired to pound some sense into Max Cady. When Cady thrashes the three goons and comes looking for the Nolte character, we realize the complexity of this movie. Unlike the simplistic version of this scene we have seen in a hundred thrillers, what Scorsese gives us is a villain who has been wronged, seeking to harm a hero who has sinned.

Cape Fear is impressive moviemaking, showing Scorsese as a master of a traditional Hollywood genre who is able to mold it to his own themes and obsessions. But as I look at this $35 million movie with big stars, special effects, and production values, I wonder whether it represents a good omen from the finest director now at work.

This is the first film in a production deal Scorsese has with Universal Studios and Steven Spielberg's Amblin Entertainment, and it represents his access to budgets much larger than those he has worked with in the past. The result seems to be a certain impersonality in a film by this most personal of directors — the Scorsese touch on a genre piece, rather than a film torn out of the director's soul. Most directors would distinguish themselves by making a film this good. From the man who made *Taxi Driver*, *Raging Bull*, *After Hours*, and *GoodFellas*, this is not an advance.

(131)

The Age of Innocence

SEPTEMBER 17, 1993

We live in an age of brutal manners, when people crudely say exactly what they mean, comedy is based on insult, tributes are roasts, and loud public obscenity passes without notice. Martin Scorsese's film *The Age of Innocence*, which takes place in 1870, seems so alien it could be pure fantasy. A rigid social code governs how people talk, walk, meet, part, dine, earn their livings, fall in love, and marry. Not a word of the code is written down anywhere. But these people have been studying it since they were born.

The film is based on a novel by Edith Wharton, who died in the 1930s. The age of innocence, as she called it with fierce irony, was over long before she even wrote her book. Yet she understood that the people of her story had the same lusts as we barbaric moderns, and not acting on them made them all the stronger.

The novel and the movie take place in the elegant milieu of the oldest and richest families in New York City. Marriages are like treaties between nations, their purpose not merely to cement romance or produce children, but to provide for the orderly transmission of wealth between the generations. Anything that threatens this sedate process is hated. It is not thought proper for men and women to place their own selfish desires above the needs of their class. People do indeed "marry for love," but the practice is frowned upon as vulgar and dangerous.

We meet a young man named Newland Archer (Daniel Day-Lewis), who is engaged to marry the pretty young May Welland (Winona Ryder).

He has great affection for her, even though she seems pretty but dim, well behaved rather than high spirited. All agree this is a good marriage between good families, and Archer is satisfied—until one night at the opera he sees a cousin who has married and lived in Europe for years. She is Ellen, the Countess Olenska (Michelle Pfeiffer). She has, he is astonished to discover, ideas of her own.

She looks on his world with the amusement and detachment of an exile.

She is beautiful, yes, but that isn't what attracts Archer. His entire being is excited by the presence of a woman who boldly thinks for herself.

The countess is not quite a respectable woman. First she made the mistake of marrying outside her circle, taking a rich Polish count and living in Europe. Then she made a greater transgression, separating from her husband and returning to New York, where she stands out at social gatherings as an extraordinary woman of undoubted fascination, whom no one knows quite what to do with. It is clear to everyone that her presence is a threat to the orderly progress of Archer's marriage with May.

This kind of story has been filmed, very well, by the Merchant-Ivory team. Their *Howard's End*, *A Room with a View*, and *The Bostonians* know this world. It would seem to be material of no interest to Martin Scorsese, a director of great guilts and energies, whose very titles are a rebuke to the age of innocence: *Mean Streets*, *Taxi Driver*, *Raging Bull*, *GoodFellas*. Yet when his friend and co-writer Jay Cocks handed Scorsese the Wharton novel, he could not put it down, and now he has filmed it, and through some miracle it is all Wharton, and all Scorsese.

The story told here is brutal and bloody, the story of a man's passion crushed, his heart defeated. Yet it is also much more, and the last scene of the film, which pulls everything together, is almost unbearably poignant because it reveals that the man was not the only one with feelings—that others sacrificed for him, that his deepest tragedy was not what he lost, but what he never realized he had.

The Age of Innocence is filmed with elegance. These rich aristocrats move in their gilded circles from opera to dinner to drawing room, with a costume for every role and every time of day.

Scorsese observes the smallest of social moments, the incline of a head, the angle of a glance, the subtle inflection of a word or phrase. And gradually we understand what is happening: Archer is considering breaking his engagement to May, in order to run away with the countess, and everyone is concerned to prevent him—while at no time does anyone reveal by the slightest sign that they know what they are doing.

I have seen love scenes in which naked bodies thrash in sweaty passion, but I have rarely seen them more passionate than in this movie, where everyone is wrapped in layers of Victorian repression. The big erotic moments take place in public among fully clothed people speaking in perfectly modulated phrases, and they are so filled with libido and terror that the characters scarcely survive them.

Scorsese, that artist of headlong temperament, here exhibits enormous patience. We are provided with the voice of a narrator (Joanne Woodward), who understands all that is happening, guides us, and supplies the private thoughts of some of the characters. We learn the rules of the society. We meet an elderly woman named Mrs. Mingott (Miriam Margolyes), who has vast sums of money and functions for her society as sort of an appeals court of what can be permitted, and what cannot be.

And we see the infinite care and attention with which May Welland defends her relationship with Newland Archer. May knows or suspects everything that is happening between Archer and the countess, but she chooses to acknowledge only certain information, and works with the greatest cleverness to preserve her marriage while never quite seeming to notice anything wrong.

Each performance is modulated to preserve the delicate balance of the romantic war. Daniel Day-Lewis stands at the center, deluded for a time that he has free will. Michelle Pfeiffer, as the countess, is a woman who sees through society without quite rejecting it, and takes an almost sensuous pleasure in seducing Archer with the power of her mind. At first it seems that little May is an unwitting bystander and victim, but Winona Ryder gradually reveals the depth of her character's intelligence, and in the last scene, as I said, all is revealed and much is finally understood.

Scorsese is known for his restless camera; he rarely allows a static shot. But here you will have the impression of grace and stateliness in his visual style, and only on a second viewing will you realize the subtlety with which his camera does, indeed, incessantly move, insinuating itself into conversations like a curious uninvited guest. At the beginning of *The Age of Innocence*, as I suggested, it seems to represent a world completely alien to us.

By the end, we realize these people have all the same emotions, passions, fears, and desires that we do. It is simply that they value $\left(135 \right)$ them more highly, and are less careless with them, and do not in the cause of self-indulgence choose a moment's pleasure over a lifetime's exquisite and romantic regret.

The *Innocence* of Martin Scorsese

MARCH 19, 1993

NEW YORK—The greatest living film director started out as a kid named Marty who I met in 1967 when he was fresh out of New York University. Now he is Martin Scorsese, the director even other directors would place first—after themselves, perhaps. No one has made more or better movies in the past quarter century, and few people have changed less. He still talks with his hands and bounces when he talks, and he uses the street-corner comedian's tactic of giving everything a punch line.

The way Scorsese talks about the movies is an education. I learn when I listen to him. He sees films in a very particular way, the emotions and the visuals all tied up together, so that when he talks about a feeling in one of his films, he is also talking about the particular kind of camera strategy he used to create it.

Listen to him talking about a moment in his great new film, *The Age of Innocence* (which opened Friday). The movie is set among the rich New York aristocrats of the 1870s, and is based on a novel by Edith Wharton in which a man is engaged to marry the right woman and falls in love with the wrong one, and society sees that as a threat and tries to stop him.

In the movie, the man has planned to travel from New York to Washington to be with his mistress. He tells his wife the purpose is business. Now the man and his wife both learn that the mistress will not be in Washington after all. The man tells his wife he has decided not to go. She guesses the reason, but is too clever to confront him with it.

"This scene was one of the reasons I wanted to make the film," Scorsese was explaining to me one afternoon in his Manhattan living room. "As they're getting into the carriage, she says, 'I'm sorry, but how can you go pick up Ellen when you have to go to Washington this afternoon?' He says, 'Oh, that's been postponed,' and they get into the carriage. Then she says, 'That's strange,' because she's learned the legal case in Washington is still being heard. And he admits, yes, it is. 'So then it's not postponed,' she says. Which is almost her way of fighting. And he says, 'No, it's not postponed, but my going is.'

"So they both know he has lied, but neither actually says it. And I found it fascinating to film that with a light touch. I asked myself how to place a hand in terms of camera placement, the size of the actors in the frame, the correct camera movement, the emotional level of performance. It was so funny; it was like painting miniatures. It was really fun."

And it is. In the hands of another director, the scene might have been assembled crudely out of big blaring close-ups and shots of narrowed eyes, so that the dimmest simpleton in the audience would know that lies and intrigues were taking place. In Scorsese's hands, the scene makes you hold your breath, because you realize what danger the characters are in. One false move, and a truth has been exposed that will end the marriage. Neither wants to make the move. Yet somehow the truth is shared without being acknowledged.

I told Scorsese that in a lot of modern movies, it's bluntly clear what the characters are saying and exactly what the scenes mean. All of the dramatic moments are punched up so that a guy watching the movie half-drunk on an airplane won't miss anything. In *The Age of Innocence*, the social fabric of the characters is being threatened with rupture, but no one wants to admit that, and the movie is about how the danger is faced and dealt with, without anyone acknowledging that there was any danger in the first place. A subtlety of language.

Scorsese laughed. "That bluntness, yeah. And losing all the color and the beauty of language and communication. They blamed me for that a few years ago. They had a wonderful article in the *New York Times*, called 'What Happened to Language in Film?' And they started quoting lines from *Raging Bull*. Now, granted, a line like 'You're gonna find your dog dead in the hallway' is not the soul of subtlety. But in that movie when the De Niro character accuses his brother of fooling around with his wife, it takes him six pages of dialogue to say what he means. It may not be drawing-room dialogue. But it's subtle.

"What has always stuck in my head is the brutality under the manners. People hide what they mean under the surface of language. In the subculture I was around when I grew up in Little Italy, when somebody was killed, there was a finality to it. It was usually done by the hands of a friend. And in a funny way, it was almost like ritualistic slaughter, a sacrifice. But New York society in the 1870s didn't have that. It was so cold-blooded. I don't know which is preferable. I grew up thinking in one way, but in my own private life the past ten years, I've started to appreciate the ability to say a little in certain emotional situations and mean a lot."

Scorsese's new film is what the industry calls a "costume drama," and great attention is paid to details of fashion, interior decoration, language, manners, and the choreography of dinner parties. Immediately under the surface, however, beats the red pulse of passion. And it is the very same passion that has inspired Scorsese in almost all of his films: the passion of a man forced to choose between what he wants, and what he knows is right.

Daniel Day-Lewis stars in the film as Newland Archer, an up-and-coming young man from a good family, who is engaged to marry May Welland (Winona Ryder). She is sweet and pretty, well connected and well behaved. Then one night at the opera, he sees a cousin who was a childhood playmate, and who married a Polish count and has now separated from him and returned to New York. She is the Countess Olenska (Michelle Pfeiffer). He desires her with his whole being. But it would be wrong to go to her—wrong to break his engagement, wrong to frustrate society's plans for him, wrong to take up with a woman who has already been married.

Watching the film, my mind strayed back to Scorsese's first film, *Who's That Knocking at My Door* (1967), in which a man falls in love with a woman and then learns she is not a virgin, and is torn between his desire and his Catholic morality. And to so many other Scorsese films—*Mean Streets*, *Raging Bull*, even the underworld of *Taxi Driver*, in which men idealize women and then cannot deal with the fact that women are human, too, and have passions, and are not perfect. Quintessentially Scorsese.

Since so many of Scorsese's films have grown out of the streets of modern New York City, out of the Italian American subculture of his youth, the announcement that he would film Edith Wharton's *The Age of Innocence* struck many people as astonishing—as surprising, say, as if Abel Ferrara had announced a film by Henry James. It is only when you see the film, and realize what it is about, that you understand how this material is quintessentially Scorsese.

The project began, Scorsese said, when the Wharton novel was given to him by his friend Jay Cocks, a former *Time* magazine film critic who became his collaborator on the screenplay.

"We became friends twenty-five years ago. So he couldn't review any of my films then; conflict of interest. We stayed friends because of our interest in film. We would introduce each other to films.

"One of the genres that I really admire is the costume piece, even the trashiest kind, like *The Count of Monte Cristo*. When I was nine or ten, my father took me to see *The Heiress*, which was the first costume piece that had a powerful impact on me. I didn't understand every detail, but I knew that something terrible had happened, a breach of trust and love—and everybody was dressed so nicely and they had such nice drawing rooms. I didn't understand how a father could talk that way to his daughter, explaining that the man was after her for her money, 'Because you're not clever and you're quite plain.' That's quite a scene.

"In 1980, Jay gave me *The Age of Innocence* and said, 'When you do your costume piece, when you do your romance, this is you.' Not meaning, of course, that I'm Archer or Ellen. It was the spirit of it—the spirit of the exquisite romantic pain. The idea that the mere

(139)

touching of a woman's hand would suffice. The idea that seeing her across the room would keep him alive for another year. That's something I guess that is part of me. He knew me, by that time, fairly well."

The Scorsese that Cocks knew is indeed a connoisseur of exquisite romantic pain. He once told me he could not go to Venice again, because of romantic associations, and that he could not see the films of a certain studio, because of memories of a woman who had worked there. He smiled when he told me, he even laughed at himself, but still, he would not go to Venice.

He did finally go to Venice in August, however, to show his film in the Venice Film Festival, and he took his mother, so they could be together after the death of his father at eighty. And he now looks at the films of all the movie studios.

"I think I've learned to . . . accept things, or at least to deal with them in terms like this book. I read a number of Wharton's other novels and they're very good, but this was the one that I said, 'Yeah, I understand this.' I was led through the labyrinth of it by the exquisite pain of not being able to consummate the relationship."

The Victorians were the sexiest generation.

"That's right. The more you had to get through all those clothes—the more he had to imagine through the clothes what was going on with her, the shade of the skin, the touch, the feel, the warmth, everything—I loved that tension, that conflict, and it's very sweet.

"And of course, it's the other thing, too. He believes that nobody notices, but everybody notices. When I read those paragraphs, I had felt that I was taken along by Edith Wharton. I felt like he did. And I realized what a fool I am. What a fool he is. I loved the way her prose just sort of dismembered him." A visual equivalent.

And then there was the problem of finding a visual equivalent for the moments when the deepest emotions strike his characters. Take, for example, the opening sequence at the opera, when Newland Archer first sees the countess through his opera glasses, realizes she has returned to New York—and realizes, almost in the same breath, that he has fallen in love with her. No dialogue is used. How can Scorsese communicate the certainty of Archer's feelings? As he explained, I felt like a student in a master class: "We look through his opera glasses, seeing what he sees. But not just in regular time. We did stop-frame photography, exposing one frame at a time and printing each frame three times and then dissolving between each three frames. It looks sort of like what you see when you look through an opera glass, but with heightened attention. He scans the audience and then backs up and stops on her. With all the different experimenting, that took almost a year to get right."

The strategy makes us feel not only that we are looking through his glasses, but that we are experiencing his feelings. What is best about the film, I think, is its feeling of complicity. There is a spoken narration (read by Joanne Woodward) that comes not from any character in the story, but as the voice of the society itself. The narrator speaks of "we," and implies all the eyes that are on Archer, May, and the countess while they conduct their private war. And the feeling that Archer is under the restraint of that "we," that he must behave as society and his wife expect him to, leads us up to the film's great last scene.

(141)

I will not describe the scene. But I will report that for Scorsese, it is not only the summation of the movie, but of his reasons for making it. In the scene there is a revelation, showing that love is more complex and hidden than we know, and that sometimes perhaps exquisite romantic loss is more precious than selfish romantic gratification. There is a line in the scene: "And to think it was his wife . . ." Think about that line, Scorsese seems to be telling us, and you will have a deeper knowledge of how life really does operate, outside the compass of our own little egos.

The afternoon was late. We sat in the living room, drinking coffee — in the second-story living room of a townhouse that was built in the age of innocence, in a room where perhaps people like Archer and May and the countess had once taken tea. Scorsese's walls were lined with books. He said he was still seeing as many movies as ever, but he was reading more, too — "much more than when I was younger. I'm getting more into the past."

Do you think as people grow older, they grow more socially conservative?

"Not the old people I'm thinking of, the old directors like Sam Fuller or Michael Powell. They speak exactly what's on their mind, as if they're aware that they don't have any time to waste."

Casino

NOVEMBER 22, 1995

If the Mafia didn't exist, it would be necessary to invent it.

The same is true of Las Vegas. There is a universal need to believe in an outfit that exists outside the rules and can get things done.

There's a related need for a place where the rules are suspended, where there's no day or night, where everything has a price, where if you're lucky, you go home a millionaire. Of course, people who go to Vegas lose money, and people who deal with the mob regret it. But hope is what we're talking about. Neither the mob nor Vegas could exist if most people weren't optimists.

Martin Scorsese's fascinating new film, *Casino*, knows a lot about the Mafia's relationship with Las Vegas. It's based on a book by Nicholas Pileggi, who had full access to a man who once ran four casinos for the mob, and whose true story inspires the movie's plot.

Like *The Godfather*, it makes us feel like eavesdroppers in a secret place.

The movie opens with a car bombing, and the figure of Sam "Ace" Rothstein floating through the air. The movie explains how such a thing came to happen to him. The first hour plays like a documentary; there's a narration, by Rothstein (Robert De Niro) and others, explaining how the mob skimmed millions out of the casinos.

It's an interesting process. Assuming you could steal 25 percent of the slot-machine take—what would you do with tons of coins? How would you convert them into bills that could be stuffed into the weekly suitcase for delivery to the mob in Kansas City? *Casino* knows. It also knows how to skim from the other games, and from food service, and the gift shops. And it knows about how casinos don't like to be stolen from.

There's an incident where a man is cheating at blackjack, and a couple of security guys sidle up to him and jab him with a stun gun.

He collapses, the security guys call for medical attention, and hurry him away to a little room where they pound on his fingers with a mallet and he agrees that he made a very bad mistake.

Rothstein, based on the real-life figure of Frank "Lefty" Rosenthal, starts life as a sports oddsmaker in Chicago, attracts the attention of the mob because of his genius with numbers, and is assigned to run casinos because he looks like an efficient businessman who will encourage the Vegas goose to continue laying its golden eggs. He is a man who detests unnecessary trouble. One day, however, trouble finds him, in the person of Ginger McKenna (Sharon Stone), a high-priced call girl.

Scorsese shows him seeing Ginger on a TV security monitor and falling so instantly in love that the image becomes a freeze-frame.

Ace showers her with gifts, which she is happy to have, but when he wants to marry her, she objects; she's been with a pimp named Lester Diamond (James Woods) since she was a kid, and she doesn't want to give up her profession. Rothstein will make her an offer she can't refuse: cars, diamonds, furs, a home with a pool, and the key to his safe-deposit box. She marries him. It is Ace's first mistake.

Another mistake was to meet Nicky Santoro (Joe Pesci) when they were both kids in Chicago. Nicky is a thief and a killer who comes to Vegas, forms a crew, and throws his weight around. After he squeezes one guy's head in a vise, the word goes out that he's the mob's enforcer. Not true, but people believe it, and soon Nicky's name is being linked with his old pal Ace in all the newspapers.

Scorsese tells his story with the energy and pacing he's famous for, and with a wealth of little details that feel just right. Not only the details of tacky 1970s period decor, but little moments such as when Ace orders the casino cooks to put "exactly the same amount of blueberries in every muffin." Or when airborne feds are circling a golf course while spying on the hoods, and their plane runs out of gas and they have to make an emergency landing right on the green.

And when crucial evidence is obtained because a low-level hood kept a record of his expenses. And when Ace hosts a weekly show on local TV—and reveals a talent for juggling.

Meanwhile, Ginger starts drinking, and Ace is worried about their kid, and they start having public fights, and she turns to Nicky for advice that soon becomes consolation, and when Ace finds out she may be fooling around, he utters a line that, in its way, is perfect: "I just hope it's not somebody who I think it might be." "It was," a narrator tells us, "the last time street guys would ever be given such an opportunity." All the mob had to do was take care of business. But when Ace met Ginger and when Nicky came to town, the pieces were in place for the mob to become the biggest loser in Vegas history. "We screwed up good," Nicky says, not using exactly those words. Scorsese gets the feel, the mood, almost the smell of the city just right; De Niro and Pesci inhabit their roles with unconscious assurance, Stone's call girl is her best performance, and the supporting cast includes such people as Don Rickles, whose very presence evokes an era (his job is to stand impassively beside the boss and look very sad about what might happen to whomever the boss is talking to).

(145)

Unlike his other Mafia movies (*Mean Streets* and *GoodFellas*), Scorsese's *Casino* is as concerned with history as with plot and character. The city of Las Vegas is his subject, and he shows how it permitted people like Ace, Ginger, and Nicky to flourish, and then spit them out, because the Vegas machine is too profitable and powerful to allow anyone to slow its operation. When the Mafia, using funds from the Teamsters union, was ejected in the late 1970s, the 1980s ushered in a new source of financing: junk bonds. The guys who floated those might be the inspiration for *Casino II*. "The big corporations took over," the narrator observes, almost sadly. "Today, it works like Disneyland." Which brings us back to our opening insight. In a sense, people need to believe a town like Vegas is run by guys like Ace and Nicky.

In a place that breaks the rules, maybe you can break some, too. For those with the gambler mentality, it's actually less reassuring to know that giant corporations, financed by bonds and run by accountants, operate the Vegas machine. They know all the odds, and the house always wins. With Ace in charge, who knows what might happen?

De Niro, Pesci, Scorsese Tell a Shocking Mob Story in *Casino*

NOVEMBER 12, 1995

NEW YORK—I've seen Martin Scorsese's movie of *Casino* and I've read Nick Pileggi's book, and what I want to know is, why are these people all still alive? Scorsese and Pileggi, I understand: they're civilians. But how did Frank "Lefty" Rosenthal, the hero of the film and book, survive to tell his story to Pileggi? How come he's enjoying retirement in Boca Raton when by all the odds (which nobody knew more about than he did), he should be pushing up cactuses?

Casino, which is being released simultaneously as Scorsese's film and Pileggi's book, tells the more or less true story of Rosenthal, the man who brought sports book betting to Las Vegas in the 1970s, and managed the Stardust at a time when a suitcase full of large bills was being dispatched on a weekly basis from that casino to the Kansas City mob, and then distributed to lucky Mafioso in Chicago, Milwaukee, and elsewhere.

Rosenthal, who is called by his real name in the book and becomes Ace Rothstein in the somewhat fictionalized movie (which opens November 22), was a Chicago bookmaker who was a genius at picking winners and figuring all of the odds having to do with gambling. He was also, on the evidence of the two *Casinos*, a competent manager and visionary businessman who presided over four Vegas casinos during the 1970s and succeeded, during his stewardship, in creating such a disaster that by the end of the decade, the mob had lost control of its Vegas casinos, and its aging bosses, who had counted on a placid and affluent old age, were being hauled before grand juries in several states.

"It was the last time street guys would ever be given such an opportunity," the film's narrator sadly observes. The era when casinos were financed by the mob-connected Teamster pension funds came to an end, and in the 1980s, a new source of funding was invented: junk bonds, championed by a new breed of financial geniuses, who could no doubt be the stars of *Casino II*.

What brought everything crashing down around Lefty Rosenthal's ears were those two virtuous impulses, love and friendship. He fell in love with a high-priced Vegas call girl named Jeri McGee. She didn't want to get married, but he persuaded her with gifts, promises, and the belief that they could work out a reasonable arrangement. Meanwhile, his childhood friend from Chicago, Tony Spilotro, journeyed west and gathered a crew of thieves around himself. He set up shop, so it seemed, as the Chicago mob's local enforcer.

He wasn't, but everyone thought he was, and every time Lefty's name appeared in the paper, it was linked with Tony's. Bad enough—but what was worse was that when things went bad between Lefty and Jeri, she turned to Tony for advice, which quickly became sympathy, and before long everyone was being shadowed and bugged by the feds, and there were messy murders and the whole thing came crashing down. One of the key lines in book and movie: "We screwed up big time."

Names have been changed in the movie to avoid lawsuits. Robert De Niro plays Ace Rothstein; Sharon Stone plays his wife, Jeri, now called Ginger McKenna; and Joe Pesci plays Tony Spilotro, now known as Nicky Santoro. Meanwhile, the real Lefty Rosenthal lives in comfortable retirement, banned forever from returning to the casinos—but alive, which is something, considering that the film opens with a shot of his Cadillac being blown up with him inside.

What is fascinating is that Scorsese and Pileggi explain exactly how the mob skimmed millions from the Vegas casinos. How, for example, would you go about stealing a third of the take of a casino's slot machines? Consider that you would have to rig the machines, and the coin scales in the locked counting room, which casino officials are not allowed to enter—and then you'd be talking about tons of coins. What would the boys in Kansas City do with twelve thousand pounds of quarters? Appear at the bank's drive-up window with a forklift?

The explanation, which is brilliant, appears in an early passage of Scorsese's film, which uses voiceover narration for much of its first hour and plays like an insider's documentary that could have been called "How to Steal from a Casino." In writing his book and the screenplay, Pileggi relied on court testimony and FBI reports, but his prime source of information was Frank Rosenthal himself, who seems to have spoken at great length and frankness about his business and personal life in Las Vegas.

"He's quite a remarkable guy," Scorsese was telling me not long ago in New York, after an early screening of the film. Throughout our talk, he referred to the characters only by their fictional names, except when I would ask him specifically about Frank Rosenthal: "He's brilliant at what he does and legally, he's clear. I mean, he's been cleared of everything, I think, and the very fact that he was able to be so open with Nick means that he's okay with talking about it. I mean, I'm sure at times Nick asked him certain things and there was no comment."

In his early days as a bookmaker, according to the book, Rosenthal would place bets only on games or races he was sure of. When friends would pressure him for a pick on a game, his answer, 98 times out of 100, was "I have no opinion on that."

"That's what he would tell Nick," Scorsese said. "I have no opinion on that."

There's no threat to him from organized crime for talking to Pileggi?

"I don't think so. I think these things happened in the past and, as Nick says, whatever arrangements had to be made I'm sure have been made."

Rosenthal has a lot he can be proud of, Scorsese said. "Let's say the guy doesn't kill anybody. He's great at numbers. He may have been a difficult boss, firing people left and right, but in terms of what he did and how he changed Vegas and opened the first sports book in a casino . . . he can be proud. It's a world and way of life that's like a microcosm. The movie deals with power and greed and respect and trust and betrayal and that goes on everywhere. It doesn't matter if you're in a village in Outer Mongolia and living in a yurt, or you're in Vegas or in the Oval Office. The big problem for me is that I had to be as true to them as possible."

The guys.

"Those people. Yeah."

Has Rosenthal seen this movie?

"Yes. From what Nick tells me, he liked it. You're dealing with characters that are 'based' on real people, you know, and they're not around to defend themselves. Like the character Nicky Santoro. I think we tried to get both sides of the issue in terms of Nicky's character. But, you know, he did what he did and that's his lifestyle."

In the film, both Santoro and his brother, a dentist, meet a horrible death in an Indiana cornfield, being beaten and then buried while still alive. "We could have made short shrift of their deaths," Scorsese said. "But I didn't feel we should have. I think it was terrible, and sad. He kind of took for everybody. That's what I think."

How did the gambling industry and Las Vegas itself react to the fact that you were shooting *Casino* there?

"Well, for the most part, they helped us. Steve Wynn (chief of the Mirage and other major casinos) helped us a lot. I think they were feeling like this was the past of Vegas, that the city is not that way now."

And the romanticism doesn't hurt, I said. When people hear some of these stories about Vegas, it seems to enhance the city, in a way. This movie won't keep one person away from Vegas.

"That may be right."

People would like to think the slots aren't rigged any more, so they have a better chance.

"How do we know?" said Scorsese.

We don't know.

"We don't know anything. I'm telling you, it's just the nature of things. It's the nature of that kind of thing, that you never know anything. It's the same in Hollywood. You never know. Who knows where the money goes? Parts of the budget could be disappearing, for all you know; people could be siphoning off money. Who knows what's going on?"

There were some difficulties, Scorsese said. "I do know that when we got a location, I worked out all my shots in a house, for example, got the actors rehearsing in the house, and suddenly, we didn't get the house."

Why not?

"In one particular case, there were these old houses, and they're very hard to find because the houses had to be from the '50s and '60s, you know, and houses that old are all gone in Vegas. We had this terrific house we were working on, and it was on a golf course. A company had bought the houses to tear them down and enlarge the golf course. And suddenly they said, 'We don't want you shooting here.' Maybe they didn't want to offend anybody who would later want to play on that course. I don't know."

Eventually, he said, his production designer found another house, also on a golf course. The golf course was essential to set up one of the funniest scenes in the movie, where FBI agents, conducting aerial reconnaissance on the casino boss, run out of gas and have to make an emergency landing on the golf green right next to his house.

"That actually happened," Scorsese said. "Their plane ran out of gas. In reality, they went into a pond, and they went back to the office soaking wet."

In many of Scorsese's films, there is a strong undercurrent of male jealousy. *Raging Bull* centers on the insane possessiveness of the boxer Jake LaMotta, and in such earlier films as *Mean Streets*, male characters exhibit what Freud called the Madonna-whore complex, in which all women seem like saints while virgins, and irreparably tarnished afterwards. In *Casino*, the Ace Rothstein character doesn't exhibit that orientation; he isn't particularly jealous on a sexual level, doesn't have a problem with the fact that Ginger was a hooker, but is *very* upset when she insults his intelligence by lying to him and trying to steal from him.

That leads to another of the movie's best scenes, between Robert De Niro and Sharon Stone. Ginger has taken some of the money from a safe-deposit box and given it to her longtime pimp and boyfriend, played by James Woods. She claims he spent the money on clothes. Ace feels that his intelligence is being insulted, and in a great verbal riff he explains why the pimp wouldn't know how to spend that much money on clothes.

Scorsese laughed as he recalled the scene, which, he said, was partly improvised by De Niro and Stone.

"She gives him the story about $25,000 for suits," he said. "He tells her, 'Look, I can't forgive the kidnapping of my kid, but I'm gonna try to. I can almost forgive the things you're doing with him and the other guys, whatever's going on, because I've got my own things I'm doing. But when you start to think that I'm such a fool that I believe $25,000 was spent on clothes in three or four days, then that's insulting my intelligence.' That's the one little extra step."

It's not his manhood, his sexual pride—it's that he's being taken for a fool.

Scorsese nodded. "That's finally the core of pride there. 'Don't treat me like a john,' he says. 'I know you think I am but I'm not.' And that was an improv. And you could see the reaction from Sharon Stone. She's really something in that."

How much of an improv?

"Most of it."

Like when he starts talking about how much he'd pay for a suit . . .

"Oh, that was written. But then he started to go off on how much a watch would cost. He figures the guy would know about a $5,000 watch, even a ten- or twelve-grand watch, but a $75,000 watch, that he wouldn't know about. De Niro started putting that stuff in because he started to work it out mentally. Here is a guy who tries to remain dispassionate, controlled, but he loses it because she doesn't take him seriously."

In all of your pictures about the mob, from *Mean Streets* to *GoodFellas* to *Casino*, has anyone *from* the outfit ever talked to you about them?

"No, I guess, would be the answer. Well, for *GoodFellas*, McDonald, who's the head of the federal task force and plays himself in the film, told me that *Mean Streets* was the task force's favorite film. And a guy from the Mafia told Pileggi that *Mean Streets* was a film they liked a lot."

Both sides.

"Both sides, yeah. That was a big compliment." He smiled. "And then for *GoodFellas*, who's the guy in Sicily who had thirty-three people killed in his family? He said the only film that was accurate about mob life was *GoodFellas*. Particularly in the scene where they're having a good time at the bar and then one guy laughs wrong and the other guy says, 'You think I'm funny?' and there's a sudden burst of violence. He said when something like that happens — this is what it's like in their life. You have to think within a few seconds whether you should kill or you should die. And it's that simple."

Part 4   Reflecting

Introduction

In February 1997, Scorsese's complete works were screened at the Wexner Center for the Arts at The Ohio State University, and the month ended with ceremonies awarding the director a medal and a round of master classes. I was asked to join him onstage for a conversation, illustrated with scenes he had chosen from his films.

The large auditorium was jammed to standing room only, and the audience was obviously very familiar with Scorsese's films. We talked on and on; I almost feel we could have never ended, and then later at a reception Scorsese held court for a few more hours with graduate students and local film people.

Reading the transcript, I was taken back to the headlong velocity of his thinking and speaking. He operates by free association, leaping between memories, no internal censor on watch. Lightly editing this transcript, I connected a few dots and eliminated a few ellipses, and otherwise just left it as it was, the full force of the director's gusto for life, work, and film.

Wexner Center for the Arts

THE OHIO STATE UNIVERSITY

FEBRUARY 28, 1997

ROGER EBERT: I didn't know what I would say when we first came out here tonight, but then I thought, I am your film student. I'll explain what I mean by that. When we go to a movie that's a good movie, for two hours we give over control of our consciousness to the director and he says look here, look there, think of this, think of that, listen to this, listen to that, feel this, feel that. And in a movie that truly absorbs me, I have a vicarious, out-of-the-body experience. And then, if it's a great movie, I go back and I see it again and again and again. Most of the things that happened to me in my life only happened once, but a great movie . . . well . . . [AUDIENCE LAUGHTER.] I didn't realize there were that many students here! [BIG LAUGHTER FROM SCORSESE.] A movie happens more than once and I have seen some of your films literally dozens of times. Last year Thelma and I were able to go through *Raging Bull* shot-at-a-time at the University of Virginia and look at all that great detail. So what has happened is . . . things that happen in *Taxi Driver* or *Raging Bull* have been absorbed into me. I refer to them when things happen in my life. They are like an experience that I learn from. And I think that's what great movies are; I think that's what people don't understand . . . it's not just killing two hours or having your mind distracted by an entertaining experience, although that's part of it too.

MARTIN SCORSESE: Yeah.

R: But a great movie actually adds to your sum of life. And that's what I think your films have done for me, more than anybody else's during the time I've been a film critic.

M: Well, as you know, I carried your review of my first film around with me when I was in Europe in 1968. It was a film I was doing that finally became *Who's That Knocking at My Door*. We started shooting it in '65, finished most of it in '67, then added the sex scene, because otherwise we couldn't get it distributed in America at the time. You had to have a nude scene in 1968 to 1970; there had to be at least one obligatory nude scene. Because there was a new freedom; it was a whole new thing, and in any event I would carry the review around with me. But I guess what I meant at the AFI thing and what I said today about the movies being me—if there is no more running away from it, if they want to give an award after twenty-five years, the AFI, I can't feel badly about some of the feelings and some of the things that the films say. Because there's a tendency to be . . . like we were saying today, can we say four-letter words tonight, you know what I'm saying? They still say that, you know: "We can't use that word! Oh, don't show that clip, they got cursing in that, you know!"

R: We said, "Can we show the *Taxi Driver* clip?" And I said, "We're both pre–Vatican II." I said, "I don't know, Marty, it's a sin, you know." [SCORSESE LAUGHTER.]

M: So the idea of saying that the films are me, I mean, we're good and bad. That's it. After being fifty-four years old I got a little more comfortable with myself, and kinda tolerate parts of myself that I didn't like, you know.

R: You mean when you saw some of your films, let's say in the first screening after the editing is finished, you thought, gee, I'm not sure I should have made this or . . .

M: Oh no. I was glad I made it.

R: But you still felt . . .

M: I was a little, you know—I didn't necessarily wanna be questioned about it—you know, do you really feel that way? Is this what you did? Did this happen to you? I'd say, "It's none of your business, that's the film," you know. [AUDIENCE LAUGHTER.] But, you know, in the era now of political correctness, there's a tendency for these pictures to be offensive at times and that sort of thing but I'm just really trying to show as much as possible in many of the films, not all of them, of course, but many of them, what I kind of knew; what I know to be as truthful and realistic as possible, emotionally, you know.

R: You talk about political correctness, you mean that people would say, "I don't approve of that film because the people in it do things I don't approve of."

M: Exactly, yeah.

R: Your answer would be, "I don't approve of them either but those are the kinds of people I know."

M: That's the people I know and I've done it. I've done it myself so condemn me, what can I tell you, you know? That's what I meant, too, anyway, so if you have a problem with the film, I guess it's a problem with me in that sense. And I have to face that and know that you can't be liked by everybody but kids wanna be liked by everyone, that sort of thing, it can't be.

R: When you look at your films, I think we see a group of films that are intensely personal and you were talking earlier today and last night about the auteur theory. About the theory that many people make a film but one person guides the film and one person inspires the vision. And then somebody asked you when we were talking to the students yesterday if you'd ever make a western. And I found your answer to be so revealing because your answer was you didn't know what a western had to do with you. And then you got a joke by saying, "Well, I've got asthma that, of course, is going to make me sneeze . . ."

M: The horses will kill me, yeah.

R: But so many directors I've talked to who—well, one director in particular, I won't mention his name, who said, "I made this movie because I always wanted to make a western." And that's a legitimate feeling for some directors, but you're not collecting genres . . .

M: Right. True, because you know why, it's very hard to make a movie. In other words, you really have to wanna be there. And you gotta get up real early in the morning. And I mean that. Like before the sun comes up sometimes, and you gotta drive out to a location and it's really hard. And what I mean by that is that when you're younger, you may wanna try doing *Boxcar Bertha* for Roger Corman, and that was an exploitation film and it had a certain, it was a subgenre of *Bonnie and Clyde*, which was a film in 1967 with Warren Beatty and all that, a watershed film which opened up everything for us, Arthur Penn's picture. And I learned how to do a film then in twenty-four days, shooting in twenty-four days; be on schedule, be on time, edit the film, all that sort of thing. But after I did *Mean Streets*, I found that even though I may have wanted to experiment with genres, because I really loved those directors who were able to do that, like Howard Hawks. They were able to do westerns, screwball comedies, musicals, thrillers . . .

R: Race cars . . .

M: Well, yeah, *Land of the Pharaohs* and *The Big Sleep*, you know—I mean, film noir. And he was excelling in every one of those genres and I would really have loved to have done that. And I found that by the time I did *New York, New York*, I realized that I had to be very, very careful as to the subject matter I choose, you know, because you just can't knock off these films once; I couldn't. The way I worked and the way I still work is a little slower, a little more deliberate, and I just found that as much as I wanted to be able to make a western or make a real musical, I mean a real musical where people sing in the middle of conversations—I'm talking about the musicals that ended in the great 1950s cycle of Arthur Fried productions, Minnelli films and Charles Walters and people like that, and Stanley Donen and Gene Kelly. But the thing about it is that as much as I wanted to do that, I realized that I was always drawn to more personal material; material that touched something in me personally, something that I felt was about myself or that I could feel the purpose of being there every day and be excited to get this on screen. It's been a process of elimination. In the case of *Raging Bull*, it took me four to five years to warm up to that project, before De Niro and I really got a very good script from Paul Schrader and then worked on it. But it took five years of . . .

R: De Niro finally brought it to you and said, "Let's make this."

M: Yeah. He brought it to me back in '73 and '74, and I played around with it for a while and then *New York, New York* was a failure and there were a lot of bad times there in Los Angeles from '76 to about '78, and during that period I lived a lot, in a way, and by the end of that period is when I realized that I just had to go back to work and he was still there with that project and Schrader had written the script by that time. And then I found what I wanted to do in that project. And we went off and that was the best collaboration we had. But then I tried one more time with *King of Comedy*. He asked me to do that too. He said, "Come on, let's just shoot it. We can do it in New York and shoot it rather quickly." And that, although I enjoyed making the film, I had to find myself while I was making the film. I had to find myself in the film while I was making it. I had to find the reason why I had to be there everyday. Which means, you know, that pressures you as a real professional, too; the reason you're there is because the actors are there, the camera's there, you gotta shoot, you know. Well, it's gotta be more than that for me. And it was there but I was kinda rehabilitating in a way and I found that, again, you just can't go off and do films for your friends. You have to try to stick to stuff you wanna do.

R: At this point in your career, you're honored, you're respected, you're famous, you're published, you're given awards, you were given the AFI Twenty-fifth Anniversary Award last week and it was pointed out you don't have an Oscar, but a lot of people have Oscars and the AFI Award, as you mentioned, includes, you know, Alfred Hitchcock, John Huston, and so forth. Yet, over the years I've interviewed you before or after and during most every film you've made. And more than once, including in connection with *Raging Bull* and again with *King of Comedy*, you told me that there was a time when you felt that that would be the last movie you would ever make.

M: Oh, no doubt.

R: . . . That you would never work again. So that your career has not been a series of professional successes as it might seem now to somebody looking back over.

M: Oh, not at all. *Raging Bull* was . . . after the failure of *New York, New York,* and then the wonderful reviews on *The Last Waltz* — everybody had a very good feeling about the film but the film was totally ignored by all the critics groups and the Academy. It was even considered ineligible for best documentary nomination, for some reason. I think it was because there was no dialog . . .

R: That's the Academy rule: no good documentary is eligible.

M: It's amazing. These guys are . . . and I can say that because 90 percent of the documentary is them singing. I put the cameras in certain places, that's it. It was really their work; The Band, Bob Dylan, Neil Young, all that. Anyway, after that, that was very disappointing and I don't know, I just . . . when I finally pulled myself together and Bob was there . . . he had a script and he had a good script this time, Schrader's script, I just realized I could do nothing else and I understood where I could find myself in that particular project because of the character Jake LaMotta and the punishment he dealt to himself and to everybody around him. And I kinda saw myself in him, just having flattened myself out completely . . . but I was still breathing, and Bob was there with the script and said, "Now, do you wanna shoot it?" I said "Okay; let's go." And I knew at that point—I gotta . . . I'd like to move out of Los Angeles. And I had an apartment in New York at the time and so I just . . . I said if you're gonna do this one it's gotta be really very, very special, I said, it's gotta be like kamikaze filmmaking. We're just gonna go in and kill; it's gonna be deadly. In other words, consider it the last picture. Bob was good about that collaboration. This is important, that he was able to get what he wanted out of the role and the film and I was able to get what I wanted, which was very often involving a man to stand in the ring for twelve hours and get hit in the head for ten weeks. And that was Bob; he needed to do it. He said, "I'll do it." I said, "I got this idea for this shot," he goes, "Oh, all right, I'll do it." And another actor, who knows, you know? But he was able to give me what I needed and it was fine with me. And so I poured everything in there thinking I was gonna go to Rome and do films for RAI Television about the lives of the saints in 16 mm. [LAUGHTER.] Another, you know, romantic notion which . . .

R: It's strange because at various times I've heard you talking about *Raging Bull* as if you felt it would be the last film you'd ever make and also you felt it was the best experience.

M: Oh, it was wonderful, yeah. It was a good experience.

R: And maybe the reason that film was so great is that you kind of worked without a net.

M: Totally. Totally. We did it in *Mean Streets* without a net too. But, you know, that was a hard one because there's only twenty-six days shooting and $650,000 and I had to fake New York in LA. So I shot certain key scenes for six days and nights in New York with a student crew of NYU and worked with Roger Corman's crew in LA for the next twenty days . . . all out of continuity. I mean, the first day in LA, the first night? The end of the picture. The cars crashing, guns . . . just, you know. Night four of shooting.

R: They're standing by with actual celluloid which they are loading into the projector at this moment . . .

M: I just like the title sequence. I like the music; I liked Phil Specter's sound of the early '60s, the girl groups, especially the Ronettes' "Be My Baby," and the 8 mm film that you see . . . well, I shot it in a camera that I bought in Italy, actually, in 1970. The idea that 8 mm was gonna have to be exactly like home movies in that there should be no interpretation. In other words, you shouldn't—at that time, you shouldn't have been able to do anything with the lens, focus—you just aim and shoot. And what you get, you get. And if you pan—it was trying to be unsophisticated. I don't know how much I got of it. I think we got some of it because actually I intercut my brother's actual home movies in there and my nephew Christopher, his christening party. So I think the cut with De Niro

(164)

and Bob and I don't know—but cut to the music and I don't know what else to say, it kinda sets the picture up.

R: Let me say about this picture as someone who was a fan of yours very early on, I was so thrilled to pick up the *New Yorker* and read Pauline Kael's review about this film because she really has been a great voice in American film criticism in our time and she was right from the get-go; just because nobody knew who you were or who anybody in the picture was . . .

M: She was very strong on it, I know.

R: . . . it didn't stop her from noticing immediately . . .

M: Yeah.

R: . . . how important the film was. She was absolutely dead-on right about it.

M: After *Taxi Driver*, then the only films she liked of mine were *Last Waltz* and *New York Stories*, and *Last Temptation*. That's it. Everything else—didn't like.

R: Oh, she was tough.

M: Yeah, she was tough.

R: We can start now.

M: Yeah, okay. Let's see the beginning of it.
   [SHOWING OF FILM.]

M: Kill it . . . kill it. Okay, thank you.
   [BIG APPLAUSE.]

R: What is interesting there is, it is apparently . . .

M: Yeah.

R: . . . home-movie footage.

M: Right.

R: Including—we were just talking here—eating the cake, it's like I'm posing for a picture of myself eating the cake in the home movie. But there's an undertone. It gets darker towards the end.

M: Yeah, it does, yeah.

R: And how did you do that? I mean, without doing anything obvious I realized that this is not gonna be a comedy by the end of that sequence. How did I know that?

M: It's, I think, the shot of De Niro. It's kinda like, he's got his hair, it's

(165)

like a really terrific kind of pompadour thing that he did and the light bulbs—you know, the old home movies of forty years ago, you had to have like photo flood lamps, they were very hot. You see in the left of the frame it comes in on his face and he has a cigarette hanging from his mouth a certain way. And there's something kinda dangerous about that, I think. But no, I edited the film myself and, you know, with the beginning with Keitel putting his head on the pillow and the music starting that way, is all worked out in the script. That was all worked out, drawn in pictures, and when I edited the home movies, the very first piece of the home movies you see is police lights. When I was shooting the film I just— anything I saw interesting, I saw in the neighborhood within the six days I was shooting there, my old neighborhood in Mulberry Street and Mott Street, I'd punch off a little bit of film; that's only maybe a half a foot of 8 mm film, and then there's the actual *Mean Streets* title card, is a freeze-frame of three frames of the 8 mm of the corner of Hester and Mulberry which is a pretty tough area, that corner. It's really a great corner. And it was only three frames that I froze it, you know. And the titles are typed up by me and blown up. Because it's a home movie; the whole picture's a home movie, you see. And it was as if you had to do it yourself, the whole thing. And every bit you see in there, even the flash frames, right before you see Keitel, there's a shot of me in there waving for two frames.

R: Right there in the beginning when you have the dots going past, right at the end of the leader, it looks like it's haphazard but yet it's cut to the music.

M: It's cut to the music, exactly.

R: So it really gets . . . it gets into you.

M: Yes.

R: And I remember when I saw the first film you made, *Who's That Knocking*, I had never heard a sound track before scored with 45 rpm hits. Now, later, *American Graffiti* became famous for doing that.

M: Yeah, yeah, yeah.

R: Correct me if I'm wrong, we know that there were underground films like *Scorpio Rising*, but I believe that your film was the first film to do what has become extremely commonplace and that is to a score a movie with pop songs.

M: I think it is. I mean, to be fair, of course, you know, as I say, I tried to do it on an 8 mm film I shot, *My Friends*, and there was no way I could sync it up, this is about 1962, and so we showed it in an evening in my mother's and father's apartment with all my friends there and I played records, you know, change the records and that sort of thing. And we read the dialog, you know. It was a very stupid little film that we shot on the roofs of Mott Street and it wasn't my camera, we couldn't afford a camera. My friend Joe's camera with 8 mm. And literally I put the music in that film. I had Lonnie Donegan, it was a skiffle group from England that John Lennon used to like, and Prokofiev's *Alexander Nevsky* and some Django Reinhart with his jazz group from France in the late '30s, quite improvisational jazz, pretty interesting. And I mixed all that music together and then I saw, I think it was in '63 or '64, I saw *Scorpio Rising* when it was banned.

R: So in fact you had actually scored a movie of yours to pop songs before you saw *Scorpio Rising*.

M: Right, right.

R: It was a small audience but the principle remained.

M: But the principle was there. I guess I'm just being technical because I like to be the first to have done it. But what I'm telling you, when you saw *Scorpio Rising*, there are three or four music cues in that picture that . . . nothing is better than "My Boyfriend's Back," for example. There's a music cue in that with a guy working on a motorcycle and there's skull in the car; it's just . . . it's unbelievable.

R: The thing is, Michael Powell, who was both your mentor and your friend—not so much a mentor as your inspiration, I think . . .

M: Exactly.

R: . . . said that your films connect directly with the audience and that very few filmmakers have that gift. Now, when I saw your first film and I guess it's true of your other films as well to various degrees,

(167)

they did connect directly; there wasn't any barrier. And the thing is, the experience of these people in Little Italy, there's no parallel with my own growing up in downstate Illinois, except maybe for Catholicism, which might be a pretty big parallel.

M: Pretty big, yeah.

R: Pre–Vatican II, anyway. But when I heard the music, when I saw the guys walking down the sidewalk in the opening shot, when I looked at these home movies, it was as if whatever separated us was gone and it was naked . . .

M: Yeah.

R: . . . in that it was my experience. It didn't have the distance of the glossy 1960s Hollywood movie.

M: Yeah. That's something I tried to do intentionally. That's one of the reasons why I don't really see my movies after I make 'em. Two, they're so personal and I'm so sensitive about seeing them, it embarrasses me in a way. I could watch sequences with music. I like the music, you know, that's kind of interesting. But, I learned it pretty much, I think my mother's a pretty good storyteller. I get a lot from her, the way she tells stories; the way she behaved was the key thing. You could see it in the documentary I did of them, *Italianamerican*, 1974. I did that, it's on laserdisc now, it's only an hour long, but my mother and father in the film, I asked them a few questions and they just took off and I learned a great deal about them. I learned about what it was like to be an Italian American, what it was like to be a Sicilian immigrant around the turn of the century, how they lived—things I didn't know. They had a whole other way of life; working at the age of nine, living in three rooms with eight kids and parents and whoever was the newest baby had to be taken care of by the eldest daughter, that is. During the day the beds were pulled up and there were chairs. At night the whole place was like a hotel, beds all over the place, kids sleeping everywhere. And everybody living together and having to get into their own pecking order with respect for the father and mother, you see. Very, very strong. And so my father's a little more reserved in that film; he has a darker side and he's more controlled when

he speaks. My mother's more open and they have a good balance
and I watch this go on during the shooting of the picture. I shot
it in three hours on a Saturday and three hours on a Sunday—six
hours, and I learned a lot about storytelling. I guess what it really
was, more than timing, it's an attitude about a certain reality and
you just say it and the hell with it and that's the way she was, you
know. She had a kind of surrealistic humor about it, too.

R: There's a feeling in that film, which I've seen several times, that
the cameras are truth machines in that things they wouldn't necessarily tell you over dinner . . .

M: Right.

R: . . . they would tell you while you were filming them because they
wanted to help Marty with his film.

M: With his film, yeah. That's right. That's right. You get this great
stuff—no, I'm just kidding. But I was surprised, you know; I was
very surprised by that. And even the moments where he gets very
upset and tells me it looks like hell, what's the matter with you;
because I just started growing a beard so he didn't like that, you
know. And all that . . .

R: The big deal they disagreed about was that they moved . . .

M: They moved.

R: Across the street!

M: Across the street. That's the punch line.

R: If you're watching the film for the first time, you think they must
have moved out of state.

M: I mean, you know . . .

R: They can see their old house from the window.

M: That's right. Literally across the street, literally, you know. I couldn't
believe it. The thing was, I learned, you know, I guess at a certain
age you wanna get out, you wanna get away from the parents, you
wanna deny, no, they're not mine. I don't have anything to do with
them. I don't know who they are. You know, you can't choose family, you know, that kind of thing. And, I don't know, they came in
with me; I don't know who they are, part of my group, just put
'em over there, you know, give 'em some drinks or something. But

by the time I did *Taxi Driver*, that was a little different, yeah, it became more open and ultimately by the time I came around to doing *Raging Bull*, is when I totally embraced it and I said that's who I am and they should come into the film, they should be in the film and they should hang around the set and . . .

R: They grew up in your life.

M: Yeah.

R: They understood that something has happened to their son that wasn't part . . .

M: That's what it was.

R: . . . but instead of denying it, they were curious about it.

M: Yeah, very curious. And they always loved movies, you know. My mother would have preferred more genre, more like the Hollywood films, at times, but then it took her a few years to begin to understand that these were different, you know. And in any event, they kind of, it kind of helped out on the set, too, because it made things more homey, I don't know; it was more like . . . it was that the other actors, people would sit down, they'd talk, they'd sit—like in *Cape Fear*, they would hang out in front of Nick Nolte's trailer. They like Nick, you know. I'd get out of my trailer and they'd be sitting there and they'd wave, "I'm fine; how're you doing?" One night she came on the set of *Taxi Driver* and we were preparing for that crane shot at the end that pulls back, which is still too long— I just, it's one of those things—I had a crane, I wanted to use it, you know. [BIG LAUGH.] You gotta be careful. I mean, I had it planned as a crane shot but it was just . . . boy, you know, to go up on that, it's so expensive. It happened because we only had it for one day, that was it, one night. And we're pulling back and we had lit the whole street, the whole thing, and she came and everybody was down there and she was watching and at one point she says, "You know, how long you're gonna keep the street lighted? You gotta get moving." I said, "What, you're working for Columbia? Who are you? Mind your business; get in the back." She's one of the studios, you know, one of the studio executives or something. But it became that way, you know. We get very, very open. A lot of food; they would make a lot of food on the set and that sort of thing.

R: She kept you in line, too. I remember the night we did a tribute to you at the Toronto Film Festival and you said, "What should I wear? What should I wear when I go on stage?" And I said, "We'll wear tuxedos because we're the presenters, but you're the star, you're a Hollywood director, you can wear your jeans." And you said, "Ah, I can wear my jeans, wear my jeans." Your mother said, "Martin, wear your tuxedo!" We're gonna get to *Taxi Driver* next. You can tell the projectionist that because you mentioned it and you kinda have a habit, a very nice habit, of making the best film of each decade.

M: Ah, I hope so.

[BIG APPLAUSE.]

R: I don't know what these critics' polls mean.

M: I know, I know.

R: It doesn't mean anything to lose one. It probably means something when you're selected, when they invite hundreds of critics to vote on the best films of a decade. And when they ask the various critics groups and assemblies about the best film of the '70s, it was *Taxi Driver*.

M: Really.

R: And we'll leave everybody in suspense as to what the best film of the '80s was; that will come later in the program. But *Taxi Driver*, to me, really represents that feeling; it's like the sum of the personal cinema. And about the time *Taxi Driver* came out, we started to get the giant multimedia blockbusters, special-effects pictures . . .

M: I know.

R: . . . all respect to people like Lucas and Spielberg . . .

M: Yeah.

R: . . . but *Jaws* and *Star Wars* . . .

M: Right.

R: . . . changed the rules, and when *Taxi Driver* was made it wasn't as unusual as it now seems.

M: I know. I know. Because you're talking about a time—you have to

(171)

understand, everybody, that the number-one box-office film of all time, for, like, since 1939 to 1972, was *Gone with the Wind*. In 1972, *The Godfather: Part I* took over. In 1976, I think, *Jaws*. And everything changed.

R: And '77 might have been *Star Wars*.

M: *Star Wars*. And that was that.

R: And then every year you get something. So this year it's *Independence Day* and last year it was *Jurassic Park* and . . .

M: So it's become like a whole other thing. It's almost like a different industry in a way. But this was, you know, a film that we really believed in, *Taxi Driver*. It's really, you know, important that everybody understand the impetus and the whole presence behind the picture is Paul Schrader. It's very important and it's not to dare to sound generous but the idea is that one has to understand that it came out of his guts in a two-week period when he was alone in LA and very depressed. [LAUGHTER FROM AUDIENCE.] So it's real; it really is real. And I was in LA and depressed a lot, too, and

. . .

R: Depression seems to be a genesis of a lot of the work of the both of you.

M: Well, yeah, it is, it is. But, no, it's not because LA is a bad place. It's when—you know, I was a kid from the Lower East Side who never went anywhere and then I'm in a strange town with no friends and I'm alone. And the only guy who would come around would be Brian De Palma and he'd take me to all these people's houses and everything. And Jay Cocks, my friend Jay, when he'd come to town, introduced me to people and that was it. But those . . . those weeks where there was no one around, it was really, really awful. You could see it in *Barton Fink* when he says, "You can't leave me in Los Angeles!" The poor guy starts crying. He was new in town, too, the poor writer, you know. So this really came out of Schrader, you see; he wants me to always point that out and I think he's right. Of course, the idea there is that when I read the script which, by the way, was given to me by Brian De Palma, when I read the script I just felt so strongly for Travis, and De Niro felt the same way. But we never sat down and talked about existentialism. In fact, I don't know what it is. I only had one philosophy course at NYU and I didn't do very well in it.

R: Schrader wrote a book called . . .

M: *Existential Style.*

R: Yes.

M: Ozu, Bresson, and Dryer. He knew what it was, Paul, yeah. He had it all in there, you know.

R: Let's look at the clip and then I have a couple of questions for you.

M: This clip is Harvey and Bob, when he first meets Harvey in the street? There's a little improvisation in this. A little bit. [CLIP.]

R: Okay, now, you were talking about De Niro when he was listening.

M: Yeah. When he's listening to Harvey give that litany of what he could do to the kid, his body . . . freezes . . . and he's so full of anger and violence—he's like a stiletto. And Harvey, the more he did that . . . if you watch Harvey, the more Harvey closed in on him. They sort of played off each other beautifully, you know. And that's why it's all in a two-shot, you see, until finally we do a closer shot of Bob and a closer shot of Harvey. And even in that closer shot you can see where he moves back this way. He does a strange thing with his back, and it's from driving the cab, too, he has this kind of interesting look of always being prepared for anything, you know. But it's containing that violence, especially when he finally says, "Okay, I'll take it. I'll take it," you know. A lot of that was improvised by Harvey, especially the stuff at the end. He says, "I'm hip." "Funny, you don't look hip." And also it's entrapment and this thing here I got from my mother, which, one time I think she told Harvey something, "Oh, yeah, that guy, he's in jail," she says like this. [BIG LAUGH.] So we threw it in, you know.

R: Looking at them in this scene, it may be a good point in the evening to talk about these two remarkable actors who have been associated with you in so many films over the years and you were the first to use Keitel. You were not the first to use De Niro but nevertheless you and De Niro are linked in everybody's mind. These two actors and your career cannot be thought about apart from each other.

M: That's right, that's right. That's what we were talking about earlier, yesterday, I think, the idea of what collaborators really are, you know. It's a blessing to have come upon this relationship, beginning with Harvey and then midway through and continuing with De Niro.

R: Harvey, the bank clerk who was mad at you for calling him back for retakes because he had a good job now at the bank.

M: No, it wasn't a bank; it was a court stenographer.

R: Court stenographer.

M: He got really mad from retakes and he would come in and would have cut his hair, it didn't match, didn't matter. We have to shoot. That was on *Who's That Knocking*, you know. There's no continuity in the film anyway; there was no plot. But, no, I really . . . with Keitel I really found, at that time in 1965, he came and he auditioned at NYU with *Waiting for Lefty*, and oddly enough, we were saying yesterday . . .

R: Wow.

M: Yeah, somebody knows it. That's great. And De Niro auditioned for De Palma for *Greetings* with *Waiting for Lefty*, the same speech, you know, about a year before. And finally . . . with Keitel, I found that we just kind of knew a lot about each other's feelings and about life and—oh, God, how to live one's life with guilt and all that sort of stuff all worked together and we kinda understood each other and trusted each other a lot. Even especially on *Last Temptation*, Harvey playing Judas, we had a really good time, you know, really good time, because in rehearsals we just couldn't stop talking about the implications and the variations of all the different levels of meaning in just the situation itself, not the book or the gospel, but the situation and the beauty of that situation. And we'd constantly get hung up enjoying the possibilities, the discussions, what if, and all that sort of thing. De Niro is similar but we find that if the script is strong enough, we don't really talk that much about the project. We usually talk about, you know, personal stuff, like when he said at the American Film Institute last week, "Marty and I talk about personal things, which are between us" and that's that. It is between us, so, you know, it's one of those things that you find—on *Taxi Driver* we became very close, I think, and—what it is, I mean really—both of them, particularly working with Bob more, I was able more to—it was—I didn't have to tell him very much about certain feelings and, well, you see it in Jake LaMotta, you see in the suffering. They got it, these guys, you know, they know it. They know it dead.

R: They are two very different people, having interviewed both of them from the journalist's point of view. With Keitel, you ask a question, you get an hour of quotes. The most interesting quote I ever got from De Niro was, "Yeah? Yeah." (175)

M: That's what I mean, yeah. The thing about De Niro is, why should he have to say it? It's up there. That's the way he feels.

R: And he should feel that way. Because it is up there.

M: It is up there and it's not easy to put it up there, that's the problem and, you know, that's where I get the problem, that's where I have the conflict of loving the old films and enjoying, I don't know, a Clark Gable or Spencer Tracy, for example, so wonderful the actors and enjoying the British actors going from John Mills, Alec Guinness, to Olivier all the way up to a lot of 'em very much now. But I would never, I guess, I could never have made movies with them, you see, where it's this kind of a situation where to even talk about the issue is like opening a wound, and it's oversensitive, and it's like a mechanism of a very, very, very, very, very delicate clock, in a way. You can't force it. You just can't force it, you know, you have to give it time.

R: When you look at *Raging Bull* you see in a fiction film, a scripted fiction film . . .

M: Yes.

R: . . . the same emotion you see in a documentary like *Crumb* where you're actually looking at human anguish on the screen and you're really seeing it. I don't know how De Niro does it, I don't know how you did it, but there are very few fiction films that have the impact of a documentary in the sense that I'm talking about, where you feel there's no performance.

M: *Raging Bull* was hard to make but we had gotten to the point where the suffering of the characters, we were able to do it without becoming a part of it, you know, ourselves; whereas, prior to that, it was rather difficult.

R: We have a *Raging Bull* clip, although if we would stick to chronology, we also have a *Last Waltz* clip. You wanna jump ahead or . . .

M: I don't know. What . . .

R: They're your films. What do I feel like? I want to see every clip on the list myself. But anyway, here's the list. Maybe you can just tell the projectionist what to cue up and I have a question while he's doing that.

M: Shall we do *Last Waltz* or . . .

R: If you want to.

M: Sure, okay, fine then. Okay, *Last Waltz*, guys.

R: Let me ask you a question while we we're waiting for the green light. I talked to Schrader not long ago and he said he's a creature of the past now.

M: He told me that, too.

R: He still believes in existentialism, the existential hero . . .

M: I know.

R: And he says now it's the ironic hero.

M: I know. He told me that too. I said what are you worried about?

R: Everything has ironic quotation marks around it now, he says.

M: I know.

R: "With my work," he said, "there's no quotation marks. I really mean it."

M: Yeah, he means it. So do I. I said, "We're victims of the past." I said, "So what?" So we're twentieth-century madmen; in a couple of years it'll be twenty-first century and we're part of the past. So maybe we're lucky to get a few more pictures out. Well, what are you gonna do? You gonna try a change for the twenty-first century? What's that? I think I know what he's talking about. Besides trying to get his pictures made, which are very hard, you know, because he's very, very unique—he can only get a certain amount of money, and he's also gotta work as a writer, too. And it's very hard to go to a studio when they say, "We want *Pulp Fiction*." And when you give it to them they say, "This is not it." You say, "Yes, it is, that's what you told me to write." You know what I'm saying? So he's more on the front lines than I am and he's seeing it really out there. But he also understands that. He wrote *Transcendental Style*. I mean, I don't even know what transcendental means, you know what I'm saying? I mean that seriously, in the sense that he really is much better educated and can really verbalize these things whereas I can't. And he told me, he said, "Don't be upset," he said, "but I said in the press that Quentin Tarantino is to Martin Scorsese as (177) David Letterman is to Johnny Carson." I said, "All right, what's that mean?" He said, "Well, Johnny Carson is like, you know, and David Letterman kind of makes fun of the situation—the actual sense of television. He goes to a donut shop and it's Mr. Donut and he interviews Mr. Donut, you know: 'Are you really Mr. Donut?' That sort of thing, which is wonderful and . . ."

R: I see where he means in a sense that Johnny Carson is really interviewing the person and David Letterman is doing a satire on the act of interviewing somebody. But at the same time, David Letterman is doing a satire on a talk show.

M: Exactly. That's it.

R: So it has the quotes around it.

M: Yeah, you always have the quotes around it, no matter what you do on the *Letterman* show, that's why some of it is so much fun.

R: Letterman will say, "What was it like to make our last movie?" as if he's making fun of the question.

M: Exactly.

R: It has the quotes on it.

M: Exactly.

R: But what Schrader also said to me was . . .

M: He said I don't have the quotes and I said, "What do you want from me? I don't know. I can't . . ."

R: Schrader said something else, though, that was interesting. He said *Taxi Driver*, if you look at it today, it's as strong as it ever was. He said, "I would be very interested in how well *Pulp Fiction* holds up in twenty-five years."

M: Oh, Paul can say that.

R: His feeling is, I'm not trying to put words in his mouth, but his feeling is that the problem with irony is, it's like satire. It's what closes Saturday night. It closes within its own time.

M: And one has to be very careful. I found out rather early in time that topical humor is the first thing to go, you know. It just references to some news event, etc., that may be funny for about twenty minutes, you know, and ten years later you say, what was that about? What the hell? You had to be there. So one has to be very careful about topical humor. We ran into that in film school and I learned right away about that. Don't even try it, you know. But Paul is very, very good. He's excellent . . . his new film, I understand, is real good and it's just that he really believes that maybe we are fifty-five years old, you know. The awards are really great at this time because I'm always looking for the encouragement to get more money to do more pictures because there was a period where I couldn't, you see, so I never take for granted anymore, you know.

R: We have a green light for *Last Waltz*. Do you want to set it up?

M: I believe this is Bob Dylan and The Band. "Forever Young," I think. And maybe "Baby, Won't You Follow Me Down," I think. After seven hours on the stage Dylan came out and they did about five songs. I was allowed to shoot the last two, "Forever Young" and "Baby Won't You Follow Me Down." And one of the things that I really enjoyed about *The Last Waltz* was—I love music and I designed for the entire seven hours all the camera positions for every song. And Robertson gave me—Robby Robertson gave me—I said, give me a grid in which the lyrics of the song are on the left and the guitar, what point the guitar is really doing something interesting, what point is the keyboard doing something interesting, who's singing what vocal where, and that sort of thing. And then I designed the light changes with the cyclorama behind them, different colors come up at different phrases and different stanzas, different verses, and I designed camera moves, or at least I knew that at the second verse I gotta be on Rick Danko, because he's gonna come in singing. And if camera number two—there was one camera on the wings here, one here, one behind, two out there, and one very big one . . . one high up in the air taking a wide shot. And so we really had one, two, three, four. If three of these cameras went down and Rick Danko was singing and I knew he's coming up, I had to make sure I could say, "Camera number two, pan over, there's Rick Danko." And you had to do this over the amplifiers, the sound was so strong. And it got a little tense at times. But what I also decided to do was to stay on the stage. In other words, never show the audience. And each song—and they've been playing for seven hours—it's very, very hard. In each song you could see the faces of Robertson and Levon Helm and Rick and Neil Young and they're giving each other looks, like, they didn't even know sometimes, "What is he gonna do?" Especially with Dylan; I don't know what song he's going into next. What riff is that? What do you think? I don't know. And they're looking, and it's almost like a round in a prize fight. By the time, especially when Van Morrison finishes, you know, Van the Man, and Robbie's, like, sweating, I mean. They didn't know what the hell he was gonna do, you know, he was capable of anything. (179)

R: What's interesting, before we see the clip, if you think of the first rock concert films from the '60s, basically it consisted of a zoom camera in the front row, zooming in and out on the singer's nostrils.

M: Yeah, yeah. Well, yeah, because they put the cameraman . . .

R: One guy.

M: Yeah, one camera on four guys, what can he get, you know?

R: Then, you were associated with *Woodstock* . . .

M: *Woodstock*, yeah, it was fun.

R: . . . which was the turning point for the whole idea of a rock documentary . . . back then.

M: Michael Wadleigh and Thelma Schoonmaker really created that.

R: But here what you just described to us, I think it's important for people to know that before you made *The Last Waltz*, there was never a rock documentary that was shot with that kind of purpose.

M: Oh, and also shot with 35 mm. This was the first one. And, in fact, we did it as an experiment, thinking that worse comes to worse, we had the money. He got the money somehow, Robbie, for the 35 mm film, and we got the best cameramen around at the time to come, just for the one day and the overall design and supervision were by Michael Chapman, though, you know, not many people realize that. Michael Chapman was making sure all the lights were fading right and everything. But Lazlo Kovacs was there, Bobbie Byrne here, Vilmos Zsigmond up there, Freddy Schuler in the middle . . . I mean, there was just . . .

R: It was like a convention of great cameramen.

M: David Myers, who shot a lot of *Woodstock*, was an excellent cinema verité cameraman, who was doing hand-held. Hiro Narita, the Japanese cameraman, who did *Never Cry Wolf* and films like that and won an Academy Award, I think, he was doing the reverse, the reverse angles. In any event, we just thought, really, just to take a chance and shoot it in 35 to see what would happen. If worse comes to worse, it would be archival. But when we put up the rushes on the cam, on the three heads, three cameras, there was something very vivid, very strong about it. But anyway, this, I think, is just one of the . . . is the last sequence. Okay. It should be played loud, too.

[EXCERPT FROM *THE LAST WALTZ*.]

R: What is new about that is you don't have the audience's eye view of the concert, which was more or less the way most concerts were always shot.

M: Right.

R: The camera is insinuated in the action, the camera is a player in the band.

M: Right. But . . . I mean, you had Michael Wadleigh doing that on *Woodstock*, in 16 mm.

R: So he kind of began it.

M: Yeah. Here, though, we were in fixed positions; we could not get on the stage.

R: But you give the impression.

M: Yeah.

R: The last shot, it's like we're standing right behind the . . .

M: Right, it's here in Narita's camera. It's right behind the drummer, right behind Levon Helm, and he had a track, and he'd go right up and down the set, in a way. And he just got the back angle that way with the light beaming at him, you could see some of the audience a little bit and you catch all the looks; to the drummer you catch the looks to Rick and Robbie and everybody trying to figure out where the hell he was gonna go, you know. And what's he gonna tell them?

R: 35 mm cameras were very heavy when you made this film.

M: Very heavy.

R: You couldn't just . . . it wasn't a hand-held situation . . .

M: No.

R: . . . it had to be moved probably by . . .

M: There was a big problem because the crystal sync motors were dying, were burning up, and I would see, like, camera number two suddenly bang somebody's hand, like the table in *GoodFellas* coming in the frame, there would be another motor going by, another one died, you know, get another one, bang, bang, bang. It was really seven hours of—we shot every song—I mean there's only a few of the songs in the film, of course, but we did get everything.

R: Isn't there going to be another laserdisc version of this coming out?

M: Yes, yeah, we hope to put out more additional material, we hope.

R: We could move on to *Raging Bull*, and I wanna just say one thing to begin. It came out in 1980. You know, when they give awards they have this persistence-of-memory thing. Like the Academy can never remember a movie they've seen earlier than December.

M: I don't know how . . .

R: When they came out, they can't remember it, frankly, they don't know it's this year's film.

(181)

M: I know, I know.

R: So *Raging Bull* came out in '80 and ten years went past and at the end of the '80s, there were three different attempts to pick the best film of the '80s. *Premiere* magazine asked everyone they could think of, and two other groups. And all three picked *Raging Bull* as the best film of the 1980s, ten years later. There hadn't been anything since like it. It is a great film. It is a film that will live as long as films are seen. And what I feel so strongly in talking to people about movies, frequently people will know I'm a movie critic, and they will discuss the subject matter as if that is what the film is about. Oh, it's a film about boxing?

M: Yeah, I know.

R: Oh, it's a film about gangsters or . . .

M: Right, right.

R: . . . whatever, you know. Like when they hear what *Breaking the Waves* is about . . . "Oh, I don't know if I want to see it." A film is not about its subject; it's about how it's about its subject.

M: Right. In fact, when . . .

R: Subject is neutral; people don't understand that. When people say, "I don't like to go to movies about . . ." and you fill in the blank, my response is anyone who makes that statement is an idiot. No, it's true.

M: It's true.

R: I don't wanna go to bad films about cowboys; I don't wanna go to bad films about boxers.

M: I know.

R: I would like to see a good film about a boxer, however.

M: I mean, when Bob gave me the book originally, it's back in 1974, I had never seen a fight. My father's a big fight fan but I didn't know anything about boxing and I wasn't interested in films about boxing, you know. But it took those years for me to go my own way to come back to understanding really what it was about.

R: It was about a boxer but it wasn't about boxing, it was about the boxer.

M: Right. It was about a man, yes, a man.

R: Do you want to talk about this scene before . . .

M: What scene? What is it?

R: It's Sugar Ray 3, Joey watches at home.

M: Oh, it's the entire Sugar Ray . . . I think this is the sixth time he fought Sugar Ray Robinson and it's the dignity he tries to retain standing up in the ring . . .

R: Able to take the punishment.

M: After taking such punishment. The punishment he takes in the ring is nothing to what he does to himself. And nothing to what he does to his family and his friends, to people who love him.

R: Could you set this up just a little bit by talking about two things. Number one, what people don't always notice, they observe viscerally but not necessarily intellectually how much technique went into the boxing sequences . . .

M: Oh . . .

R: . . . from the slow motion and lenses and movement of camera.

M: Well, what happened with the boxing sequences, once I saw De Niro perform the nine fights — Jake LaMotta and Jimmy Nickerson worked on blocking from nine fight scenes and he showed 'em to me in Gleason's Gym on 14th Street and was stunned. In fact, Bob came over to me, he says, "Are you watching? Because I'm killing myself." I say, yeah, I am. And I realized he thought I was hanging around not watching. I'm watching, I realize we can't shoot this. We can't shoot this from my angle. I said we have to be in there with him and it's gotta be *The Wild Bunch*. Every punch has to be worked out in such a way, or, let's say, not every punch, but you have to do it like music. You have to do it like it's from the musical sequences in *New York, New York* where three bars of music was one shot, literally. Not four cameras then you cut 'em together in the editing room. That's selecting, not directing; it's a different thing, you know. But directing is, you know . . . these four punches . . . one, two, three, four, camera tracks from left to right, swings around over the shoulder of the guy who's getting hit, and we see a close-up of LaMotta hitting him. And it's gotta be a knock, shoom, like this, and as fast as the punch is. Then do it, then on the set we

(183)

realized, in certain cases we realized, in certain cases we began to understand we couldn't even see the punches, they were so fast; we had to go higher speed, on 3, 6, 48, 96, that sort of thing, just to see them and you see all the speeds. But primarily what happened was that I drew out every shot for each fight scene; there are nine fight scenes in the film. One I didn't draw up a shot; it was the second Sugar Ray fight, but I decided that I was doing it with long lenses and we put a bar of fire in front of the lens so . . . heat ripples. And the most important thing was that the camera never, as much as possible, never goes outside the ring. That you're always in the ring with him. His vision becomes your sensibility. In other words, what he perceives in the ring. Sometimes I open the ring up. We had a ring that I built special where I made it longer and sometimes wider and it was like — imagine being punched in the head, what you hear and what you perceive. You don't know where you are.

R: It's all hallucinatory; breaking glass . . .

M: Breaking glass.

R: . . . animal noises.

M: Animal noises; that's something Fred Weiler did. He wouldn't tell us after a while what he was using. He said, "I'm not gonna tell anybody," you know, whatever it is, it's great, you know, that sort of thing. Pulling out the sound, putting in the sound, we even changed speeds during a shot, which now you can do very easily with a button, but then you had to actually change the motor and also the left stop with two assistants, that sort of thing. But many of them, what I'm saying there was all designed and they were all designed, shot A, B, C, D; one, two, three, four, five; they were all cut together . . . some of the cutting of the fight scenes was easiest to do because it was all laid out. But we had planned five and a half weeks of shooting and it did take ten weeks. And it was very specific and De Niro would have on the side of the camera a very big punching bag, one of those cylinder ones, that looks like a cylinder, and when we're ready to yell, we're ready to go for a roll, we'd have the slate ready, you know, and start rolling and you hear off camera, he's punching the bag, punching the bag, then he'd jump into frame, sweating, you know, and then to slate, so he came in already heated, bang, ready to go. It wasn't like, you know, wasting any footage. But the physical stamina it took him to sustain ten weeks of that was amazing, because he believed in the shots I wanted to get, you know. And it was hard. Irwin Winkler and Bob Chartoff, my producers, after about the sixth week they said, "What are you doing? We gotta get going here." I said, yeah, well, whatever. They liked the footage; we cut some together and they said, "Oh, I see, I see." So they left us, you know. It took us another ten weeks to do the dialog scenes and then about ten days to shoot the scenes where he was heavier. But what you see here is the final, the final battle, in a way, and the punishment he takes, especially the montage when he gets beaten up by Sugar Ray is based, in a way, the drawings I made were based on the shower scene from *Psycho*. And I shot it in that way in thirty-nine shots and it took ten days just to shoot those shots, because there were applications and all kinds of makeup problems and, just to get the angle right, was like ten days and then when we edited them together in order, we started to play around with the film and we started re-editing that whole little sequence where it just became visceral; that was a case where shot one did not go to shot two and shot three. It just became shot thirty-eight, by the last time we were cutting the film. There's even a shot in there Sam Fuller told me about. He said, "Put the lens in somebody's hand and just swing, this way. You'll see." We even put the camera on the boxing glove and the glove is in the foreground; it comes flying at 'em this way. It's all in there for, like, maybe five frames, six frames, you know.

R: Thelma Schoonmaker told me, when we went through this film a shot at a time at Virginia, she felt as much work, preparation, shooting, and postproduction, went into the fight scenes in *Raging Bull* as any footage of any film ever shot.

M: Yeah. Well, I mean, of the films we did.

R: Well, or maybe . . . I don't know, who knows?

M: We did a lot of preparation and you have to understand, too, there's

(185)

only about nine or ten minutes of fight footage in the film, you know. I have the drawings, you know. Some people never believed us; no, I got the drawings to show you, just look, you know.

[CLIP OF *RAGING BULL*.]

M: One thing I forgot to say before it started was that the announcer's voice, that's the actual announcer of the actual fight. The phrases he used, it was hard to get his voice out through the stereo and that sort of thing, it's hard to hear sometimes, but the lines he uses are amazing. No man could take this punishment. That's all real. That's actually as it was happening, you know.

R: Obviously, this film is in black and white. It came at a time when you were involved in a battle with Eastman over the fading color stock but apart from that, didn't you believe that this film had to be in black and white?

M: Yeah. I believed that. Remember *Sweet Smell of Success*? That's a great film by Alexander Mackendrick with Burt Lancaster and Tony Curtis, really sort of based on Walter Winchell. It had extraordinary black-and-white photography of New York—James Wong Howe photography, 1950-something, '55, I think, '56, '57. Anyway, I thought of that and I also knew that there were four or five other boxing films coming out that year. There was *A Main Event*, with Barbra Streisand and—well, a comedy . . . and there was *Rocky II* or *Rocky III*, I think, and there were a couple of others and there was even *Matilda, the Boxing Kangaroo* in color. Think of it, I said, ours is the only one in black and white; it's gotta be different, you know. But the studio was extremely nervous about that and we had a meeting with David Field and Steven Bach, I think, from UA, at my apartment in New York at the time. I was living in both places at the time, in New York and LA, and I think it's in that book *Final Cut*, it describes the meeting. Interesting about Irwin as a producer, he's really quite good and he never let me know the difficulties surrounding the picture as I was working. For example, he told me, he said, "Guys, you know, they're very nice guys actually, David and Steven. They just wanna come up and see you and Bob at the apartment, just to talk to you and just, you know, check in

(186)

on the script and see how things are going; just something purely personal. It's a hello-goodbye meeting, that's all it is." I read *Final Cut* and they're coming up in the elevator thinking they're gonna cancel the picture. I said I didn't know that; this is amazing, you know. And then one of them said something about who cares about boxing, and they were very nice about it but they really wanted to know, and I explained the black and white to them and they went with that. And then they wanted to know why we'd want to make a film about this guy, this guy is like a cockroach, and De Niro just looks and says, "He's not a cockroach." And they bought that.

R: Oh, thank you for explaining . . .

M: Yeah.

R: . . . exactly.

M: They saw that we genuinely cared about it and Irwin didn't tell me any of what led to the meeting. He's never told me that, in fact. He also recently told me that while we were editing the film, UA was trying to sell it and they couldn't sell it. They couldn't sell it. Now, you have to understand that there's a little delicate political problem there. The UA that was trying to sell the film was not the UA that greenlit the film. The men who greenlit it were really wonderful; it was Arthur Krim and Eric Pleskow.

R: And they were gone.

M: And they left because of the fight with whatever . . . Transamerica . . . and they formed Orion and there was a new interim regime at UA at the time and they inherited this picture, you know. They didn't know what to do with it, you know.

R: There's a tradition, too, that if you inherit someone's picture and it's a success, it makes them look good.

M: And it makes them look really bad.

R: Makes you look bad.

M: Yeah. *King of Comedy* was that way too. Sherry Lansing, who believed in the film so much, head of Fox, she loved the picture; gave us all the time in the world to do it. She shouldn't have—she had to leave the studio six weeks before the opening. And that was the end of that, you know.

R: The other thing about the picture might have been that the blood in color would have been . . .

M: Well, that's one of the reasons. I really felt that the blood was too much . . . in black and white it was better. I also felt that, you know, I was learning about what was happening to the older films, the color fading was such a problem. When I was young a special film was made in color. That was a special thing. By the time the '60s came around, late '60s, special films were being made in black and white and everything was color and just when you got to all the films being made in color, the stock wasn't as good anymore, so that the color after about ten years looked lousy. This was before video, so if you went to see a retrospective of a director's work or an actor's work, you know, you'd see—I'll never forget about going to the Regency Theatre in New York, they showed a retrospective of Minnelli's films and I wanted to go see *Lust for Life*, the one on Van Gogh, which they really use the Van Gogh paintings in widescreen and color. And I was shooting *Taxi Driver*. I went actually after a day of shooting to go to Regency to see that film in color. It was magenta, pink, the whole picture. Beautiful stereo track, by the way. You know, who cares if they—why should they worry about it, it's a movie about a painter. I mean, the color in the original images was gone. And that's all, by the way, changed right now. I mean, that's in 1975, so it's been changed since then. But that's what got me understanding that nobody was there watching, or taking care of the store, in a way, and nobody's taking care of the archives and if you take care of the archives, it's money in the bank for them. But there was no video at the time, you see, so they really didn't know that, so the only thing I could do was, during the editing of *Raging Bull*, was to complain to Eastman Kodak and get names on a petition of filmmakers and people in . . .

R: Francis has also made a black-and-white film at that time . . .

M: *Rumblefish*.

R: *Rumblefish*.

M: Right after, yeah. And what eventually happened was that we met with Eastman Kodak and Kodak actually came through beautifully—a year later, two years later, what you have now to-day; they print everything, including rushes, on a stock called LPB, which is a low-fade stock which they claim would fade in sixty to one hundred years, but you have to keep 'em in the right conditions. Prior to that, the regular processing was maybe, if you're lucky, ten years, six years, two years. In the right wrong conditions you could lose it in six months, they told me. And that was the kind of thing we were doing so we were trying to study these films without video. We'd have to go to these theatres and the print would come up, they looked like hell. We couldn't see anything. And I got very angry about it because just when we designed something in color, when color becomes so important that every film is being made in color, the color of the jacket, the tie, is important, you choose it, you go crazy with all this sort of thing. *New York, New York*, we did that. We painted makeup on the people to try to look like the old Technicolor and that's exactly when the color is gonna go. There's another technical point, too, that the three-strip Technicolor made in the '30s and '40s was printed in a process called dye transfer. And the last film to be printed that way—that print, by the way—when a film's printed that way, it doesn't matter what stock it's shot on, the print will always survive, the color will always stay that way. And the last film to be printed that way was *Godfather II*, 1974. And the machines were sold to China . . .

R: Which then went on to make some beautiful color films.

M: Absolutely. But, you know . . . what's happened now is that Techni-color is—it's always a killer, Technicolor for the past few years now. It's terrific because they're coming back with IB; they're coming back with the dye-transfer prints. They released *Giant*, re-released *Giant* in five prints made in Technicolor, the real old Technicolor, so that no matter when you see the print projected, the color will still be there. So it's gotten better.

R: Well, you started the Film Preservation Foundation to help . . .

M: Yeah, yeah.

R: We have . . . the next clip that we have marked is over here on

(189)

page two but, you know, I think we oughta stop at a film on our way, don't you?

M: Sure, why not?

R: *Last Temptation of Christ*, if you could wrap that.

M: Right.

R: The thing about home video is despite the fact that it's great, isn't it great to look at this celluloid?

M: Amazing, amazing.

R: At least what home video has done, people can see the movie . . .

M: Yes.

R: . . . and it provides an economic incentive for the studios to preserve them.

M: Yeah, I think the number of pictures I've made earned back their money for the studio just on video. Video and European distribution, you know.

R: Roman Catholicism has been very important to you throughout your entire career. You studied to be a priest at one time. Did I tell you that I did too?

M: How old were you?

R: High school. I didn't really study, but they had a kind of a summer camp at the seminary . . .

M: Ah ha.

R: . . . and it was real thrilling when you got to smoke with the seminarians. I remember that better than any of the religion part of it. My mother made me take Latin in high school because I would have to have it if I ever regained my vocation, which I'd lost, you see. And *The Last Temptation of Christ* is the most overtly religious of your pictures, in terms of its subject matter. And probably comes out of a lot of feelings you have about the passion and death of Christ, growing up as a Catholic in this world.

M: Yeah, yeah. There's no doubt that the most incredible theatrical experience, without being disrespectful, for an eight-year-old, was going into St. Patrick's Holy Cathedral for the first time and seeing a Mass and seeing those statues — the plaster saints and the body of Christ lying in the sepulcher, you know. I believe after they shot *Godfather*, they changed the statues and things; they got some money, you know, sort of modernized it in a way, but the older saints, the older plaster statutes of the saints, the old Italians, the old Sicilians and Calabrese grew up with those saints, so great. And it was so vivid, you know. And the use of color and the suffering of the saints; it was really something, that seven- or eight-year-old who was going there and see a High Mass. It was quite a theatrical experience but, I mean, religious, but also at the same time something that has never left my consciousness, and I guess by the time we got to do this scene in *The Last Temptation of Christ*, I think I got carried away because Paul Schrader's original script was very short, very short. And what he wanted was the story of Jesus, the known story of Jesus from the Gospels. Of course, we're in Kazantzakis's book which, as we have to say again, is purely a story; it's not the Gospel. But you take everything that you kind of know about Jesus up to the point of the crucifixion and that's only, like, an hour and fifteen minutes into the film and the audience would be wondering what's gonna happen because that's the end of the story; there's a resurrection and that's it. And instead, you go into the last temptation. But Jay Cocks and I rewrote the script about seven times, actually, and there are lots of things in Kazantzakis's book that I wanted to put in, particularly a scene between Jesus and a monk, played by Barry Miller, where Jesus confesses to the monk, because I felt that what was interesting was that there should be a direct connection between Jesus as a man and God to the man in the street. I mean, he should be preaching on 8th Avenue and 52nd Street, this Jesus, you see. And in the worst part of town, you know. And healthy and taking care of the beggars and the prostitutes, the killers and everything. That's the Jesus that we wanted to do because in the Gospels it is, as far as our interpretation. Many friends of mine that are priests say that that's Jesus, that's the way he behaved. He was criticized for it, in fact. But what happened was that I think I got also very much carried away in the passion week, the scene with Pilate, cutting thorns, whipping up the column, the posts . . .

R: Stations of the cross.

M: There are some stations of the cross. There is no way I could get away from those—the imagery, and I wanted to do my impression of it. We started making the film in 1983, in January in pre-production. By December the film was cancelled by Paramount Pictures, for good reason. The UA theatres would not show it and if you spend $19 or $20 million on a picture, it'd be nice to have a place to show it. As I said, you can't complain about Barry Diller, it's understandable, okay. Michael Eisner and Jeff Katzenberg leave Paramount; they form Touchstone Pictures, you know. In the meantime I go with them. We do *Color of Money* at Touchstone. I meet Mike Ovitz. Mike Ovitz says, "What film do you wanna get made?" I said, "*The Last Temptation of Christ.*" And he had me meet Tom Pollack at Universal and Garth Drabinsky, who ran Cineplex Odeon theatres, and within four weeks, Barbara De Fina and I had the picture made. And we didn't believe them. But, you see, the big difference was this: it was no longer $19 million; it was $7 million, fifty-five days shooting in Morocco, and no pay for anybody and a full delivery . . . delivering the picture at $7 million. And we found ourselves in Morocco in the summer, scouting, and literally I used my drawings from '83 and then finished them in Morocco, so every shot in this picture is either drawn or notated because we had no time to think on the set. And we got there and the sun . . . as soon as the sun broke, we were shooting. And in the case of this crucifixion you're gonna see, we shot in two days, from sun up to sun down, and we did seventy-five set-ups, you know. Actually, I had about one hundred set-ups but we cut them down.

R: A typical day of shooting on average by another director might get four . . .

M: Six to ten. Ten's a good day. What we did here, too, is Michael Ballhaus, because he worked with Fassbinder, and he did a film called *Beware the Holy Whore*, which after three days of shooting, he needed another four days to finish, Fassbinder, but he didn't like the actor; he cancelled the actor, he put himself in the part. He said they were going to reshoot everything in one day. So he did it this way. He said okay, at 7:52, we shoot by the window. At 8:01, we're up . . . and they literally did it that way. That's the way we did this crucifixion scene.

R: Fassbinder was the only director who made films that took less time to shoot than to see.

M: To see! I know, he got . . . But over here, I think the shot that we allowed the most time for, forty minutes, was a shot where the camera goes on its side and he says, "Father, why have you forsaken me?" And because Michael had to shoot that and not look through the lens, there was no way, we had no video assist so we shot that way and kinda hoped that he was in the right. That took forty-five minutes to an hour; we went ten minutes over that one.

R: Okay.

M: So let's take a look.

[THE LAST TEMPTATION OF CHRIST, "FATHER, WHY HAVE YOU FORSAKEN ME" SCENE.]

M: Thank you. I just wanna make it clear that those were edited; those sequences were edited, actually. There's more to that. I think Thelma put, like, three sections together but there's a lot more going on. But it was a . . . it was very difficult to shoot the picture. It's still, to this day, I think it's the hardest thing we've ever done. Because of the limit of money and time and difficulty with the dialog and whether those scenes should be longer or shorter. We never really . . . well, we finished it, but we had to release it two or three weeks before its real completion.

R: Because of the controversy.

M: Because of the controversy. So the only thing we could do is to show the film and let people decide for themselves. And maybe it's the way it should have been, which is never really finished, in a way. It's a little long for me, it's two hours and forty-six minutes, and I believe Criterion's going to do a laserdisc version of it soon; like they got the way to get me to do an interview on it . . . but the next few weeks, I think.

R: There was an international protest against the film from some fundamentalist Christians.

M: Fundamentalist Christians, yeah. Which is a different . . .

R: But I remember getting calls because I thought it was a great film and people said things like, "They showed him nude on the cross." And I was saying, "It's okay to crucify him as long as he's wearing a jock strap, right?"

M: Exactly. Well, you said it. I mean, all of a sudden they're gonna put nails in the oak, let's cover him up.

R: It's okay to put the nails in because . . .

M: Yeah. I said no, I've seen that in art. I saw it when I was a kid at the Metropolitan Museum. There was an incredible — I don't know who did it — a wooden sculpture of the three crosses and the two thieves and Jesus naked on the crucifix. That's obviously the truth. Can you imagine on the cross for three days, you know?

(194)

R: I think that people compartmentalize Jesus to such a degree that your film, which I think was done in total spirit of the story . . .

M: Yeah.

R: . . . was too much for people because they want to tame it somehow into more palatable images.

M: It raises a lot of questions. We just wanted to make him one of us, in a sense. The film Christologically is as a member of the religious . . . there's an archbishop of New York, Episcopalian, and a number of my friends are Catholic priests, talk about the correct . . . Christologically correct, they call it, that Jesus is God and man in one. That's the one thing we assume, okay, bang, we go in with that and Kazantzakis too, you know, in the book. And the idea that if it's man, then he has to be afraid of dying.

R: And he has to be capable of lust.

M: And he has to be capable of everything. And what I thought was so great — so great — about Kazantzakis's book was that the last temptation is not for riches or whatever; it's just to live a life of a common man, to have a family, to die in bed and that sort of thing. It's almost a love that he has for mankind, you see. The love he has for us. That's the idea. And in order to die he has to know what we go through. If he doesn't know what we go through, what good is God, you see.

R: Either God or man, then you have to be completely man.

M: Yeah, completely man. That's the trick. So it's not there and it is in all the other things that were coming out, all these different heresies were suddenly being talked about. It was very interesting. It had to be provocative but when you also have to be a movie that, although I'm fond of the old Hollywood epics, you know, dialog written by Christopher Pride, Gore Vidal—just beautiful dialog in many cases—of course, the actual quotes from the Bible, from the Gospel itself, the King James version—the New English Bible is very good. All the different versions. It's just beautiful lines. We use correctly the quotes in the Bible in *Mean Streets*, but not from here. Here, here, I wanted to make it . . . break down—unfortunately break down the poetry of the Bible so that it's, like, literally. Instead of "Live by the sword, you die by the sword," he says, "You live by this, you die by it. Put it down," you know. It's more colloquial and the message is told directly to you in the audience and you deal with it, as told in the voice. Because what happened when you see the older epics, which I love, curtains would open, there'd be widescreen and color, stereophonic sound and everybody is speaking with a British accent.

R: It looked like a holy card.

M: I mean, basically, they say, okay, this is a defense, in a way. We don't have to get too emotionally involved because this happened a long time ago and people spoke funny. We said, no, this guy talks like you, talks like me, some guy has a Brooklyn accent, another guy has a Canadian accent, I mean, it was interesting. One of the tabloids in England, in England it was a real mess. They really got very upset by it. And one of the tabloids, this one writer, I gotta find that piece, hated it. He hated it. But there is one thing, he said, everybody's talking about the accents, the accents in the film, he says, where does it say that everybody in ancient Judea spoke by listening to the BBC? Because you are powered . . . you know, you're powered down by art with a capital *A*, you know. Like, you know, very often it has to have a British accent for you to accept it as something genuine. That's not true. And I'm a great, great,

(195)

great admirer and get so much inspiration from British films. But you know, come on guys, just because it's English doesn't mean it's always the . . .

R: Of course, the subtext in WWII was that Americans spoke with an American accent and Nazis spoke with a British accent.

M: British accent, I know. They can't win, poor guys, I know, it's terrible, okay.

R: Let's move . . . we don't wanna be rushing things, we'd like to be here all night. But the next scene that we have here, which is gonna be *GoodFellas* . . . the projectionist is doing a great job . . .

M: He's great, this guy, yeah.

R: The thing about this scene, this particular scene when Henry and Karen enter the Copacabana, is famous because it's all one take and you can talk abut that . . .

M: Yeah.

R: . . . but it's also illustrative of another thing and that is your constant use throughout your career of a moving camera. And the moving camera in my way of thinking is subjective and involving just as the steady camera is objective and distancing. Your camera often is moving even if the audience isn't aware of it . . .

M: That's right.

R: . . . in this film, it's to implicate the audience in the action. Can you talk about that?

M: It draws you emotionally and psychologically into the action. I mean, I find that one of the key things, for example, in *Taxi Driver* was that you have to see practically everything from Travis's point of view. Otherwise, you wouldn't go with him when he killed those people. You wouldn't know why. Not that you do know why, but you'd have to understand the feeling. You know that something terrible is gonna happen and here it goes and I'm with you because I'm inside him, you see, as much as you can get. And therefore I used lots of point-of-view shots and very often when we did the point-of-view shots, his point of view, we slowed up, higher speeds, lower speeds, that sort of thing. If you look at *Taxi Driver*, rarely, I think—say it's a two-shot and I'm De Niro and this is Albert Brooks or Keitel, on Brooks or Keitel we're over the shoulder of De Niro; he's in the frame. But when we cut to the reverse, it's only Bob; it's only De Niro. He couldn't pose himself into their world because he's always an outsider. And I think that helps to psychologically set him apart from the other people. And the same thing, for example, in the film about the Dalai Lama I'm doing now. It starts with a two-year-old boy to a six-year-old to a twelve-year-old to an eighteen-year-old. And we start with the lower camera; we start with the boy's point of view, mainly. And it's kind of an interesting—that's kind of a tricky thing in how a point of view puts you in the mind-frame of the person. But if the moving camera kind of, for me, is more like choreography and dance, and involves you with the people emotionally . . . that doesn't mean that the objective camera doesn't . . . you know, sometimes you hold back . . . some great directors, Ozu, you know, will just hold like that, and William Wyler to a certain extent in *Little Foxes* and *Best Years of Our Lives*, where you get a solid image and hold that, you know. The return of Fredric March from the war; you see his wife all the way in the background and she doesn't know he's there and the kids see him first. It's beautiful. Watch how he uses his wide shots, and he holds that image.

R: Ozu will even start the scene before the people enter and . . .

M: Oh, yeah. It's beyond me.

R: . . . hold it up till they've left the scene, to insist on the objectivity. He makes it work.

M: Yeah. I guess he makes it work. So what I must say is that my taste for film is catholic with a small *c* and I love most of them but it's taken me years to love the Ozu, Bresson, and Dryer that Schrader wrote about . . .

R: That's Schrader's book. You're still trying to read that book, right?

M: I still . . . I can't read it. I still prefer Dryer. I still prefer Dryer because somehow his emotion got me right away. I don't care whether the camera was static or not, he got me. Then I began to

(197)

understand Bresson. And I still now have Ozu to look forward to. You follow? So, anyway . . .

R: You want to set this up or . . .

M: Yeah, this is Henry taking out his wife-to-be, to the Copacabana, and in a sense, it had to be like royalty arriving; make straight the path where you take stones off the rock, the rocks off the path so the king could come by. And he's seated in the front seat, the best seats in the house. And it's probably the only time in the picture where you see his reward, or what he thinks is a reward . . .

R: For being a wiseguy.

M: . . . for being a wiseguy.

R: But let me ask you one more question. I was asked today, after this was shown earlier, well, doing it in one take, was that just a stunt to prove that you could do it?

M: No.

R: I have an answer to that but I'm not interested in my answer, excellent as it was, but . . .

M: No, no, you see, the whole point, the whole point was that the camera has to go with him so that it takes you through the labyrinth and then finally you come out and you're treated like a king. And it all has to be in one take, and when you think it's just about over, because the place is crowded, the camera pans at a table that's floating through the air and they put the table in front of some other guys and when you sit down then you think it's over, then, well, Mr. Tony just sent us some champagne so you gotta pan over to see Mr. Tony, wave to him, bang, bat. And it finally lands on Henny Youngman saying, "Take my wife, please," you know. And the point is that it had to be a kind of virtuosity that reflected exhilaration of that lifestyle because that's the danger, you see, that's the danger of that lifestyle.

R: To some degree isn't it also Karen's POV. She sees what his gift is . . .

M: Yeah.

R: . . . to her.

M: Yeah.

R: If I go with this guy, the waters will part for him and I can walk along in his footsteps.

M: Oh, yeah, she admits it. Later she says, "I got excited by him," you know, by hiding the gun. She liked it, you know, it turned her on. [CLIP OF *GOODFELLAS*.]

M: You know, I gotta tell you one thing, one thing that I didn't make clear is that, you know, for me, when I was growing up, the Copacabana was like a palace; you couldn't get any higher in style and class. I mean, you know, to see Frank Sinatra at the Copa. My friend who passed away last year on Good Friday, we're the same age, Dominick, his father was the bartender at the Copa Lounge and months and months they would go, on the house, to see the show, you know, and they'd see Sinatra there many times. It was just amazing; I never got to see Sinatra there. But we would go and it was really, like, I mean, you couldn't get any higher. In my mind, this was the epitome of everything; this was what I aspired to. And every now and then, a number of times we went, and we'd have seats and it was "Nice to see you," and the fellow with blue jacket . . . who, by the way, is the real maitre d' of the Copa in the late '50s, and we'd have seats up there. We could see the show; it wasn't too bad. But sometimes we'd get seats down in front and, oh, boy, this is great, this is great. All of a sudden the table would come in. Up. Right in front of us, two tables, and Mr. So-and-so and who knows, you know, and they'd have Big Tony here and then, God forbid, the big problem, as Nick Pileggi would tell you, the big problem is one set of wiseguys were upstaged by another set. Then there was a war and a lot of trouble sometimes. We were, like, you know, hoping that we could at least see the show. But my graduation prom night at the Cardinal Hayes High School we went there, we saw Bobby Darin there . . . It was a wonderful place. I mean, there was . . . it was really fantastic. Great Chinese food.

R: When you said "action" in this scene, you set into motion a lot of actors because you were just telling me during the shot that all the extras standing outside in line to get in, the moment that the

(199)

camera goes inside, they all run in because they're the extras inside too.

M: Well, I didn't know that, you see. What happened was that I was doing . . . like, I think, take fourteen or take fifteen, and by the end I would say, okay, let's do one more. And by the fifteenth take I heard the whole audience go, "oh." I said, "What's the matter with them, they're sitting down, what's their problem?" And Barbara then told me . . . Joe Reidy, who was my AD who set up the shot, said, "We ran out of extras, they're the people waiting in line outside. While the camera's going through, they're running down and getting into the chairs."

R: Let's do a bunch more takes, let's go . . .

(200) M: Well, that was Barbara. I didn't know. I remember we didn't have enough extras. We had . . . we made the film for $25 million, and when I told it to Spielberg, he said, "Oh, still working low budget, huh?"

R: Another thing about that shot that I noticed, as he's grinning to people behind him, the last one he's greased, the guy in the blue suit, sits down slowly and looks at him. Now he's just an extra but it was a great performance because it showed that he felt this person was to be feared and . . .

M: Oh, powerful, powerful. He knew powerful people and although Henry himself was a nice guy, the people he's connected with are very powerful and you oughta be very respectful of him because it could be war any second, you gotta be very careful. Now, also what's interesting about those extras, they're not really extras. These are guys from my neighborhood, my old neighborhood, that—Nicky, what's his name—oh, a nice guy—oh, whatever, he became an extra and he acted in a few of my films and he works in a lot of films in New York now. Frank Aquillino, I think, and then, Butchy, his name is. He has a hat—like Bob wears in *Mean Streets*. And he went down into the neighborhood, and another guy, Johnny Cha Cha, went down and they gathered up all these guys and they brought them up there. And they said they'd be in a film, you know. But the problem was they'd never been in a film before. They'd been sitting all day and the problem was they understood that they were then going to be like actors and they'd get SAG cards and everything. And it was hard to explain to them when they would grab the AD and say, "When do we get our cards?" It doesn't work that way.

R: For you it works that way.

M: Putting money in the AD's pocket. "No, no, no, don't . . . take it back, please." My poor AD, Joe Reidy, is trying to explain to them it doesn't work that way, it's a process we have to go through, it's just a beginning, you know, that sort of thing. And you pay a fine for that, too, but their faces are so strong and they're so good. And you also have to understand that what I did was Nick Pileggi and I wrote that in the script, a paragraph, and I said we do it in one shot. And then I lined it up with Ballhaus and Joe Reidy, Michael Ballhaus on camera, and basically kind of lined it up in certain areas and said here, here this should happen, here's where we should pan from here to the table, that sort of thing. And we have to go around the kitchen in a circuitous way because there was a man next door who wouldn't allow us to go past his door. So it made the shot a little more interesting, actually, thank him. No amount of money, nothing; he was angry at the guys who ran the Copa and that was that. So we had to rearrange the shot, redo all that; all that happening in one day. They set it up for about six hours while I waited and then called me in when they kind of roughed it in. So all that action you saw is designed by my ADs, the guys in the kitchen, all that stuff that they were doing, making cakes and swans and that sort of thing. I just basically gave the outline . . . here's where they walk in, make sure you see the hand giving money here, make sure the maitre d' calls him over this way, make sure you pan over, the pan's gotta be nice and leisurely like a piece of music on choreography, the table comes in, go all the way down, then we pan, you pan over nice to Mr. Tony this way, go right back and then wind up on Henny Youngman. And literally they set it up for me.

R: In *GoodFellas*, which spans a period of time, you shot in different styles to reflect the times . . .

(201)

M: Yeah.

R: . . . so you have more speed-up at the end . . .

M: Yes. Well, no, the more speed-up at the end is due to the drugs.

R: . . . through his drugs.

M: Yes.

R: Subjective cocaine . . .

M: Oh, yes, yes. That will speed it up, yeah.

R: Apart from that, there is a stylistic progression through the film.

M: I think so. I'm not sure, I'm not sure. I think what we did there, what we did with the story, was almost like a documentary, in a sense. But make it very enticing at first and dangerously exhilarating as a lifestyle and then when Spider gets shot is where everything turns and they get to see what you have to pay for this.

R: Starts with the kid looking out the window just as you perhaps were looking out the window when you were a kid.

M: Yeah, oh, yeah. Exactly.

R: I think maybe we have time for one more. Can we choose from these two, whichever . . .

M: What is that? *Casino*, maybe.

R: Okay, *Casino*.

M: I mean, we could do, yeah . . .

R: With Pileggi again.

M: With Pileggi, yeah. In this case, in the case of *Wiseguy*, the book, Nick had written a wonderful book and Henry Hill's voice spoke to an entire book. In fact, there'd be another five or six movies in that book that you can do. I just told one story. One thing about *GoodFellas* that Pauline Kael complained about, saying it's like *Scarface* without Scarface. I said well, why shouldn't it be? Why can't we just have *Scarface* without Scarface? Why do you have to have Paul Muni running around? I mean, I think *Scarface* is an extraordinary film but, you know, I must say, looking at it now, Paul Muni's performance is more theatrical. The great acting there is George Raft in that film; I'm talking about the Howard Hawks one. No, I wanted to take you to the lifestyle, you know, so that Henry Hill is just one of a number of an ensemble of people headed by Uncle

Jimmy, you know. Jimmy Conway, played by Bob. And so by the time we got to do *Casino*, there was another look at this group, or the lifestyle, but in Vegas and with an American touch, the idea of what Vegas and the desert is for the soldiers when they came back from World War II, the idea of dreams being just a spin of the roulette wheel, bang, your whole life changes. And in the meantime they're taking you for suckers. You're giving them money, you know. You put your money in there, they take your money. The odds are against you, totally.

R: What I love about both these films is the documentary information in it.

M: Yeah.

R: Where you find out little things . . .

M: Yes.

R: . . . details.

M: Details make it work, details make it work. It makes it more personal. The first time I realized it is when I saw *The Rise of Louis XIV* by Rossellini, in which at the end of the film the display and demonstration of the power that Louis XIV finally pulled together was in refusing to eat the pork at dinner and you have to see the way the pork is presented to him, you know. And it goes on and on, that scene, when the food comes to the table and he takes something and they go back and then they bring it down and finally the guy says, "I would advise you to eat pork," he sends it away; everybody watches. And he suddenly—he's the man, he's taken total control, you know, he's arrested Fouquet and all that, all that sort of thing. It's really quite—all the documentary detail in the Rossellini films is what led me to play around with that in *GoodFellas*, and of course with *The Age of Innocence* and *Casino*.

R: One thing in *Casino* that I love is that the mob is skimming from the casino.

M: Probably, yeah.

R: And this is something you know.

M: Yes.

R: Even I know this.

M: Yes.

R: They're taking casino money.

M: They have to, yes. They do.

R: What's fascinating is you deal with the problem of what you do with the money after you've stolen it. How you physically get it out. It never occurred to me. You can't just say, okay, here's a large mailbag full of $100 bills, and it's ours now and we're gonna walk out through the front door, and hail a cab. But what about the quarters? If you're gonna steal a ton of quarters, now you've got them, what do you do with them?

M: Yeah, I know, I know.

[*casino* CLIP.]

(204) M: There's more to that scene. Unfortunately . . .

R: Yeah, I know.

M: . . . we don't have it with us tonight but . . .

R: He's mesmerized by that woman.

M: Yeah. And that's actually where Frank Rosenthal, who the story's based upon, told us that he saw her do that one night, you know. She was chip hustling, you know, and a guy caught her and she didn't give a damn anyway; she had a few brandies in her and knocked everything around. The place was pandemonium, he said. He fell madly in love with her, madly.

R: It was even more attractive because it was dangerous and forbidden.

M: Totally.

R: Big trouble for him to do that.

M: Yeah. And that's the one mistake he makes. Because he had so much control; he controlled everything—numbers, figures, he had it all worked out. He was what they call a handicapper. The last time I saw Sam Fuller in New York, somebody asked at the table, "What's a handicapper? You mean, he's a gambler?" Sam Fuller says "No, no, he's not a gambler—handicapper." He says, "A gambler plays games," he says, "The handicapper knows the temperature of the game." Fuller, you know, he's such a great writer and all the newspapers that he worked on in the '20s and '30s, you know, across the country. But he knows the temperature of the game, he knows who watches the weather channel now. You know, you watch because then you'll know what the conditions are. When he bet horses he would go and understand what the jockey was doing, understand if the jockey wasn't feeling well, if he had a personal problem, would go and feel the horse, feel the actual muscles of the horse, you know. And that was the difference between him and the character Joe Pesci plays, where out of ten or fifteen races, Bob's character would play one race and win $25,000. And Joe's character would bet every race and not care about it and lose the money and curse and complain, but have a lot of fun.

R: This film as well as in *Raging Bull*, you used the slow motion to show the erotic obsession.

M: Yeah.

R: We're almost out of time. Let me just ask you a final question that probably won't take you long to answer since it probably cannot be answered. What have you learned or what do you know for sure about it all now, as, in my opinion, the best director we have, what can you tell us?

M: Actually, it's a hard one because, of course, "best director" is certainly relative toward a lot of things but I appreciate it greatly because in the '80s things were kinda down for me, it was really difficult before . . .

R: Made some awfully good films for somebody having a down decade.

M: It was really hard. It was really hard. Thank you. But I guess I learned . . . I mean, what I learned is to be aware of myself, to be wary of myself, and to be wary of becoming complacent about what I can do. And it's so freeing, I'm so free when I realize that ultimately, I'll go on a set, I'll have a script, and I'll see something, bang, it hits this way. *Age of Innocence*, shoot this, shoot that way, and then go—but there's always something as you're trying to transfer that thought, and that note and the little drawing from paper to a lens and then from the lens, my God, what size lens, where do you go, you know. Very often I know what size lens but still, what's in front of the lens? Is there something wrong? You realize that once you know all possibilities are there, it's open, wide open, be prepared, be prepared for everything and anything. The idea is you can't be prepared for anything, you can't be prepared for everything, but what you could be prepared for is not to feel shocked when you don't know. Because if you start to get nervous with yourself, you'll only get irritable with everybody around you and say, you know, I knew it, and I should have done it this way. Be okay with yourself. If you don't know it, just go with it and try to find it. Try to find it with the actor, try to find it with the director of photography, and take it a little easier on yourself. That's the one thing. It makes it scarier but it makes it also more interesting; it's scarier but more relaxing.

R: You know, I think that people don't realize how hard it's been for you. How many films didn't get made or didn't get made with enough money or didn't get made with enough fees or didn't get made at all or almost didn't get made. You're talking about shooting *The Lives of the Saints*. I have a feeling that if you had done, you wouldn't have started with St. Francis. I think you would have started with St. Sebastian.

M: Oh, absolutely, yeah.

R: That's the guy that had all the arrows.

M: He had all the arrows, yeah.

R: But the arrows aside, you still stayed the course and kept your faith.

M: Thank you.

Part 5 Venturing

Introduction

In the most recent decade, only *The Departed*, the film that finally won Martin Scorsese a long-deserved Oscar as best director, was a traditional Scorsese project. The others showed a director looking for new directions to take his work. There is nothing to prepare us for *Kundun*, for example. *Bringing Out the Dead* is like *After Hours* made darker, an existential dread trip. *The Aviator* is a full-dress, big-budget Hollywood biopic. *No Direction Home* is a documentary about Bob Dylan. Then with *The Departed* we return to his familiar world of cops and robbers—or not quite so familiar, because the film, inspired by a Hong Kong police drama, is set in Boston and not New York.

Yet you can see Scorsese themes coiling beneath the surface of all the films, least easily identified, to be sure, in *Kundun*. This lush and poetic story of the childhood and young manhood of the Dalai Lama shows a youth consecrated to spiritual matters, and perhaps speaks to that part of Scorsese that studied for the priesthood. It shows a child willingly submitting to elders who told him who he was, what his destiny was, what his spiritual duties were, and his importance as a spiritual being. Every Catholic school child has been exposed to similar instruction, and found greater or less consolation from it. I may of course be reaching much too far in this parallel; in a reconsideration after the review, I write about other reasons this story, seemingly so unlikely for Scorsese, may have exerted a powerful attraction.

Curiously, of the films in this decade, the one I admired the most got the least enthusiastic reviews. *Bringing Out the Dead* scored only 71 percent on the Tomatometer, and let this be the first and last time we refer to that meter in this book, however intriguing it may be. I thought it was a dark story of redemption sought and lost, a powerful performance by Nicholas Cage as Frank, a man driven into a desperate occupation as an emergency-response worker in the Hell's Kitchen district of Manhattan.

The film contains special effects that would have been unavailable to Scorsese earlier, such as tumbling vehicles and emergencies fraught with sensational events. But at its heart is a man doggedly pursuing his vocation in the face of unremitting doubt and discouragement. "I came to realize that my work was less about saving lives than about bearing witness," Frank says in a voiceover. "I was a grief mop." He is like one of the angels in Wim Wenders's *Wings of Desire*, sorrowing over the mortal suffering of those he moves among. It has driven him mad, this ceaseless labor among the maimed, the dying, the dead, and those few who loved them and whom he is powerless to comfort.

The screenplay is once again by Paul Schrader, based on a novel by Joe Connelly, who was himself an emergency-response worker. The emotional undercurrents linking the film to Schrader's *Taxi Driver* screenplay are obvious. The Cage character is like a man on a rescue mission in the same vein as Travis Bickle. Travis thought he was on a rescue mission, too, and both men in their different ways fixate on a woman they hope can save and redeem them. The story in *Bringing Out the Dead*, which spans three days, has obvious references, even in the title, to the work of Jesus Christ, and Frank, like the Jesus of *The Last Temptation of Christ*, is torn by doubt about his purpose and mission. Is it significant that the woman he focuses on (Patricia Arquette) is named Mary? Well, is it not significant?

I talked about the film with Schrader in 2007, and, forthright as always, he told me: "I'm not as big a fan as you are, because I feel the movie was miscast and I don't think it survived that miscasting. It was written for an actor in his early twenties who has a nervous breakdown as an EMS paramedic. And Nick Cage wanted to do it and he was ten years too old. I wanted Ed Norton to do it and I thought that a man under that kind of pressure wouldn't still be putting himself through it at Nick's age. He would have been dead, insane, or in another job."

I wonder if Schrader's doubts spring from his own strong image of the character as he was creating him. I saw the movie with no preconceptions, accepted the casting of Cage as a given, and reflected how well this actor can convey intense suffering, either overt (*Leaving Las Vegas*) or interior (*The Weatherman*). For me, the film advanced at a white heat, hurdling headlong into grief, showing an angry and despairing redeemer. If Scorsese's human Christ had survived the crucifixion, he might have ended like this, at about Frank's age.

Gangs of New York is a hugely ambitious project, a historical recreation of the underbelly of New York in the 1800s, a portrait of a city opposite in every way from the one in *The Age of Innocence*. In a sense, its bloody gang battles are like the sudden fight at the beginning of *Who's That Knocking*, made epic, ruthless, and fatal. Never before had Scorsese used such elaborate sets and special effects, as he created that lost time. The performances are focused and dedicated, the energy is awesome, the sense of history palpable, and the performance by Daniel Day-Lewis as Bill the Butcher creates one of the great characters in Scorsese's work.

And yet, as I write in my review, the film somehow falls short of greatness. It is too big to be nimble. We sense that Scorsese is more interested in the overarching story than in the individual characters. Unusually for him, there is no one on the screen we can be sure he identifies with; all of the characters operate outside his psychic realm. Even the deliberate Catholic symbolism, as when the Liam Neeson character prepares for battle as for celebrating the Mass, lacks a purpose in the plot; it is just there. No one else could have made this film, and perhaps Scorsese should not have, either. I suspect he was so fascinated by the story that he neglected to find fascination in a character—not interest, complexity, color, but fascination with the person inside.

There is no lack of that fascination in Scorsese's *The Aviator*, a long-contemplated biopic about Howard Hughes. I speculate in my review about the parallels in the story arcs of this and some of his other films,

(211)

and in Hughes's life and Scorsese's, although their later chapters were so different. The film shows Scorsese mastering a production no less ambitious and complex than *Gangs of New York*, but illuminated from within by a character he feels a deep instinct for. Like *New York, New York*, it recaptures an era of nightclubs, great stars, glamorous women, playboys, Hollywood legends.

Leonardo DiCaprio seemed an unlikely choice as Howard Hughes, but here again he exorcised the curse of his absurd fame after *Titanic*, and proved he is a gifted actor and has been ever since his remarkable early work in *This Boy's Life* (1992) and *What's Eating Gilbert Grape* (1993). One of his challenges is to convince us of Hughes's seductiveness and charm in his early years, and do that in a way that we are somehow not surprised by his deterioration. Hughes proceeds to madness step by reluctant step, fighting all the way, sensing what is happening, powerless to prevent it.

Of course, everyone going into the movie knew how the life ended; the legendary recluse, shielded from the world by his minders, victim of obsessive-compulsive disorder, paranoid about germs. I am of two minds on the question of whether Scorsese should have fully followed him down those lonely, dark corridors. On the one hand, they represented half of the life. On the other, they were all the same scene. If Hughes had not achieved what he did in the years before his decay, he would have been just another inmate in an institution. Scorsese made a movie about the man in his full glory, and he was correct: that's where the story is.

Next came *No Direction Home*, the documentary about Bob Dylan, arguably the central figure in pop and rock of the last fifty years. Dylan is notoriously elusive and mercurial, and Scorsese captured that essence. He also found, yet once again, a protagonist as reluctant messiah. For me, the film was a revelation; Scorsese's sympathy with his subject persuaded me I had been focused on the wrong one of the many Dylans.

The film continued the director's interest in music that was revealed in the opening moments of *Who's That Knocking*, flowered in *Woodstock*, filled his sound tracks, inspired *The Last Waltz*. At the time of this writing, Scorsese is in postproduction on a concert film of the Rolling Stones that employed no less than eighteen Academy Award–winning cinematographers. We can see the flowering of an approach introduced by Wadleigh of putting the camera on the stage with the performers in *Woodstock*, refined by Scorsese in mapping specific shots to the music in *The Last Waltz*, and now choreographing music, performers, and cameras in one complex visual and sound ballet.

The Departed, his most recent feature before my book deadline, was inspired by *Infernal Affairs*, the 2002 Hong Kong production by Alan Mak and Andrew Lau. It is obvious what interested Scorsese. The film begins with two characters not unlike Henry Hill in *GoodFellas* and requires both to lead public lives in opposition to their inner natures. The cop as an undercover gangster has to be a good gangster to be a good cop. The same is true in reverse for the gangster as an undercover cop. Both are living within lies. The plot allows the development of enormous suspense and the constant threat of betrayal (consider the scene where a character is told he was given the wrong address but went to the right address anyway). That the two men are assigned to uncover each other is the crowning twist: each has to investigate himself, through the looking glass. This moral ambiguity must have been irresistible to Scorsese.

I begin my review of the film, "Most of Martin Scorsese's films have been about men trying to realize their inner image of themselves." *The Departed* is not merely the opposite of that theme, but even more ironically, assigns each man to betray another who *does* embody his inner image. For the fake cop is a dedicated cop, and the fake gangster is a dedicated gangster, and the better they perform their missions, the better they must betray themselves. Here is the soul conflict from the earliest days of Scorsese's work now turning on itself in a cruel paradox; one can hardly imagine a more complex degree of guilt. There is another element hidden in plain view. Coincidentally, both men end up in association with the same psychiatrist (Vera Farmiga). Her character's name is not Magdalene, but, well, Madolyn. And she is attracted to both men because of the opposite sides of their characters.

At this point in this book, I should provide a summary of what I know, or think I know, or believe, about Martin Scorsese. I know and believe he is one of the greatest of all film artists. Beyond that, I find I have already written such a summary, and you will find it in the last paragraph of my review of *The Departed*.

Kundun

JANUARY 16, 1998

At a midpoint in Martin Scorsese's *Kundun*, the fourteenth Dalai Lama reads a letter from the thirteenth, prophesying that religion in Tibet will be destroyed by China—that he and his followers may have to wander helplessly like beggars. He says, "What can I do? I'm only a boy." His advisers say, "You are the man who wrote this letter. You must know what to do." This literal faith in reincarnation, in the belief that the child at the beginning of *Kundun* is the same man who died four years before the child was born, sets the film's underlying tone. *Kundun* is structured as the life of the fourteenth Dalai Lama, but he is simply a vessel for a larger life or spirit, continuing through centuries. That is the film's strength, and its curse. It provides a deep spirituality, but denies the Dalai Lama humanity; he is permitted certain little human touches, but is essentially an icon, not a man.

Kundun is like one of the popularized lives of the saints that Scorsese must have studied as a boy in Catholic grade school. I studied the same lives, which reduced the saints to a series of anecdotes. At the end of a typical episode, the saint says something wise, pointing out the lesson, and his listeners fall back in amazement and gratitude. The saint seems to stand above time, already knowing the answers and the outcome, consciously shaping his life as a series of parables.

In *Kundun*, there is rarely the sense that a living, breathing and (dare I say?) fallible human inhabits the body of the Dalai Lama. Unlike Scorsese's portrait of Jesus in *The Last Temptation of Christ*, this is not a man striving for perfection, but perfection in the shape of a man. Although the film is wiser and more beautiful than Jean-Jacques Annaud's recent *Seven Years in Tibet*, it lacks that film's more practical grounding; Scorsese and his writer, Melissa Mathison, are bedazzled by the Dalai Lama.

Once we understand that *Kundun* will not be a drama involving a plausible human character, we are freed to see the film as it is: an act of devotion, an act even of spiritual desperation, flung into the eyes of twentieth-century materialism. The film's visuals and music are rich and inspiring, and like a mass by Bach or a Renaissance church painting, the film exists as an aid to worship: it wants to enhance, not question.

That this film should come from Scorsese, master of the mean streets, chronicler of wiseguys and lowlifes, is not really surprising, since so many of his films have a spiritual component, and so many of his characters know they live in sin and feel guilty about it. There is a strong impulse toward the spiritual in Scorsese, who once studied to be a priest, and *Kundun* is his bid to be born again.

The film opens in Tibet in 1937, four years after the death of the thirteenth Dalai Lama, as monks find a young boy who they sense may be their reincarnated leader. In one of the film's most charming scenes, they place the child in front of an array of objects, some belonging to the thirteenth, some not, and he picks out the right ones, childishly saying, "Mine! Mine! Mine!" Two years later, the monks come to take the child to live with them and take his place in history. Roger Deakins's photography sees this scene and others with the voluptuous colors of a religious painting; the child peers out at his visitors through the loose weave of a scarf and sits under a monk's red cloak as the man tells him, "You have chosen to be born again." At his summer palace, he sees dogs, peacocks, deer, and fish. He is given a movie projector, on which a few years later he sees the awful vision of Hiroshima. Soon the Chinese are invading Tibet, and he is faced with the challenge of defending his homeland while practicing the tenets of nonviolence. There is a meeting with Chairman Mao, at which the Dalai Lama hears that religion is dead. The Dalai Lama can no longer look in the eyes of a man who says such a thing, focusing instead on Mao's polished Western shoes, which seem to symbolize the loss of older ways and values.

The film is made of episodes, not a plot. It is like illustrations bound into the book of a life. Most of the actors, I understand, are real Tibetan Buddhists, and their serenity in many scenes casts a spell. The sets, the fabrics and floor and wall coverings, the richness of metals and colors, all place them within a tabernacle of their faith. But at the end I felt curiously unfulfilled; the thing about a faith built on reincarnation is that we are always looking only at a tiny part of it, and the destiny of an individual is froth on the wave of history. Those values are better for religion than for cinema, which hungers for story and character.

I admire *Kundun* for being so unreservedly committed to its vision, for being willing to cut loose from audience expectations and follow its heart. I admire it for its visual elegance. And yet this is the first Scorsese film that, to be honest, I would not want to see again and again. Scorsese seems to be searching here for something that is not in his nature and never will be. During *The Last Temptation of Christ*, I believe Scorsese knew exactly how his character felt at all moments. During *Kundun*, I sense him asking himself, "Who is this man?"

Scorsese Learns from Those Who Went before Him

JANUARY 11, 1998

NEW YORK—There is no greater American filmmaker right now than Martin Scorsese, and hasn't been for some time, perhaps since Welles and Hitchcock and Ford died, and yet to talk with him is like meeting this guy who hangs out all the time at the film society.

We spoke for an hour or two about *Kundun*, his new film, and our conversation kept jumping the tracks and heading for his loves and enthusiasms. When I mentioned, for example, that his life story of the fourteenth Dalai Lama reminded me of the lives of the saints that we read in Catholic grade school, that started him on Rossellini's *Flowers of St. Francis*, and when I talked about how he got interested in the subject matter—the fall of Tibetan culture to Chinese imperialism—he began telling me about a 1952 film named *Storm Over Tibet*, and Frank Capra's *Lost Horizon*, and the Tyrone Power version of *The Razor's Edge*. We started on his camera moves in *Kundun*, and that led to his camera moves in *Taxi Driver*, and how its greatest influence was the way Hitchcock moved his camera in *The Wrong Man*.

This is a voluptuary, a sensualist. Instead of describing beautiful women or old masters, exotic cuisines or great wines, hoards of jewels or the effects of forbidden potions, he is describing movies. Scorsese tells you about a shot in an old film, and it's like listening to Sidney Greenstreet telling Bogart that he must have the Maltese falcon. Perhaps the reason he is the greatest director is because he has spent the most time learning from those who went before him.

Listen to him here, in a breathless passage that I supply for you word
by word:

> I heard that the opening shot in *Boogie Nights* is like the shot in *Good-*
> *Fellas* where the camera tracks through the nightclub. Well, why not?
> I mean, we did tons of that. Myself and DePalma and Spielberg and
> Coppola; in so many of our films we did things that relate to earlier
> films. There are several shots in *Taxi Driver* that are inspired by *Shane*.
> It's homage—the self-consciousness of saying, hey, here's a little nudge
> in the ribs to Truffaut; that's a nudge to Fellini; that's one to George
> Stevens; that's one to John Ford. You find yourself looking at old films
> a lot. The Hitchcock pictures I like looking at repeatedly, repeatedly,
> repeatedly. Very often without the sound. The Powell-Pressburger
> films, John Ford, Welles, of course.
>
> What happens is that you find, through these images, a way of
> writing with the camera that stays in your mind. *The Wrong Man* by
> Hitchcock has more to do with the camera movements in *Taxi Driver*
> than any other picture I can think of. It's such a heavy influence be-
> cause of the sense of guilt and paranoia. Look at the scenes where
> Henry Fonda has to go back to the bank with the police and just walk
> up and down while the tellers look at him. They're deciding a man's
> fate. And watch the camera moves. Or the use of color in Michael
> Powell and Emeric Pressburger's *The Red Shoes*. I think there's that
> kind of . . . influencing. It's not necessarily direct stealing. Each film
> is interlocked with so many other films. You can't get away. Whatever
> you do now that you think is new was already done in 1913.

Scorsese is sitting in the screening room of his offices in Midtown
Manhattan. This is not simply the room were he looks at his daily
rushes or the rough cuts assembled by his editor, Thelma Schoonmaker.
It's also where he screens old movies, many of them rare prints from
his own archive. Who else among active directors would take the
time he did, to assemble and narrate a long television documentary
on great films, and then write a book to go with it?

Now that *Kundun* is being released, Scorsese is in the same strangely
objective mindset he often is after finishing a movie. I've been talking

with him since his first film thirty years ago, and I suspect that if I looked back through all of my notes I would find him saying the same thing after every film: "I don't know if anyone will want to see this." He truly doesn't, and there is a reason for that: he doesn't make a film just because people will want to see it.

Most filmmakers work in a two-stage process: (1) read public's mind; (2) duplicate findings in next movie. Not Scorsese. "We're making this film for ourselves," he told Schoonmaker during *Raging Bull*, which was widely considered the best film of the 1980s. "It's a home movie."

Kundun would seem to be at right angles to most of his work. It's about the childhood and young manhood of Tibet's spiritual leader, who is believed to have lived thirteen times before his present reincarnation. This looks like a radical departure for Scorsese, whose films are often about Italian Americans, not infrequently mobsters, living on the mean streets. Upward mobility for his characters means moving to Vegas (*Casino*) or Miami (*Raging Bull*) and continuing to lead the same lives.

But there is another thread to Scorsese's work that is perfectly consistent with *Kundun*, and that's his obsession with spirituality—which is usually linked with guilt, but not (significantly) this time. His hero in *Mean Streets* holds his hand in the flame of a votive candle, trying to imagine the fires of hell. The overhead shots in *Taxi Driver* are inspired by how priests array the implements of the Mass on an altar. *The Last Temptation of Christ* is the story of man's struggle between the carnal and the exalted (for if God became man, did he not feel the same lust as any other man?).

Kundun is the story of a man who has achieved mastery over his ignoble emotions, who has found spiritual peace, and who carries that treasure out into a hostile world. The film begins with a small child being chosen by monks, who are seeking the new human vessel into which the thirteenth Dalai Lama, having died, will reappear. There is a magical scene in which the little boy tries to pick out "his" possessions from the earlier life, as they are scattered on a tabletop with others. As a young man he grows serene in the practice of his faith, and then must deal with postwar Red China, whose leaders covet the territory of Tibet and are scornful of its religion and tradition.

"I always wanted to make a series of films on the lives of the saints," Scorsese mused. "To try to understand their choices. I remember a film by Maurice Cloche, *Monsieur Vincent* (1947), about St. Vincent de Paul. The greatest one is Rossellini's *Flowers of St. Francis* (1950), which is daunting because of its simplicity and compassion and heart. I've been watching that film for twenty-five years, and I always wanted to make something like it, about a human being who by exemplary action shows us how to live. Where nonaction becomes action; where a decision not to make a decision is the decision. It may not be what Western audiences expect, but I believe the Dalai Lama and Gandhi and Martin Luther King, people who stood on the line for passive resistance and got hit for it, have a lotta guts."

Scorsese, who has made so many films about violent men, erupting tempers, and sudden death, told a "little parable" he came across while preparing this film: "An army came into town and marched up to the monastery door and the general took his sword out, and the head of the monastery opened the door and just stood there. The general looked at him and said, 'Don't you realize I can kill you without blinking an eye?' And the monk replied, 'Don't you realize I can die without blinking an eye?' That's where I'd like to get to."

Now watch the way Scorsese's mind works, how all of his films, even those that seem opposites, are directed by the same man. His parable would seem to be far outside the universe of Jake LaMotta, the hero of *Raging Bull*, but a little later, as we talked, he said:

> I want to feel like Jake does at the end of *Raging Bull*, a stage I've never gotten to. He's at peace with himself, by the end, looking at himself in the mirror, rehearsing his act, repeating "my kingdom for a horse." I knew when I was doing it that I wasn't there. Up to that point I was with him, but I couldn't get beyond that point until finally, maybe, oh, when I did *Color of Money* (1986), I kind of got used to myself. I realized, I'm gonna be this way all my life, and I better calm down, take it easy, don't waste the energy and burn up that fuel of yourself

and everybody else around you. So I just got used to myself, and what can I do? I'm stuck.

He looked content to be stuck, at that place already occupied by Gandhi, Dr. King, LaMotta, and the Dalai Lama, which, apart from anything else, would be the makings of an interesting dinner party.

"It has always made me feel a little comfortable that human beings may be capable of evolving spiritually," he said. "The Tibetans are not the only ones. There are modern people who have a compassionate heart, like Dorothy Day in New York, or Mother Teresa. There was a book recently that was critical of her, but the people who write that stuff, I wonder when was the last time they helped somebody to die?"

Scorsese cast his film only with nonactors, including many Tibetans who knew the Dalai Lama. And from them, he said, he absorbed some of the spirit that he tried to communicate in *Kundun*.

"Some of the older ones had been part of his retinue back in 1949, before they left Tibet. So they understood everything and very often in the picture I'd walk onto the set and they'd be meditating and it was like a painting out of the Renaissance. There was a reverence and a spirituality that pervaded the set, which was interesting. I wanted to be part of that world. Whether I took something away with me, I'm not sure, but I think I have.

"And then working with the little boy who played the Dalai Lama as a child, that was a contact with reality. The kid was terrific, he had a great face. But we had to do a lot of tricks to get that performance. Like the scene where they put him in front of the table and ask him to choose 'his' possessions, from his previous reincarnation, so they'll know it's really him.

"The Tibetans in the scene, and his own mother and the father and the other kids, really helped out a lot. But if a two-year-old kid doesn't want to play, he doesn't want to play; that's it. He wants to take a nap, the crew waits until he wakes up. But I found that I was anchored in his behavior, because he wasn't acting, and neither were the other Tibetan actors. Some of the best acting in the movie takes place at the edges of the screen, with the extras, because you look at their faces and you see they are really truly in the moment."

And so here is this film about peace and spirituality, filmed in the lush colors that Scorsese has always loved in the older films he studies, and expressing his own sense of connection and growth. And now what will he make next? He is discussing a film about the life of Dean Martin. Now that would seem like an absolute change in direction, a fundamental shift in tone. But if he makes it, we will, I suspect, still be able to sense the same vision, the same search, the same filmmaker. Come on in, Dino; have you met everyone else here tonight? Mother Teresa, you know . . .

Kundun

In all of the representations I have seen, the Buddha gazes at the world impassively, enveloped in serenity. That might also describe the performances of the four actors who portray the Dalai Lama at various ages between two and twenty-four in Scorsese's *Kundun*. Consider a passage in which the young man holds court for a delegation of Chinese Communist officials. One after another, they exhort and lecture him, and to each he says no word, looking at them not with hostility but with polite interest. As a manifestation of Buddhist detachment and acceptance of the moment, this is admirable, but when it defines the central character of a film, it is problematical. My difficulty with the film has always been that I have more curiosity about the character than he apparently has about himself.

What would it be like, to be identified while a young child as the fourteenth reincarnation of the leader of the ancient Gelug sect of Buddhism? To be worshipped with reverence from that early age? To be raised and trained within a religion that does not impose itself upon you because you are, after all, its embodiment? I have met Buddhist monks and know that it is possible to be perfectly happy living such a life, but those I have met have chosen it for themselves. What does it require of a child, what does it take from a child, to grow up entirely contained within an ages-old tradition that you did not choose, but that defines your thoughts, beliefs, and actions, and that you are told springs from your very self?

Kundun doesn't ask such questions. Its hero rarely seems like a real little boy, more like a child whose gaze can leave adults with shaking hands. Contrast this little boy with the Dalai Lama depicted in Jean-Jacques Annaud's *Seven Years in Tibet* (also 1997), the story of his friendship with a tutor from Austria. That film, not very good, makes the mistake of growing preoccupied with the foreigner, perhaps because he is played by Brad Pitt. But at least the Dalai Lama seems more like a plausible real boy, who asks some natural questions.

What I have seen of the fourteenth Dalai Lama, now in his early seventies, gives me no reason to believe he is dissatisfied with his life. He seems a commendable man. But is there more to it than that? *Kundun* doesn't ask. What was it about this story that attracted Scorsese, when it has nothing in common with any other story that has ever interested him, certainly not the life of Christ? There is the possibility, of course, that the Dalai Lama really is the fourteenth reincarnation of, literally, the same man. But to the degree that he has spiritual beliefs, Scorsese's are Roman Catholic, and they specifically reject the possibility of reincarnation. There is the possibility that Scorsese was attracted to Buddhism as a worthy spiritual discipline. Certainly it has been associated with less mischief and misery than other world religions. But Scorsese has not become a Buddhist. Perhaps Scorsese admires the Dalai Lama as a man worthy of a film evoking his life. But then what life does *Kundun* evoke? We come full circle to the passive gaze, detached, serene.

Scorsese has made other films based on real lives, notably *The Aviator*, about Howard Hughes; *Casino*, about Frank Rosenthal; *Raging Bull*, about Jake LaMotta; *GoodFellas*, about Henry Hill; and, of course, *The Last Temptation of Christ*, which goes to pains to seek the real man beneath the image. In documentaries like *Italianamerican*, about his parents; *American Boy: A Profile of Stephen Prince*; and *No Direction Home*, about Bob Dylan, he tries in various ways to look beneath the surface. He has been planning a life of Theodore Roosevelt. Only in *Kundun* is the subject taken at, literally, face value.

Very near the end of the film, the Dalai Lama is asked, "Are you the Lord Buddha?" Of course the answer is no, because he is not thought to be the Lord Buddha. But the answer he gives is more provoking: "I believe I am a reflection, like the moon on water. When you see me, and I try to be a good man, you see yourself." That is true if the questioner is a good man. If he is a bad man, what does he see reflected? I am drawn irresistibly to a few lines by e. e. cummings:

> for whatever we lose (like a you or a me)
> it's always ourselves we find in the sea

Is it always ourselves that we find in *Kundun*, the Scorsese film that some critics, like my friend Jonathan Rosenbaum, think is his finest? It may indeed be near the top of his work in terms of "pure cinema," which is how it's often described, but "pure cinema" too often means "pure visuals" without such qualities as the messiness of human life. Can *Taxi Driver* be described as pure cinema? *GoodFellas*? No, but I think they are better films. Scorsese and his screenwriter, Melissa Mathison, were, I suspect, baffled by the Dalai Lama, but powerfully attracted to him. He is, Scorsese told me in 1998, "a human being who by exemplary action shows us how to live. Where nonaction becomes action; where a decision not to make a decision is the decision." Exemplary lessons in how to live a life, but not in how to write a screenplay. I wonder if Scorsese wanted not so much to understand the Dalai Lama as to become him, or at the least learn from his serenity? Perhaps what Scorsese needed in making *Kundun* he was able to find, even if it was not what we were looking for.

Of all his films, *Kundun* is Scorsese's most sumptuous. The screen is drenched with rich reds and golds, with panoply and ritual. He makes no journalistic attempt to explain what we are seeing: maybe it's an ancient tradition they're practicing, he said of scenes in his film, or maybe it's breakfast. This from the man who made the steak-cooking episode in *Raging Bull* into a sociological microscope. Here his "pure cinema" seems poured on with reverence, as a true believer might sing a hymn more loudly. In the concluding passages, as the Philip Glass score underlines the increasing solemnity, the Dalai Lama's departure from Tibet is turned from a journey into a royal progress; not a victory, certainly, but somehow not a defeat. That was in 1959. Today, "he still hopes to return." A case could be made that his life since 1959 has been more important and influential than his early years.

Scorsese used only nonprofessional actors in his film, many of them relatives or contemporaries of the Dalai Lama. He'd come on the set to find them meditating, he said. A mood of veneration must have suffused some of the shooting days. That mood seems reflected in the unusual restraint of his camera; no other Scorsese film moves the camera with less curiosity, or more sedately. It often centers the Dalai Lama in compositions, like the subject of a religious icon. It regards an empty throne, and observes the Dalai Lama entering the room to occupy it. It doesn't follow him into the room, hand-held, the way it follows Henry Hill into the Copacabana in *GoodFellas*.

Scorsese is willing in *Kundun* to let images speak for themselves. (227) When the little boy separates two beetles, were they fighting, or copulating? When the adult Dalai Lama notices the shiny black shoes of Chairman Mao (I wrote confidently in my original review) they "seem to symbolize the loss of older ways and values." Do they? Or is he remembering an earlier scene in the film, when in the storeroom of the thirteenth Dalai Lama, he comes across a handsome pair of brown wingtips? In that case, is he thinking that Mao's shoes represent clunky collectivist factory products? Either reading is possible.

In the last shot but one in the movie, the Dalai Lama pauses on a peak in India and uses his telescope to look back toward Tibet, which he has left for the first time. A black cloud hangs over the sacred land. It's clear what the cloud symbolizes. But notice how specific Scorsese is to *avoid* giving us a POV shot. The Dalai Lama looks, and then the camera looks, and it is the camera that holds full-screen on the black cloud, with no telescope iris to suggest we are seeing exactly what the Dalai Lama sees. Scorsese observes the cloud, and we draw our conclusions. Perhaps the Dalai Lama sees it not as a symbol of Chinese occupation, but simply accepts it as the weather, doing what the weather will do.

Bringing Out the Dead

OCTOBER 22, 1999

The speaker is Frank, a paramedic whose journeys into the abyss of human misery provide the canvas for Martin Scorsese's *Bringing Out the Dead*. There may be happiness somewhere in the city, but the barking voice on Frank's radio doesn't dispatch him there. His job is to arrive at a scene of violence, or collapse, and try to bring not only help but encouragement.

"Do you have any music?" he asks the family of a man who seems dead of a heart attack. "I think it helps if you play something he liked." As the old man's Sinatra album plays in the background, he applies the defibrillator to his chest and shouts, "Clear!" The corpse jumps into life like a movie monster. The psychology is sound: Sinatra may not bring the dead to life, but he will give the family something to do, and the song will remind them of their dad's happier times.

Frank is played by Nicolas Cage, seen in the movie's close-up with his eyes narrowed in pain. He cruises the streets of Hell's Kitchen with a series of three co-pilots, in a three-day stretch during which he drifts in and out of sanity; he has hallucinations of an eighteen-year-old homeless girl named Rose, whose life he failed to save, whose death he wants to redeem. Like Travis Bickle, the hero of Scorsese's *Taxi Driver* (1976), Frank travels the night streets like a boatman on the River Styx, while steam rises from manholes as if from the fires below. Travis wanted to save those who did not want saving. Frank finds those who desperately want help, but usually he is powerless.

The movie is based on a novel by Joe Connelly, himself once a New York paramedic. The screenplay by Paul Schrader is another chapter in the most fruitful writer-director collaboration of the last quarter century (*Taxi Driver*, *Raging Bull*, *The Last Temptation of Christ*). The film wisely has no real plot, because the paramedic's days have no beginning or goal, but are a limbo of extended horror. At one point, Frank hallucinates that he is helping pull people's bodies up out of the pavement, freeing them.

To look at *Bringing Out the Dead* — to look, indeed, at almost any Scorsese film — is to be reminded that film can touch us urgently and deeply. Scorsese is never on autopilot, never panders, never sells out, always goes for broke; to watch his films is to see a man risking his talent, not simply exercising it. He makes movies as well as they can be made, and I agree with an observation on the Harry Knowles Web site: you can enjoy a Scorsese film with the sound off, or with the sound on and the picture off.

Now look at *Bringing Out the Dead*. Three days in Frank's life.

The first day his co-pilot is Larry (John Goodman), who deals with the grief by focusing on where his next meal is coming from. To Larry, it's a job, and you can't let it get to you. Day two, Frank works with Marcus (Ving Rhames), who is a gospel Christian and uses emergencies as an opportunity to demonstrate the power of Jesus; bringing one man back to life, he presents it as a miracle. He drives as if he hopes to arrive at the scene of an accident by causing it. On the third day, the day Christ rose from the dead, Frank's partner is Walls (Tom Sizemore), who is coming apart at the seams and wreaks havoc on hapless patients.

Haunting Frank's thoughts as he cruises with these guys are two women. One is Rose, whose face peers up at him from every street corner. The other is Mary (Patricia Arquette), the daughter of the man who liked Sinatra. After her dad is transferred to an intensive-care unit, his life, such as it is, consists of dying and being shocked back to life, fourteen times one day, until Frank asks, "If he gets out, are you gonna follow him around with a defibrillator?" Mary is a former druggie, now clean and straight, and Frank — well, I was going to say he loves her, but this isn't one of those autopilot movies where the action hero has a romance in between the bloodshed. No, it's not love, it's need. He thinks they can save each other.

Scorsese assembles the film as levels in an inferno. It contains some of his most brilliant sequences, particularly two visits to a highrise drug house named the Oasis, where a dealer named Cy (Cliff Curtis) offers relief and surcease. Mary goes there one night when she cannot stand any more pain, and Frank follows to save her; that sets up a later sequence in which Frank treats Cy while he is dangling near death.

All suffering ends at the same place, the emergency room of Our Lady of Perpetual Mercy (nickname: Perpetual Misery), where the receiving nurse (Mary Beth Hurt) knows most of the regulars by name.

Nicolas Cage is an actor of great style and heedless emotional availability: he will go anywhere for a role, and this film is his best since *Leaving Las Vegas*. I like the subtle way he and Scorsese embody what Frank has learned on the job, the little verbal formulas and quiet asides that help the bystanders at suffering. He embodies the tragedy of a man who has necessary work and is good at it, but in a job that is never, ever over.

Bringing Out the Dead is an antidote to the immature intoxication with violence in a film like *Fight Club*. It is not fun to get hit, it is not redeeming to cause pain, it does not make you a man when you fight, because fights are an admission that you are not smart enough to survive by your wits. *Fight Club* makes a cartoon of the mean streets that Scorsese sees unblinkingly.

Bringing Out Scorsese

OCTOBER 21, 1999

Martin Scorsese's new movie, *Bringing Out the Dead*, is one of his best. That means a lot when you are arguably the greatest active American director. The film, which opens Friday, stars Nicolas Cage as a paramedic whose runs through Hell's Kitchen are like a bus route through Dante's Inferno.

I telephoned Scorsese earlier this week, plunging once again into his rapid-fire Walter Winchell dialog. To deconstruct his verbal riffs into the forms of a traditional interview would lose the music. Here are some of the notes he hit:

1. "The first things I thought of, when I read Joe Connelly's book, were Nic Cage's face and his eyes. His uncle Francis [Ford Coppola] had us meet a few years ago. You know, you meet some people sometimes, you don't wanna spend five months with them on the set, you know what I'm saying? Well, this guy seemed to be polite. He was a nice guy to be around, and then Brian De Palma told me he was great to work with. I know his films over the years. He's inventive and he goes from an expressive style, almost like silent film, like Lon Chaney, whom he adores, to something extremely internal. So I thought immediately of Nic for this."

2. "Some people keep asking, 'Gee, New York looks a little different now.' And I say, 'But you're looking at the surface. This is not about New York. This is about suffering, it's about humanity. It's about what our part is in life.' This whole thing about how New York is changing,

getting better. It goes in cycles. Some people are saying, 'The movie is representative of New York in the early 1990s. It's different now.' I say it's not so. We were there; we were shooting in that area. They were out; they were there . . . those people. And if some of them aren't on the streets, believe me, they gotta be someplace. I saw some of the places where they are. You don't wanna know. It's like underneath the city in a hole. Under the railroads. It's the end of life. It's the dregs. It's down. You can't get any lower."

3. "The Nic Cage character has three co-pilots, a different partner every night. John Goodman is probably in the best shape. Goodman basically worries about where he's gonna eat, takes a few minutes off, takes a nap. Ving Rhames, he gets religion. But the thing about Ving's character is that you can't make him work more than two nights, or he gets overexcited. And then, of course, the Tom Sizemore character, he's a paramilitary, he's in there. He knows what to do when he gets there, but he freaks out from time to time."

4. "The people they're carrying in their ambulance, I saw it like that in the Bowery. I saw it happening to some of the people in my old neighborhood. I grew up with them, in a way. Some of them, when they weren't drinking, were kinda nice. They worked for people in the grocery store. But when they got drunk, there was no dealing with them. And people would just become frustrated and hit them. I saw it happen all the time."

5. "That title, *Bringing Out the Dead*—Joe Connelly chose that title with a sense of humor. It's based on a reference to *Monty Python and the Holy Grail*. You remember? 'Bring out your dead,' John Cleese tells them. He takes out one person, and the guy says, 'I'm not dead yet.' He says, 'Don't be a baby. Come on.' Remember, he puts him on the cart? He says, 'He's very ill. He's gonna die any second.'"

6. "When I read the galleys of the book I told [producer] Scott Rudin, who gave me the book, 'the only man who could write a script of this is Paul Schrader.' [Schrader also wrote Scorsese's *Taxi Driver*, *Raging Bull*, and *The Last Temptation of Christ*.] The last scene that Paul wrote, it's not that way in the book. Nic says, 'Rose, forgive me. Forgive me, Rose.' And she says, 'Nobody told you to suffer. It was

your idea.' And when Schrader wrote that, I said, 'Oh—of course.' And that's the connection between us. We never really discuss it, but over the years, we've had this similarity to each other. I said to him, 'It's so beautiful. And you're right, because you can't forgive yourself. You want everybody else to forgive you.' We're tied to each other with this sort of thing."

7. "When you bring somebody back to life, you feel like God, you are God. But one has to get past the idea of the ego and the pride. Hey, the job isn't about bringing people back to life, it's about being there, it's about compassion for the suffering, suffering with them."

8. "Right after we finished shooting, another guy fell on a fence in New York. This happens all the time. Every few months there's an impaling like that. We shot in the emergency room in Bellevue on the ground floor; we built the set down there. A few stories above, one of the doctors had a section of the fence they took out of the man, as a showpiece in his office. That was the incident that inspired the scene in the movie."

9. "Helen [Morris, his wife, a book editor] told me last night there was a big deal on the Web about the *New York Times* walking out of the movie. But it wasn't a critic. It was Bernie Weinraub, their Hollywood columnist. And I said, 'Well, Bernie, I know him a little bit.' He liked *Casino*. He hurt us very badly on *Age of Innocence* in an article he wrote in the *Times* where he complained about us having a big budget on *Age of Innocence*, and he hit Daniel Day-Lewis and Michelle Pfeiffer for not taking less than their usual fee. By the way, they did take less, I don't know how much, but they did. We were compared unfavorably to *Remains of the Day* and pictures like that because they're made for a good price, and we were wasting money. And that was it. They gave us $32 million; we went a little bit over, but not a lot, and $32 million was the average amount for a film being made at that time. If somebody wanted to give us $30 million, and somebody else wanted to give us $32 million, I'd take the thirty-two."

10. "I'm still going to make *Dino*, the Dean Martin picture, with Tom Hanks. We're gonna hopefully do it right after *Gangs of New York*, which I've been trying for years to get done. Jay Cocks and I

have been rewriting the script since January. We got Leonardo Di-Caprio, we may have Bob De Niro to play the archvillain, hero-villain, whatever. It's taken ten months to make the deal, mainly because it's a lot of money in the film, and you gotta be careful and you have to get the right amount of star power in it. It's only become real since Monday [of last week]. We're ready to go. And then deal with *Dino* right after, I hope. Tom Hanks and I were speaking about it only a couple of weeks ago."

Gangs of New York

DECEMBER 20, 2002

Martin Scorsese's *Gangs of New York* rips up the postcards of American history and reassembles them into a violent, blood-soaked story of our bare-knuckled past. The New York it portrays in the years between the 1840s and the Civil War is, as a character observes, "the forge of hell," in which groups clear space by killing their rivals. Competing fire brigades and police forces fight in the streets, audiences throw rotten fruit at an actor portraying Abraham Lincoln, blacks and Irish are chased by mobs, and navy ships fire on the city as the poor riot against the draft.

The film opens with an extraordinary scene set beneath tenements, in catacombs carved out of the Manhattan rock. An Irish American leader named Priest Vallon (Liam Neeson) prepares for battle almost as if preparing for the Mass—indeed, as he puts on a collar to protect his neck, we think for a moment he might be a priest. With his young son Amsterdam trailing behind, he walks through the labyrinth of this torchlit Hades, gathering his forces, the Dead Rabbits, before stalking out into daylight to fight the forces of a rival American-born gang, the Nativists.

Men use knives, swords, bayonets, cleavers, cudgels. The ferocity of their battle is animalistic. At the end, the field is littered with bodies—including that of Vallon, slain by his enemy, William Cutting, aka Bill the Butcher (Daniel Day-Lewis). This was the famous gang fight of Five Points on the Lower East Side of Manhattan, recorded in American history but not underlined. When it is over, Amsterdam disappears into an orphanage, the ominously named Hellgate House of Reform. He emerges in his early twenties (now played by Leonardo DiCaprio) and returns to Five Points, still ruled by Bill, and begins a scheme to avenge his father.

The vivid achievement of Scorsese's film is to visualize this history and people it with characters of Dickensian grotesquerie. Bill the Butcher is one of the great characters in modern movies, with his strangely elaborate diction, his choked accent, his odd way of combining ruthlessness with philosophy. The canvas is filled with many other colorful characters, including a pickpocket named Jenny Everdeane (Cameron Diaz), a hired club named Monk (Brendan Gleeson), the shopkeeper Happy Jack (John C. Reilly), and historical figures such as William "Boss" Tweed (Jim Broadbent), ruler of corrupt Tammany Hall, and P. T. Barnum (Roger Ashton-Griffiths), whose museum of curiosities scarcely rivals the daily displays on the streets.

Scorsese's hero, Amsterdam, plays much the same role as a Dickens hero like David Copperfield or Oliver Twist: he is the eyes through which we see the others, but is not the most colorful person on the canvas. Amsterdam is not as wild, as vicious, or as eccentric as the people around him, and may not be any tougher than his eventual girlfriend, Jenny, who like Nancy in Oliver Twist is a hellcat with a fierce loyalty to her man. DiCaprio's character, more focused and centered, is a useful contrast to the wild men around him.

Certainly, Day-Lewis is inspired by an intense ferocity, laced with humor and a certain analytical detachment, as Bill the Butcher. He is a fearsome man, fond of using his knife to tap his glass eye, and he uses a pig carcass to show Amsterdam the various ways to kill a man with a knife. Bill is a skilled knife artist, and terrifies Jenny, his target for a knife-throwing act, not only by coming close to killing her but also by his ornate and ominous word choices.

Diaz plays Jenny as a woman who at first insists on her own independence; as a pickpocket, she ranks high in the criminal hierarchy, and even dresses up to prey on the rich people uptown. But when she finally caves in to Amsterdam's love, she proves tender and loyal, in one love scene where they compare their scars, and another where she nurses him back to health.

The movie is straightforward in its cynicism about democracy at that time. Tammany Hall buys and sells votes, ethnic groups are delivered by their leaders, and when the wrong man is elected sheriff he does not serve for long. That American democracy emerged from this cauldron is miraculous. We put the founding fathers on our money, but these founding crooks for a long time held sway.

Scorsese is probably our greatest active American director (Robert Altman is another candidate), and he has given us so many masterpieces that this film, which from another director would be a triumph, arrives as a more measured accomplishment. It was a difficult film to make, as we know from the reports that drifted back from the vast and expensive sets constructed at Cinecitta in Rome. The budget was enormous, the running time was problematical.

The result is a considerable achievement, a revisionist history linking the birth of American democracy and American crime. It brings us astonishing sights, as in a scene that shows us the inside of a tenement, with families stacked on top of one another in rooms like shelves. Or in the ferocity of the Draft Riots, which all but destroyed the city. It is instructive to be reminded that modern America was forged not in quiet rooms by great men in wigs, but in the streets, in the clash of immigrant groups, in a bloody Darwinian struggle.

All of this is a triumph for Scorsese, and yet I do not think this film is in the first rank of his masterpieces. It is very good but not great. I wrote recently of *GoodFellas* that "the film has the headlong momentum of a storyteller who knows he has a good one to share." I didn't feel that here. Scorsese's films usually leap joyfully onto the screen, the work of a master in command of his craft. Here there seems more struggle, more weight to overcome, more darkness. It is a story that Scorsese has filmed without entirely internalizing. The gangsters in his earlier films are motivated by greed, ego, and power; they like nice cars, shoes, suits, dinners, women. They murder as a cost of doing business. The characters in *Gangs of New York* kill because they like to and want to. They are bloodthirsty, and motivated by hate. I think Scorsese liked the heroes of *GoodFellas*, *Casino*, and *Mean Streets*, but I'm not sure he likes this crowd.

Gangs All Here for Scorsese

DECEMBER 15, 2002

NEW YORK—In 1977, right after he made *Taxi Driver*, Martin Scorsese took out a two-page ad in *Variety* to announce his next production: *The Gangs of New York*.

"It's been on my mind for many, many years," Scorsese was saying the other day. We were having lunch in his hotel suite, and he was eating a bowl full of something that looked like puppy chow but which he said was on the Zone Diet.

He asked his longtime collaborator Jay Cocks to do a screenplay about the incredibly violent years between 1830 and the Civil War, when gangs ruled New York's streets and engaged in warfare. But then he made *Raging Bull*, and then *The King of Comedy*, and then *The Last Temptation of Christ*, and by then, he said, the moment had passed and Hollywood wasn't making pictures like *Gangs* any more. By which he meant, although he didn't say it, that Hollywood had turned to formulas and was afraid of such an ambitious project.

So twenty years passed and he never stopped thinking about the film, and now here it is, a year after it was first scheduled to be released, surrounded by rumors of power struggles, *The Gangs of New York*.

Scorsese's film, which opens Friday, stars Leonardo DiCaprio as Amsterdam Vallon, a tough Irish kid whose father was martyred while leading the Dead Rabbits, a gang of recently arrived immigrants. Daniel Day-Lewis plays William Cutting, also known as Bill the Butcher, leader of a gang called the Nativists, who hate immigrants. Cameron

Diaz is Jenny Everdeane, pickpocket and con woman, who was once Bill's woman but now loves Amsterdam.

The film was made at a cost of untold millions (the figure changes from story to story) on enormous sets built at Rome's Cinecitta to duplicate the notorious Five Points area of New York in the decades before the war. No movie has ever depicted American poverty and squalor in this way: immigrants huddle on shelves in a rooming house, starving children die in the streets, there is no law except the rule of the mighty, and each immigrant or racial tribe battles the others.

"It's not about guys with wigs writing with feathers," Scorsese said, chuckling over his gruel. He is quick to explain, however, that his movie should be seen as an "opera, not a documentary"—that he played with the facts to tell a better story. He has a scene, for example, when navy ships fire their cannons on rioting draft resisters. "Actually, they unloaded some howitzers and fired from land," he said. "They were joined by army troops fresh from fighting at Gettysburg—I had to cut out the part explaining that—and these troops were impatient at draft resisters and also feared they might be facing a British-led rebellion."

Scorsese tells me these things and many more during our lunch. He is not one of those film promoters who sticks to sound bites and is focused on selling his picture. He talks about whatever comes into his mind, and I learn that he thinks *The River* is Jean Renoir's best movie, that he would love to make a film from a book by Joseph Conrad, that he has finally gotten through James Joyce's *Ulysses*, that he needs to work because he plugged half of his salary back into *Gangs of New York*, and that there will not be a "director's cut" of the film on DVD.

That last he makes particularly clear, because of all the controversy over reported arguments he had with Miramax chief Harvey Weinstein about the length of the film. "The debate was about how you get a picture to play, not about how long it was," he said. He talked about a long process with his editor, Thelma Schoonmaker, who has worked on all of his pictures, as they made versions that ran from three hours and forty minutes to as little as two hours and thirty-six minutes. They screened before test audiences: "This is a film that needed to be screened that way because it contains a lot of information. How much was getting across? How much wasn't getting across? How much was getting across that you didn't need to get across, because you could just drop or forget it?"

At one point, he said, it was too short. Scenes played too fast. "I added three or four minutes, clarified certain other things. The rhythm was still off, I felt. This went on and on over a period of about a year. At one point I put too much back in."

His discussions with Weinstein, he said, were always about finding the length where the picture worked. When that got to the press, it was translated into fights. The movie is currently 168 minutes long, he said, and that is the right length, and that's why there won't be any director's cut—because this is the director's cut.

Scorsese explains these things in a torrent of enthusiasm. I have known him thirty-five years, and this has never changed: he loves movies to an unreasonable, delirious degree, and he has unalloyed zeal for making them and talking about them. Words pour from him. Let me provide statistics. I tape-recorded exactly forty-five minutes of our conversation. It contained 8,731 words, which means he was speaking at 194 words a minute—but even faster, actually, because some of the tape is me, speaking more slowly. I say that just to illustrate that in a time when many people in the film business speak guardedly or even with paranoia, Scorsese wears it all on his sleeve.

The film's art director, Dante Ferretti, created catacombs carved from the rock of Manhattan for the opening scenes. Scorsese said they are based on fact. "Right now in Chinatown they have sweatshops beneath the basements," he said. "A friend of mine did some research a few years ago, going through the underground areas in Chinatown. He actually saw sweatshops below."

Are any of the catacombs like those shown in the movie still down there?

"Oh, I think they're there. Just covered over. And I know for a fact that the basements of the Lower East Side where I grew up, you could go in a basement on Elizabeth Street and come out somewhere on Mott Street. That was mainly to get away from the police. And also the Italians used it a lot for making wine down there, which was against the law. The city has a whole . . . underneath. I was trying to employ that with these caves."

Now, Scorsese said, he needs to go to work again. "I have a three-year-old to feed," he smiles. What will he make? Two projects are in his mind. One is a biopic based on Dean Martin, which he has been talking about for years. Another is *The Aviator*, based on the early life of Howard Hughes, who has an earth-shaking love affair with Katharine Hepburn.

"You know who looks uncannily like young Howard Hughes?" Scorsese mused. "Leonardo DiCaprio."

The Aviator

DECEMBER 24, 2004

Howard Hughes in his last two decades sealed himself away from the world. At first he haunted a penthouse in Las Vegas, and then he moved to a bungalow behind the Beverly Hills Hotel. He was the world's richest man, and with his billions bought himself a room he never left.

In a sense, his life was a journey to that lonely room. But he took the long way around: as a rich young man from Texas, the heir to his father's fortune, he made movies, bought airlines, was a playboy who dated Hollywood's famous beauties. If he had died in one of the airplane crashes he survived, he would have been remembered as a golden boy. Martin Scorsese's *The Aviator* wisely focuses on the glory years, although we can see the shadows falling, and so can Hughes. Some of the film's most harrowing moments show him fighting his demons; he knows what is normal and sometimes it seems almost within reach.

The Aviator celebrates Scorsese's zest for finding excitement in a period setting, re-creating the kind of glamour he heard about when he was growing up. It is possible to imagine him wanting to be Howard Hughes. Their lives, in fact, are even a little similar: heedless ambition and talent when young, great early success, tempestuous romances, and a dark period, although with Hughes it got darker and darker, while Scorsese has emerged into the full flower of his gifts.

The movie achieves the difficult feat of following two intersecting story arcs, one in which everything goes right for Hughes and the other in which everything goes wrong. Scorsese chronicled similar life patterns in *GoodFellas*, *Raging Bull*, *The King of Comedy*, *Casino*, actually even *The Last Temptation of Christ*. Leonardo DiCaprio is convincing in his transitions between these emotional weathers; playing madness is a notorious invitation to overact, but he shows Hughes contained, even trapped, within his secrets, able to put on a public act even when his private moments are desperate.

His Howard Hughes arrives in Los Angeles as a good-looking young man with a lot of money, who plunges right in, directing a World War I aviation adventure named *Hell's Angels*, which was then the most expensive movie ever made. The industry laughed at him, but he finished the movie and it made money, and so did most of his other films. As his attention drifted from movies to the airplanes in his films, he began designing and building aircraft and eventually bought his own airline.

Women were his for the asking, but he didn't go for the easy kill. Jean Harlow was no pushover, Ava Gardner wouldn't take gifts of jewelry ("I am not for sale!"), and during his relationship with Katharine Hepburn, they both wore the pants in the family. Hepburn liked his sense of adventure, she was thrilled when he let her pilot his planes, she worried about him, she noted the growing signs of his eccentricity, and then she met Spencer Tracy and that was that. Hughes found Jane Russell and invented a pneumatic bra to make her bosom heave in *The Outlaw*, and by the end he had starlets on retainer in case he ever called them, but he never did.

DiCaprio is nobody's idea of what Hughes looked like (that would be a young Sam Shepard), but he vibrates with the reckless spirit of the man. John C. Reilly plays the hapless Noah Dietrich, his right-hand man and flunky, routinely ordered to mortgage everything for one of Hughes's sudden inspirations; Hughes apparently became the world's richest man by going bankrupt at higher and higher levels.

Scorsese shows a sure sense for the Hollywood of that time, as in a scene where Howard, new in town, approaches the mogul L. B. Mayer at the Coconut Grove and asks to borrow two cameras for a big *Hell's Angels* scene. He already had twenty-four, but that was not enough.

Mayer regards him as a child psychiatrist might have regarded the young Jim Carrey. Scorsese adds subtle continuity: every time we see Mayer, he seems to be surrounded by the same flunkies.

The women in the film are wonderfully well cast. Cate Blanchett has the task of playing Katharine Hepburn, who was herself so close to caricature that to play her accurately involves some risk. Blanchett succeeds in a performance that is delightful and yet touching; mannered and tomboyish, delighting in saying exactly what she means, she shrewdly sizes up Hughes and is quick to be concerned about his eccentricities. Kate Beckinsale is Ava Gardner, aware of her power and self-protective; Gwen Stefani is Jean Harlow, whose stardom overshadows the unknown Texas rich boy; and Kelli Garner is Faith Domergue, "the next Jane Russell" at a time when Hughes became obsessed with bosoms. Jane Russell doesn't appear in the movie as a character, but her cleavage does, in a hilarious scene before the Breen office, which ran the Hollywood censorship system. Hughes brings his tame meteorology professor (Ian Holm) to the censorship hearing, introduces him as a systems analyst, and has him prove with calipers and mathematics that Russell displays no more cleavage than a control group of five other actresses.

Special effects can distract from a film or enhance it. Scorsese knows how to use them. There is a sensational sequence when Hughes crash-lands in Beverly Hills, his plane's wing tip slicing through living-room walls seen from the inside. Much is made of the *Spruce Goose*, the largest airplane ever built, which inspires Sen. Owen Brewster (Alan Alda) to charge in congressional hearings that Hughes was a war profiteer. Hughes, already in the spiral to madness, rises to the occasion, defeats Brewster on his own territory, and vows that the plane will fly—as indeed it does, in a CGI sequence that is convincing and kind of awesome.

By the end, darkness is gathering around Hughes. He gets stuck on words and keeps repeating them. He walks into a men's room and then is too phobic about germs to touch the doorknob in order to leave; with all his power and wealth, he has to lurk next to the door until someone else walks in, and he can sneak through without touching

anything. His aides, especially the long-suffering Dietrich, try to protect him, but eventually he disappears into seclusion. What a sad man.
What brief glory. What an enthralling film, 166 minutes, and it races
past. There's a match here between Scorsese and his subject, perhaps
because the director's own life journey allows him to see Howard
Hughes with insight, sympathy—and, up to a point, with admiration.
This is one of the year's best films.

Howard's End

SCORSESE AND *THE AVIATOR*

DECEMBER 12, 2004

LOS ANGELES—Martin Scorsese is not a creature of the sound bite. In an age when directors and stars are trained by their publicists to stay on message and repeat glowing mantras about their movies, Scorsese is all over the map. He loves his new movie, *The Aviator*, you can tell that, but he's finished with it. It's in the can. He's straining at the bit.

He's talking out loud about ideas for his next movie. He'll make a Boston police picture, starring DiCaprio for the third time in a row. Then maybe he'll adapt Endo's *The Silence*, about a Jesuit missionary in Japan in the sixteenth century. Or maybe Boswell's *London Journal*—he loves that book, about a young man from Scotland, on the make in the big city: "I love it when he gets the clap from that actress and after he's treated, he goes around and presents her with the doctor's bill."

We are having lunch in the Beverly Wilshire Hotel. He is eating a piece of chicken that has been prepared to his specifications. Flattened. Seasoned. Breaded. His mother was a great cook. He once included her recipe for tomato sauce in the credits of a movie. He knows how he wants his chicken.

His hair is gray now. His face is lined. I met him when we were in our twenties. He had a mane of hippie hair and a beard, wore the jeans and the beads, was editing *Woodstock* in a loft in SoHo. We went down to Little Italy on the Feast of San Gennaro and ate pasta, and he told me about a project that would become, a few years later, *Mean Streets*.

I cannot look at Martin Scorsese and see a man who is sixty-two. I see the kid. Certainly I hear the kid.

"I've never been that interested in Howard Hughes's life, beginning to end," he said, talking about the subject of *The Aviator*, opening December 25. He was interested in the middle. Then he saw a screenplay by John Logan, who is good at finding the story line in an epic life; he wrote *Gladiator* and *The Last Samurai*.

"What Logan chose not to show, that's what interested me," Scorsese said. "You can't do the whole life. The last twenty years, it's a guy locked in a room watching movies. I went through a phase like that myself, movies all day long, all night long; my friends would say I was walking around with the Kleenex boxes on my feet again. Just like Howard Hughes.

"What I liked was the young Howard Hughes who came to Hollywood with the money his dad made on drill bits, and bet the store. He had energy and lust. I saw him walking into the Coconut Grove, beautiful girls on swings above the dance floor, L. B. Mayer standing there with his flunkies, asking Mayer if he could borrow a couple of cameras. 'Cause he's got twenty-four cameras for this scene, but he needs two more. He needed twenty-six cameras to film the aerial fights in *Hell's Angels*.

"Mayer gave him excellent advice. 'Go back to Houston. You'll go broke here.' But even *Hell's Angels*, then the most expensive picture ever produced, eventually made its money back. He was a genius at getting rich, he had a visionary sense, but always there was that fatal flaw eating away at him, consuming him."

Hughes spent his last decades as a mad recluse, but Scorsese's film only takes him to the point where he is about to shut the door on the world. There are episodes of madness, but also flashes of triumph. We know Hughes is falling to pieces, but the world doesn't guess; he faces down a congressional hearing that tries to paint him as a war profiteer but fails.

"Most of the Senate stuff, that's what he really said, verbatim," he said. "He won. He really did say if the *Spruce Goose* didn't fly, he would leave the country and never come back again. And it flew."

It flew, in one of several special-effects scenes Scorsese integrates with eerie realism into the film; another is a scene where Hughes crash-lands in Beverly Hills, the wing of his plane slicing through the wall of a house.

"You want my guess?" Scorsese said. "Ultimately, when he looks in the mirror at what he has become, he would do it all again. It was worth it."

And the girls. Harlow, Hepburn, Jane Russell and the pneumatic brassiere he personally designed to assist her bosom in its heaving.

"Breasts!" Scorsese said. "He embraced them so passionately. I am appreciative of that part of the female form, but it's not my point of view. But he loved them!"

There came a time when Scorsese had to decide between two films: (249) Alexander the Great or Howard Hughes. "Alexander or Howard? But Alexander would take years of preproduction; I'm not getting any younger. And Oliver Stone told me it was the passion of his life. And the Logan script about Hughes was so attractive."

And you worked again with Harvey Weinstein and Miramax, I said, despite all those stories about how you were at each other's throats during *Gangs of New York*.

"Harvey? A difference of opinions. Issues of taste. No blood-letting. And ultimately, it came down to a hard, cold case of production costs and how much we could spend." Scorsese hinted, almost under his breath, that *Gangs of New York* had fallen a little short of what he had dreamed, but in the real world of production money and how much it can buy, Scorsese made the best movie it was possible to make.

More to the point, I thought, was the movie before that, *Bringing Out the Dead* (1999), with Nicolas Cage as an ambulance driver in Hell's Kitchen. This I thought was a brilliant film, a descent into the underworld. "But it failed at the box office," Scorsese said, "and was rejected by a lot of the critics."

I was astonished by its energy and dark vision, by its portrait of a man venturing nightly into hell to rescue the dying and the damned. "I had ten years of ambulances," he said. "My parents, in and out of hospitals. Calls in the middle of the night. I was exorcising all of that.

Those city paramedics are heroes—and saints, they're saints. I grew up next to the Bowery, watching the people who worked there, the Salvation Army, Dorothy Day's Catholic Worker Movement, all helping the lost souls. They're the same sort of people."

Saints, I said. A lot of saints in your films.

"Despite everything, I keep thinking I can find a way to lead the spiritual life," he said. "When I made *The Last Temptation of Christ*, when I made *Kundun*, I was looking for that. *Bringing Out the Dead* was the next step. Time is moving by. I'm aware of that."

Do you still read all the time, and watch movies all the time?

"Both of them, all of the time. On our top floor, I have a projection room, a big screen. I'm always watching something, and my daughter's bedroom is at the other end of the hall. She knocks on the door: 'Daddy, turn the movie down!' It's supposed to be the daddy who tells the kid to turn down the noise. And reading. George Eliot. All of Melville— everything he wrote. I'm fascinated by whale boats, but I'm afraid of a picture on the water, so many technical problems. Then I got sidetracked by Ovid, and he took me back to Propertius."

He spells "Propertius" for me.

"You gotta read Propertius."

The movies? He sighed. "It's almost like I've seen enough of some of the old films. *Citizen Kane*, it's a masterpiece, I'm in awe of it, but I know it. I know it. It comes up on TV, I don't stop. Now *The Trial*, by Welles, *Touch of Evil*, I'll stop and watch. And music. Leadbelly. If you sit through all the credits after *The Aviator*, we play a song written and performed by Leadbelly:

> Get up in the morning
> Put on your shoes
> Read about
> Howard Hughes.

"He wrote that. Leadbelly wrote that."

No Direction Home: Bob Dylan

SEPTEMBER 20, 2005

It has taken me all this time to accept Bob Dylan as the extraordinary artist he clearly is, but because of a new documentary by Martin Scorsese, I can finally see him freed from my disenchantment. I am Dylan's age, and his albums were the sound track of my college years. I never got involved in the war his fans fought over his acoustic and electric styles: I liked them all, every one.

Then in 1968, I saw *Don't Look Back* (1967), D. A. Pennebaker's documentary about Dylan's 1965 tour of Great Britain. In my review, I called the movie "a fascinating exercise in self-revelation," and added, "The portrait that emerges is not a pretty one." Dylan is seen not as a "lone, ethical figure standing up against the phonies," I wrote, but is "immature, petty, vindictive, lacking a sense of humor, overly impressed with his own importance, and not very bright."

I felt betrayed. In *Don't Look Back*, he mercilessly puts down a student journalist, and is rude to journalists, hotel managers, fans. Although Joan Baez was the first to call him on her stage when he was unknown, after she joins the tour, he does not ask her to sing with him. Eventually she bails out and goes home.

The film fixed my ideas about Dylan for years. Now Scorsese's *No Direction Home: Bob Dylan*, a 225-minute documentary that will play in two parts September 26–27 on PBS (and comes out today on DVD), creates a portrait that is deep, sympathetic, perceptive, and yet finally leaves Dylan shrouded in mystery, which is where he properly lives.

The movie uses revealing interviews made recently by Dylan, but its subject matter is essentially the years between 1960, when he first came into view, and 1966, when after the British tour and a motorcycle accident, he didn't tour for eight years. He was born in 1941, and the career that made him an icon essentially happened between his twentieth and twenty-fifth years. He was a young man from a Minnesota town who had the mantle of a generation placed, against his will, upon his shoulders. He wasn't at Woodstock; Arlo Guthrie was.

Early footage of his childhood is typical of many Midwestern childhoods: the town of Hibbing, Minnesota, the homecoming parade, bands playing at dances, the kid listening to the radio and records. The early sounds he loved ran all the way from Hank Williams and Webb Pierce to Muddy Waters, the Carter Family, and even Bobby Vee, a rock star so minor that young Robert Zimmerman for a time claimed to be Bobby Vee.

He hitched a ride to New York (or maybe he didn't hitch; his early biography is filled with romantic claims, such as that he grew up in Gallup, New Mexico). In Greenwich Village, he found the folk scene, and it found him. He sang songs by Woody Guthrie, Pete Seeger, and others, and then was writing his own. He caught the eye of Baez, and she mentored and promoted him. Within a year he was . . . Dylan.

The movie has a wealth of interviews with people who knew him at the time: Baez, Pete Seeger, Mike Seeger, Liam Clancy, Dave Von Ronk, Maria Muldaur, Peter Yarrow, and promoters like Harold Leventhal. There is significantly no mention of Ramblin' Jack Elliott. The documentary *The Ballad of Ramblin' Jack* (2000) claims it was Elliott who introduced Dylan to Woody Guthrie, and suggested that he use a harmonica holder around his neck, and essentially defined his stage persona; "There wouldn't be no Bob Dylan without Ramblin' Jack," says Arlo Guthrie, who is also not in the Scorsese film.

Dylan's new friends in music all admired the art but were ambivalent about the artist. Van Ronk smiles now about the way Dylan "borrowed" his "House of the Rising Sun." The Beat Generation, especially Jack Kerouac's *On the Road*, influenced Dylan, and there are many observations by the beat poet Allen Ginsberg, who says he came back from

252

India, heard a Dylan album, and wept, because he knew the torch had been passed to a new generation.

It is Ginsberg who says the single most perceptive thing in the film: for him, Dylan stood atop a column of air. His songs and his ideas rose up from within him and emerged uncluttered and pure, as if his mind, soul, body, and talent were all one.

Dylan was embraced by the left-wing musical community of the day. His "Blowin' in the Wind" became an anthem of the civil rights movement. His "Only a Pawn in the Game" saw the killer of Medgar Evers as an insignificant cog in the machine of racism. Baez, Seeger, the Staple Singers, Odetta, Peter, Paul & Mary all sang his songs and considered him a fellow warrior.

But Dylan would not be pushed or enlisted, and the crucial passages in this film show him drawing away from any attempt to define him. At the moment when he was being called the voice of his generation, he drew away from "movement" songs. A song like "Mr. Tambourine Man" was a slap in the face to his admirers, because it moved outside ideology.

Baez, interviewed before a fireplace in the kitchen of her home, still with the same beautiful face and voice, is the one who felt most betrayed: Dylan broke her heart. His change is charted through the Newport Folk Festival: early triumph, the summit in 1964 when Johnny Cash gave him his guitar, the beginning of the end with the electric set in 1965. He was backed by Michael Bloomfield and the Butterfield Blues Band in a folk-rock-blues hybrid that his fans hated. When he took the new sound on tour with the Hawks (later The Band), audiences wanted the "protest songs," and shouted "Judas!" and "What happened to Woody Guthrie?" when he came onstage. Night after night, he opened with an acoustic set that was applauded, and then came back with the band and was booed.

"Dylan made it pretty clear he didn't want to do all that other stuff," Baez says, talking of political songs, "but I did." It was the beginning of the Vietnam era, and Dylan had withdrawn. When he didn't ask Baez onstage to sing with him on the British tour, she says quietly, "It hurt."

But what was happening inside Dylan? Was he the jerk portrayed in *Don't Look Back*? Scorsese looks more deeply. He shows countless news conferences where Dylan is assigned leadership of his generation and assaulted with inane questions about his role, message, and philosophy. A photographer asks him, "Suck your glasses" for a picture. He is asked how many protest singers he thinks there are: "There are 136."

At the 1965 Newport festival, Pete Seeger recalls, "The band was so loud, you couldn't understand one word. I kept shouting, 'Get that distortion out! If I had an ax, I'd chop the mike cable right now!'" For Seeger, it was always about the words and the message. For Dylan, it was about the words and then it became about the words and the music, and it was never particularly about the message.

Were drugs involved in these years? The movie makes not the slightest mention of them, except obliquely in a scene where Dylan and Johnny Cash do a private duet of *I'm So Lonesome I Could Cry*, and it's clear they're both stoned. There is sad footage near the end of the British tour, when Dylan says he is so exhausted: "I shouldn't be singing tonight."

The archival footage comes from many sources, including documentaries by Pennebaker and Murray Lerner (*Festival*). Many of the interviews were conducted by Michael Borofsky, and Jeff Rosen was a key contributor. But Scorsese provides the master vision, and his factual footage unfolds with the narrative power of fiction.

What it comes down to, I think, is that Robert Zimmerman from Hibbing, Minnesota, who mentions his father only because he bought the house where Bobby found a guitar, and mentions no other member of his family at all, who felt he was from nowhere, became the focus for a time of fundamental change in music and politics. His songs led that change, but they transcended it. His audience was uneasy with transcendence. They kept trying to draw him back down into categories. He sang and sang, and finally, still a very young man, found himself a hero who was booed. "Isn't it something, how they still buy up all the tickets?" he asks about a sold-out audience that hated his new music.

What I feel for Dylan now and did not feel before is empathy. His music stands and it will survive. Because it embodied our feelings, we wanted him to embody them, too. He had his own feelings. He did not want to embody ours. We found it hard to forgive him for that. He had the choice of caving in or dropping out. The blues band music, however good it really was, functioned also to announce the end of his days as a standard-bearer. Then after his motorcycle crash in 1966, he went away into a personal space where he remains.

Watching him singing in *No Direction Home*, we see no glimpse of humor, no attempt to entertain. He uses a flat, merciless delivery, more relentless cadence than melody, almost preaching. But sometimes at the press conferences, we see moments of a shy, funny, playful kid inside. And just once, in his recent interviews, seen in profile against a background of black, we see the ghost of a smile.

The Departed

JULY 6, 2007 (RELEASED 2006)

Most of Martin Scorsese's films have been about men trying to realize their inner image of themselves. That's as true of Travis Bickle as of Jake LaMotta, Rupert Pupkin, Howard Hughes, the Dalai Lama, Bob Dylan, or, for that matter, Jesus Christ. *The Departed* is about two men trying to live public lives that are the radical opposites of their inner realities. Their attempts threaten to destroy them, either by implosion or fatal betrayal. The telling of their stories involves a moral labyrinth, in which good and evil wear each other's masks.

The story is inspired by *Infernal Affairs* (2002) by Alan Mak and Andrew Lau, the most successful Hong Kong film of recent years. Indeed, having just reread my 2004 review of that film, I find I could change the names, cut and paste it, and be discussing this film. But that would only involve the surface, the plot, and a few philosophical quasi-profundities. What makes this a Scorsese film, and not merely a retread, is the director's use of actors, locations, and energy—and its buried theme. I am fond of saying that a movie is not about what it's about; it's about how it's about it. That's always true of a Scorsese film.

This one, a cops-and-gangster picture set in Boston rather than, say, New York or Vegas, begins with a soda-fountain scene that would be at home in *GoodFellas*. What is deliberately missing, however, is the initial joy of that film. Instead of a kid who dreamed of growing up to be a mobster, we have two kids who grow up as imposters: one becomes a cop who goes undercover as a gangster, and the other becomes a gangster who goes undercover as a cop.

Leonardo DiCaprio and Matt Damon star. Damon is Colin Sullivan, the kid spotted in that soda fountain by mob boss Frank Costello (Jack Nicholson). He enlists in the state police after Costello handpicks him so many years before as a promising spy. DiCaprio is Billy Costigan, an ace police cadet who is sent undercover by Captain Queenan (Martin Sheen) to infiltrate Costello's gang. Both men succeed with their fraudulent identities; Colin rises in the force, and Billy rises in the mob.

The story's tension, which is considerable, depends on human nature. After several years, both men come to identify with, and desire the approval of, the men they are deceiving. This may be a variant of the Stockholm syndrome; for that matter, we see it all the time in politicians who consider themselves public servants even though they are thieves. If you are going to be a convincing gangster, you have to be prepared to commit crimes. If a convincing cop, you have to be prepared to bust bad guys, even some you know. Protect your real employers and you look fishy. *The Departed* turns the screw one more time because each man is known to only one or a few of the men on the side he's working for. If Billy's employer, Captain Queenan, gets killed, who can testify that Billy is really a cop?

Ingenious additional layers of this double-blind are added by the modern devices of cell phones and computers. When the paths of the two undercover men cross, as they must, will they eventually end up on either end of the same phone call? And when the cops suspect they have an informer in their midst, what if they assign the informer to find himself? The traps and betrayals of the undercover life are dramatized in one of my favorite moments, when one of the characters is told, "I gave you the wrong address. But you went to the right one."

Although many of the plot devices are similar in Scorsese's film and the Hong Kong "original," this is Scorsese's film all the way, because of his understanding of the central subject of so much of his work: guilt. It is reasonable to assume that Boston working-class men named Costigan, Sullivan, Costello, Dignam, and Queenan were raised as Irish

American Catholics, and that if they have moved outside the church's laws they have nevertheless not freed themselves of a sense of guilt. The much-married Scorsese once told me that he thought he would go to hell for violating the church's rules on marriage and divorce, and I believed him. Now think of the guilt when you are simultaneously (1) committing crimes, and (2) deceiving the men who depend on you. Both Billy and Colin are doing that, although perhaps only a theologian could name their specific sin. A theologian, or Shakespeare, whose advice from Polonius they do not heed: "To thine own self be true, and it must follow, as the night the day, thou canst not then be false to any man."

Another amateur theologian, Hemingway, said it's good if you feel good afterwards, and bad if you feel bad afterwards. Colin and Billy feel bad all of the time, and so their lives involve a performance that is a lie. And that is the key to the performances of DiCaprio and Damon: it is in the nature of the movies that we believe most characters are acting or speaking for themselves. But in virtually every moment in this movie, except for a few key scenes, they are not. Both actors convey this agonizing inner conflict so that we can sense and feel it, but not see it; they're not waving flags to call attention to their deceptions. In that sense, the most honest and sincere characters in the movie are Queenan (Sheen), Costello (Nicholson), and Costello's right-hand man, French (Ray Winstone, that superb British actor who invests every line with the authority of God dictating to Moses).

It's strange that Jack Nicholson and Scorsese have never worked together, since they seem like a natural fit; he makes Frank Costello not a godfather, not a rat, not a blowhard, but a smart man who finally encounters a situation no one could fight free of, because he simply lacks all the necessary information. He has a moment and a line in this movie that stands beside Joe Pesci's work at a similar moment in *GoodFellas*.

There is another character who is caught in a moral vise, and may sense it although she cannot for a long time know it. That is Madolyn (Vera Farmiga), a psychologist who works for the police, and who coincidentally comes to know both Colin and Billy. Her loyalty is not to her employer but to her client—but, oh, what a tangled web that becomes.

It is intriguing to wonder what Scorsese saw in the Hong Kong movie that inspired him to make the second remake of his career (after *Cape Fear*, 1991). I think he instantly recognized that this story, at a buried level, brought two sides of his art and psyche into equal focus. We know that he, too, was fascinated by gangsters. In making so many films about them, about what he saw and knew growing up in Little Italy, about his insights into their natures, he became, in a way, an informant.

I have often thought that many of Scorsese's critics and admirers do not realize how deeply the Catholic Church of pre–Vatican II could burrow into the subconscious, or in how many ways Scorsese is a Catholic director. This movie is like an examination of conscience, when you stay up all night trying to figure out a way to tell the priest: I know I done wrong, but, oh, Father, what else was I gonna do?

Shine a Light

APRIL 4, 2008

Martin Scorsese's *Shine a Light* may be the most intimate documentary ever made about a live rock-and-roll concert. Certainly it has the best coverage of the performances on stage. Working with cinematographer Robert Richardson, Scorsese deployed a team of nine other cinematographers, all of them Oscar winners or nominees, to essentially blanket a live September 2006 Rolling Stones concert at the smallish Beacon Theater in New York. The result is startling immediacy, a merging of image and music, edited in step with the performance.

In brief black-and-white footage opening the film, we see Scorsese drawing up shot charts to diagram the order of the songs, the order of the solos, and who would be where on the stage. This was the same breakdown approach he used with his documentary *The Last Waltz* (1978), which would hopefully enable him to call his shots through earpieces of the cameramen, as directors of live TV did in the early days. The challenge this time was that Mick Jagger toyed with his list in endless indecision; we look over his shoulder at titles scratched out and penciled back in, and hear him mention casually that of course the whole set might be changed on the spot. Apparently after playing together for forty-five years, the Stones communicate their running order telepathically.

This movie is where Scorsese came in. I remember visiting him in the postproduction loft for *Woodstock* in 1970, where he was part of a team led by Thelma Schoonmaker that was combining footage

from multiple cameras into a split-screen approach that could show
as many as three or four images at once. But the footage the team had
to work with was captured on the run, while *The Last Waltz* had a shot
map and outline, at least in Scorsese's mind. *Shine a Light* combines
his foreknowledge with the versatility of great cinematographers so
that it essentially seems to have a camera in the right place at the right
time for every element of the performance.

It helped, too, that the Stones songs had been absorbed by Scorsese into his very being. "Let me put it this way," he said in a revealing
August 2007 interview with Craig McLean of the *London Observer*.
"Between '63 and '70, those seven years, the music that they made I
found myself gravitating to. I would listen to it a great deal. And ultimately, that fuelled movies like *Mean Streets* and later pictures of mine,
Raging Bull to a certain extent and certainly *GoodFellas* and *Casino* and
other pictures over the years."

Mentioning that he had not seen the Stones in concert until late
1969, he said the music itself was ingrained: "The actual visualization
of sequences and scenes in *Mean Streets* comes from a lot of their music,
of living with their music and listening to it. Not just the songs I use
in the film. No, it's about the tone and the mood of their music, their
attitude . . . I just kept listening to it. Then I kept imagining scenes
in movies. And interpreting. It's not just imagining a scene of a track-
ing shot around a person's face or a car scene. It really was [taking]
events and incidents in my own life that I was trying to interpret into
filmmaking, to a story, a narrative. And it seemed that those songs
inspired me to do that . . . To find a way to put those stories on film.
So the debt is incalculable. I don't know what to say. In my mind, I
did this film forty years ago. It just happened to get around to being
filmed right now."

The result is one of the most engaged documentaries you could
imagine. The cameras do not simply regard the performances; in a
sense, the cameras are performers too, in the way shots are cut together by Scorsese and his editor, David Tedeschi (who also edited
The Last Waltz). Even in their sixties, the Stones are the most physical
and exuberant of bands. Compared to them, watching the movements

(261)

of many new young bands on *Leno, Letterman*, and *SNL* is like watching jerky marionettes. Jagger has never used the mechanical moves employed by many lead singers; he is a dancer and an acrobat, and a conductor, too, who uses his body to conduct the audience. In counterpoint, Keith Richards and Ron Woods are loose-limbed, angular, like way-cool backup dancers. Richards in particular seems to defy gravity as he leans so far over; there's a moment in rehearsal when he tells Scorsese he wants to show him something, and leans down to show that you can see the mallet of Charlie Watts's bass drum, visible as it hits the front drumhead. "I can see that because I'm down there," he explains.

The unmistakable fact is that the Stones love performing. Watch Ron lean an arm on Keith's shoulder during one shared riff. Watch the droll hints of irony, pleasure, quizzical reaction shots, which so subtly move across their seemingly passive faces. Notice that Keith smokes onstage not simply to be smoking, but to use the smoke cloud, brilliant in the spotlights, as a performance element. He knows what he's doing. And then see it all brought together and tied tight in the remarkably acrobatic choreography of Jagger's performance. I've seen the Stones in Chicago in venues as large as the United Center and as small as the Double Door, but I've never experienced them this way, because the cameras are as privileged as the performers on stage.

And the music? What do I have to say about the music? What is there *left* to say about the music? In that interview, Scorsese said, "'Sympathy for the Devil' became this score for our lives. It was everywhere at that time, it was being played on the radio. When 'Satisfaction' starts, the authority of the guitar riff that begins it is something that became anthemic." I think there is nothing useful for me to say about the music except that if you have been interested enough to read this far, you already know all about it, and all I can usefully describe is the experience of seeing it in this film.

Part 6 Masterpieces

Introduction

In 1997 I began to write a longer review every other week about a great movie from the past. The Great Movies Collection is now approaching three hundred titles and a third book, and it includes the following five titles by Scorsese. Bergman also has five; Hitchcock has six. I've often been asked for my definition of a great movie, and find I cannot improve on the words of the London critic Derek Malcolm: "A great movie is a movie I cannot bear the thought of never seeing again."

Three of the films are unquestioned masterpieces. *Raging Bull* has now been accepted as one of the greatest of all films, and the impact of *Taxi Driver* remains undiminished. For some people *GoodFellas* is a more accurate, less operatic portrait of Mafia life than the *Godfather* films. *Mean Streets* has never reached the audience of those three, and *The Age of Innocence*, although it springs directly from Scorsese's deepest feelings, is sometimes not thought of as one of his films. Merchant-Ivory, maybe? Not on your life.

I think *Raging Bull* approaches perfection. Howard Hawks once said a good movie has "three good scenes, no bad scenes." There are no bad scenes in *Raging Bull*. The fierce energy of Robert De Niro creates a man driven, consumed, by jealousy. It is one of the finest performances in movie history, backed by the writing to make it Shakespearian. I look at it over and over again, and it never grows familiar. I have heard it said that we remember facts more accurately than feelings. Although the film's events are known to me, the emotion is newly powerful every time. When you see what is happening to Jake LaMotta, when you see the pain in the eyes of his brother and the resentment in the eyes of his wife, all distance from the film falls away and you look in pity.

De Niro's Travis Bickle is equally possessed in *Taxi Driver*, although more shielded by madness from the strength of his feelings. Does that closing scene even happen at all? It is impossible to say. Paul Schrader is not even sure. It brings closure but not a solution or an "ending." Certainly it involves the unlikely coincidence of who gets into his cab. But given that, could the rest happen? We would say no, but then came the case of Bernhard Goetz, the "subway vigilante," less than ten years later.

If *Who's That Knocking at My Door* shows young men entering the mob culture more or less unthinkingly, almost playfully, *GoodFellas* watches similar characters as they grow into the hard realities of their trade. The world is at the feet of Henry Hill to begin with; the famous nightclub scene is his fifteen minutes as a master of the universe. He is a man who commands respect and deference in the circles he chooses, but by the end he can barely move out of his house. The vise has tightened.

You can follow these threads of emotional development (and in *Casino*, too) because they have been supplied from life to the filmmaker. I love *The Godfather*, but I believe Mario Puzo knew little enough about the Mafia and Francis Ford Coppola not as much. Maybe that helps their films become more entertaining. "When the legend becomes fact, print the legend," we hear in John Ford's *The Man Who Shot Liberty Valance*, a film, along with *The Searchers*, that J. R. cites to The Girl in the first extended conversation Scorsese ever filmed. Scorsese's gangsters seem more based on fact, indeed on the real lives of Frank Rosenthal and Henry Hill and the guys he grew up with in Little Italy.

Mean Streets centers on Charlie (Harvey Keitel), who is obviously interchangeable with J. R., the autobiographical hero of *Who's That Knocking*. We know that because Scorsese has told us, but also because he marks Charlie as his own in the film with its first words, a voiceover: "You don't make up for your sins in church. You do it in the streets. You do it at home. All the rest is bullshit and you know it." Then we fade in on Charlie. The words being quoted were probably said to Charlie by a priest, but the voice is Scorsese's own.

The Age of Innocence begins for our purposes when Newland Archer sees the Countess Ellen Olenska in another box at the opera. It is a shot like Jake's first look at Kathy, or Rosenthal's first sight of Geraldine in the casino, or J. R. noticing The Girl in the ferry terminal. Scorsese was asked by Gene Siskel at the Toronto tribute if he could name one "master shot" that held the key to his cinema. He named the title sequence in *Raging Bull*, with Jake LaMotta dancing in slow motion behind the ropes of the ring — ropes, he said, like the lines on a musical score — while the sad intermezzo from Pietro Mascagni's *Cavalleria Rusticana* is heard. It is an opera, yes, about jealousy. That will serve as a master shot, but I submit that the shots of four men seeing the woman who will obsess them will serve as well.

(267)

Derek Malcolm's definition applies to all five of these films. I could not bear the thought of never seeing them again. There are more "great movies" circling to land: *The Last Temptation of Christ*, certainly, and perhaps *After Hours* and *Bringing Out the Dead*. And of course there are films still unmade.

Mean Streets

MARCH 15, 1998 (RELEASED 1973)

Martin Scorsese's *Mean Streets* is not primarily about punk gangsters at all, but about living in a state of sin. For Catholics raised before Vatican II, it has a resonance that it may lack for other audiences. The film recalls days when there was a greater emphasis on sin—and rigid ground rules, inspiring dread of eternal suffering if a sinner died without absolution.

The key words in the movie are the first ones, spoken over a black screen: "You don't make up for your sins in church. You do it in the streets. You do it at home. All the rest is bullshit and you know it." The voice belongs to Scorsese. We see Charlie (Harvey Keitel) starting up in bed, awakened by a dream, and peering at his face in a bedroom mirror. The voice was Scorsese's, but it possibly represents words said to him by a priest.

Later Charlie talks in a voiceover about how a priest gave him the usual "Ten Hail Marys and ten Our Fathers," but he preferred a more personal penance; in the most famous shot in the film, he holds his hand in the flame of a votive candle before the altar, testing himself against the fires of hell.

"The clearest fact about Charlie," Pauline Kael wrote in her influential review launching the 1973 film, "is that whatever he does in his life, he's a sinner." The film uses lighting to suggest his slanted moral view. The real world is shot in ordinary colors, but then Charlie descends into the bar run by his friend Tony, and it is always bathed in red, the color of sex, blood, and guilt.

He enters the bar in a series of shots at varying levels of slow motion (a Scorsese trademark). He walks past his friends, exchanging ritual greetings, and eventually he gets up on the stage with the black stripper, and dances with her for a few bars of rock and roll. He fantasizes about the stripper (Jeannie Bell), and later in the movie even makes a date with her (but fears being seen by his friends with a black woman, and stands her up). He also dreams of his cousin Teresa (Amy Robinson), who is Johnny's sister. They have sex, but when she says she loves him, he says, "Don't say that."

For him both women—any woman he feels lust for—represent a possible occasion of sin, which invests them with such mystery and power that sex pales by comparison. (Immediately after dancing with the stripper, he goes to the bar, lights a match, and holds his finger above it—instant penance.)

Charlie walks through the movie seeking forgiveness—from his Uncle Giovanni (Cesare Danova), who is the local Mafia boss, and from Teresa, his best friend Johnny Boy (Robert De Niro), the local loan shark, Michael (Richard Romulus), and even from God. He wants redemption. Scorsese, whose screenplay has autobiographical origins, knows why Charlie feels this way: he knows in his bones that the church is right, and he is wrong and weak. Although he is an apprentice gangster involved with men who steal, kill, and sell drugs, Charlie's guilt centers on sex. Impurity is the real sin; the other stuff is business.

The film watches Charlie as he uneasily tries to reconcile his various worlds. He works as a collector for Giovanni, hearing the sad story of a restaurant owner who has no money. Charlie is being groomed to run the restaurant, but must obey Giovanni, who forbids him to associate with Johnny Boy ("honorable men go with honorable men") and with Teresa, whose epilepsy is equated in Giovanni's mind with madness.

Trouble is brewing because Johnny Boy owes money to Michael, who is growing increasingly unhappy about his inability to collect.

(269)

De Niro plays Johnny almost as a holy fool: a smiling jokester with
no sense of time or money, and a streak of self-destruction. The first
time we see him in the film, he blows up a corner mailbox. Why?
No reason. De Niro and Keitel have a scene in the bar's back room
that displays the rapport these two actors would carry through many
movies. Charlie is earnest, frightened, telling Johnny he has to pay
the money. Johnny launches on a rambling, improvised cock-and-bull
story about a poker game, a police raid, a fight—finally even losing
the thread himself.

Scorsese first displayed his distinctive style in his first feature, *Who's
That Knocking at My Door* (1967), which was also set in Little Italy and
also starred Keitel. In both films he uses a hand-held camera for scenes
of quick movement and fights, and scores everything with period rock-
and-roll music (a familiar tactic now, but unheard of in 1967).

The style is displayed joyously in *Mean Streets* as Charlie and friends
go to collect from a pool-hall owner, who is happy to pay. But then
Johnny Boy is called a "mook," and although nobody seems quite sure
what a mook is, that leads to a wild, disorganized fight. These are not
smooth stuntmen, slamming each other in choreographed action, but
uncoordinated kids in their twenties who smoke too much, drink
too much, and fight as if they don't want to get their shirts torn. The
camera pursues them around the room, and Johnny Boy leaps onto a
pool table, awkwardly practicing the karate kicks he's learned in 42nd
Street grind houses; on the sound track is "Please, Mr. Postman" by
the Marvelettes. Scorsese's timing is acute: cops barge in to break up
the fight, are paid off by the pool-hall owner, leave, and then another
tussle breaks out.

Underlying everything is Charlie's desperation. He loves Johnny
and Teresa, but is forbidden to see them. He tries to be tough with
Teresa, but lacks the heart. His tenderness toward Johnny Boy is shown
in body language (hair tousling, back slapping) and in a scene where
Johnny is on the roof, "shooting out the light in the Empire State
Building." Charlie essentially feels bad about everything he does; his
self-hatred colors every waking thought.

At one point, late in the film, he goes into the bar, orders scotch, and holds his fingers over the glass as the bartender pours, copying the position of the priest's fingers over the chalice. That kind of sacramental detail would also be a motif in *Taxi Driver*, where overhead shots mirror the priest's-eye-view of the altar, and the hero also places his hand in a flame. Everything leads, as it must, to the violent conclusion, in which Michael, the loan shark who feels insulted, drives while a gunman (Scorsese) fires in revenge. Who can be surprised that Charlie, after the shooting, is on his knees?

Seen after twenty-five years, *Mean Streets* is a little creaky at times; this is an early film by a director who was still learning, and who learned so fast that by 1976 he would be ready to make *Taxi Driver*, one of the greatest films of all time, also with De Niro and Keitel. The movie doesn't have the headlong flow, the unspoken confidence in every choice, that became a Scorsese hallmark. It was made on a tiny budget with actors still finding their way, and most of it wasn't even shot on the mean streets of the title, but in disguised Los Angeles locations. But it has an elemental power, a sense of spiraling doom, that a more polished film might have lacked.

(271)

And in the way it sees and hears its characters, who are based on the people Scorsese knew and grew up with in Little Italy, made it an astonishingly influential film. If Francis Ford Coppola's *The Godfather* fixed an image of the Mafia as a shadow government, Scorsese's *Mean Streets* inspired the other main line in modern gangster movies, the film of everyday reality. *The Godfather* was about careers. *Mean Streets* was about jobs. In it you can find the origins of all those other films about the criminal working class, like *King of the Gypsies*, *GoodFellas*, *City of Industry*, *Sleepers*, *State of Grace*, *Federal Hill*, *Gridlock'd*, and *Donnie Brasco*. Great films leave their mark not only on their audiences, but on films that follow. In countless ways, right down to the detail of modern TV crime shows, *Mean Streets* is one of the source points of modern movies.

Taxi Driver

MARCH 16, 1998 (RELEASED 1976)

Are you talkin' to me? Well, I'm the only one here.

—Travis Bickle in *Taxi Driver*

It is the last line, "Well, I'm the only one here," that never gets quoted. It is the truest line in the film. Travis Bickle exists in *Taxi Driver* as a character with a desperate need to make some kind of contact some-how—to share or mimic the effortless social interaction he sees all around him, but does not participate in.

The film can be seen as a series of his failed attempts to connect, every one of them hopelessly wrong. He asks a girl out on a date, and takes her to a porno movie. He sucks up to a political candidate, and ends by alarming him. He tries to make small talk with a Secret Service agent. He wants to befriend a child prostitute, but scares her away. He is so lonely that when he asks, "Who you talkin' to?" he is addressing himself in a mirror.

This utter aloneness is at the center of *Taxi Driver*, one of the best and most powerful of all films, and perhaps it is why so many people connect with it even though Travis Bickle would seem to be the most alienating of movie heroes. We have all felt as alone as Travis. Most of us are better at dealing with it.

Martin Scorsese's 1976 film (re-released in theaters and on video in 1996 in a restored color print, with a stereophonic version of the Ber-nard Herrmann score) is a film that does not grow dated, or overfamiliar.

I have seen it dozens of times. Every time I see it, it works; I am drawn into Travis's underworld of alienation, loneliness, haplessness, and anger.

It is a widely known item of cinematic lore that Paul Schrader's screenplay for *Taxi Driver* was inspired by *The Searchers*, John Ford's 1956 film. In both films, the heroes grow obsessed with "rescuing" women who may not, in fact, want to be rescued. They are like the proverbial Boy Scout who helps the little old lady across the street whether or not she wants to go.

The Searchers has Civil War veteran John Wayne devoting years of his life to the search for his young niece, Debbie (Natalie Wood), who has been kidnapped by Comanches. The thought of Debbie in the arms of an Indian grinds away at him. When he finally finds her, she tells him the Indians are her people now, and runs away. Wayne then plans to kill the girl, for the crime of having become a "squaw." But at the end, finally capturing her, he lifts her up (in a famous shot) and says, "Let's go home, Debbie."

The dynamic here is that Wayne has forgiven his niece, after having participated in the killing of the people who, for fifteen years or so, had been her family. As the movie ends, the niece is reunited with her surviving biological family, and the last shot shows Wayne silhouetted in a doorway, drawn once again to the wide open spaces. There is, significantly, no scene showing us how the niece feels about what has happened to her.

In *Taxi Driver*, Travis Bickle also is a war veteran, horribly scarred in Vietnam. He encounters a twelve-year-old prostitute named Iris (Jodie Foster), controlled by a pimp named Sport (Harvey Keitel). Sport wears an Indian headband. Travis determines to "rescue" Iris, and does so, in a bloodbath that is unsurpassed even in the films of Scorsese. A letter and clippings from the Steensmas, Iris's parents, thank him for saving their girl. But a crucial earlier scene between Iris and Sport suggests that she was content to be with him, and the reasons why she ran away from home are not explored.

The buried message of both films is that an alienated man, unable to establish normal relationships, becomes a loner and wanderer, and

assigns himself to rescue an innocent young girl from a life that offends his prejudices. In *Taxi Driver*, this central story is surrounded
by many smaller ones, all building to the same theme. The story
takes place during a political campaign, and Travis twice finds himself with the candidate, Palatine, in his cab. He goes through the
motions of ingratiating flattery, but we, and Palatine, sense something wrong.

Shortly after that Travis tries to "free" one of Palatine's campaign
workers, a blonde he has idealized (Cybill Shepherd), from the Palatine
campaign. That goes wrong with the goofy idea of a date at a porno
movie. And then, after the fearsome rehearsal in the mirror, he becomes a walking arsenal and goes to assassinate Palatine. The Palatine
scenes are like dress rehearsals for the ending of the film. With both
Betsy and Iris, he has a friendly conversation in a coffee shop, followed
by an aborted "date," followed by attacks on the men he perceived as
controlling them; he tries unsuccessfully to assassinate Palatine, and
then goes gunning for Sport.

There are undercurrents in the film that you can sense without
quite putting your finger on them. Travis's implied feelings about
blacks, for example, which emerge in two long shots in a taxi drivers' hangout, when he exchanges looks with a man who may be a
drug dealer. His ambivalent feelings about sex (he lives in a world
of pornography, but the sexual activity he observes in the city fills
him with loathing). His hatred for the city, inhabited by "scum." His
preference for working at night, and the way Scorsese's cinematographer, Michael Chapman, makes the yellow cab into a vessel by
which Travis journeys the underworld, as steam escapes from vents
in the streets, and the cab splashes through water from hydrants—a
stygian passage.

The film has a certain stylistic resonance with *Mean Streets* (1973),
the first Scorsese film in which Keitel and De Niro worked together.
In the earlier film Scorsese uses varying speeds of slow motion to suggest a level of heightened observation on the part of his characters,
and here that technique is developed even more dramatically; as the
taxi drives through Manhattan's streets, we see it in ordinary time,

but Travis's point-of-view shots are slowed down: he sees hookers and pimps on the sidewalks, and his heightened awareness is made acute through slow motion.

The technique of slow motion is familiar to audiences, who usually see it in romantic scenes, or scenes in which regret and melancholy are expressed—or sometimes in scenes where a catastrophe looms, and cannot be avoided. But Scorsese was finding a personal use for it, a way to suggest a subjective state in a POV shot. And in scenes in a cab drivers' diner, he uses close-ups of observed details to show how Travis's attention is apart from the conversation, is zeroing in on a black who might be a pimp. One of the hardest things for a director to do is to suggest a character's interior state without using dialog; one of Scorsese's greatest achievements in *Taxi Driver* is to take us inside Travis Bickle's point of view.

There are other links between *Mean Streets* and *Taxi Driver* that may go unnoticed. One is the "priest's-eye-view" often used in overhead shots, which Scorsese has said are intended to reflect the priest looking down at the implements of the Mass on the altar. We see, through Travis's eyes, the top of a taxi dispatcher's desk, candy on a movie counter, guns on a bed, and finally, with the camera apparently seeing through the ceiling, an overhead shot of the massacre in the red-light building. This is, if you will, the final sacrifice of the Mass. And it was in *Mean Streets* that Keitel repeatedly put his finger in the flame of a candle or a match, testing the fires of hell: here De Niro's taxi driver holds his fist above a gas flame.

There has been much discussion about the ending, in which we see newspaper clippings about Travis's "heroism," and then Betsy gets into his cab and seems to give him admiration instead of her earlier disgust. Is this a fantasy scene? Did Travis survive the shoot-out? Are we experiencing his dying thoughts? Can the sequence be accepted as literally true?

I am not sure there can be an answer to these questions. The end sequence plays like music, not drama: it completes the story on an emotional, not a literal, level. We end not on carnage but on redemption, which is the goal of so many of Scorsese's characters. They despise

(275)

themselves, they live in sin, they occupy mean streets, but they want to be forgiven and admired. Whether Travis gains that status in reality or only in his mind is not the point; throughout the film, his mental state has shaped his reality, and at last, in some way, it has brought him a kind of peace.

Raging Bull

MAY 10, 1998 (RELEASED 1980)

Raging Bull is not a film about boxing but about a man with paralyzing jealousy and sexual insecurity, for whom being punished in the ring serves as confession, penance, and absolution. It is no accident that the screenplay never concerns itself with fight strategy. For Jake LaMotta, what happens during a fight is controlled not by tactics but by his fears and drives.

Consumed by rage after his wife, Vickie, unwisely describes one of his opponents as "good-looking," he pounds the man's face into a pulp, and in the audience a Mafia boss leans over to his lieutenant and observes, "He ain't pretty no more." After the punishment has been delivered, Jake (Robert De Niro) looks not at his opponent, but into the eyes of his wife (Cathy Moriarty), who gets the message.

Martin Scorsese's 1980 film was voted in three polls as the greatest film of the decade, but when he was making it, he seriously wondered if it would ever be released: "We felt like we were making it for ourselves." Scorsese and De Niro had been reading the autobiography of Jake LaMotta, the middleweight champion whose duels with Sugar Ray Robinson were a legend in the 1940s and '50s. They asked Paul Schrader, who wrote *Taxi Driver*, to do a screenplay. The project languished while Scorsese and De Niro made the ambitious but unfocused musical *New York, New York*, and then languished some more as Scorsese's drug use led to a crisis. De Niro visited his friend in the hospital, threw the book on his bed, and said, "I think we should make this." And the making of *Raging Bull*, with a screenplay further sculpted by Mardik Martin (*Mean Streets*), became therapy and rebirth for the filmmaker.

The movie won Oscars for De Niro and editor Thelma Schoonmaker, and also was nominated for best picture, director, sound, and supporting actor (Joe Pesci) and actress (Moriarty). It lost for best picture to *Ordinary People*, but time has rendered a different verdict.

For Scorsese, the life of LaMotta was like an illustration of a theme always present in his work, the inability of his characters to trust and relate with women. The engine that drives the LaMotta character in the film is not boxing, but a jealous obsession with his wife, Vickie, and a fear of sexuality. From the time he first sees her, as a girl of fifteen, LaMotta is mesmerized by the cool, distant blonde goddess, who seems so much older than her age, and in many shots seems taller and even stronger than the boxer.

Although there is no direct evidence in the film that she has ever cheated on him, she is a woman who at fifteen was already on friendly terms with mobsters, who knew the score, whose level gaze, directed at LaMotta during their first date, shows a woman completely confident as she waits for Jake to awkwardly make his moves. It is remarkable that Moriarty, herself nineteen, had the presence to so convincingly portray the later stages of a woman in a bad marriage.

Jake has an ambivalence toward women that Freud famously named the Madonna-whore complex. For LaMotta, women are unapproachable, virginal ideals—until they are sullied by physical contact (with him), after which they become suspect. During the film he tortures himself with fantasies that Vickie is cheating on him. Every word, every glance, is twisted by his scrutiny. He never catches her, but he beats her as if he had; his suspicion is proof of her guilt.

The closest relationship in the film is between Jake and his brother Joey (Joe Pesci). Pesci's casting was a stroke of luck; he had decided to give up acting, when he was asked to audition after De Niro saw him in a B movie. Pesci's performance is the counterpoint to De Niro's, and its equal; their verbal sparring has a kind of crazy music to it, as in the scene where Jake loses the drift of Joey's argument as he explains,

"You lose, you win. You win, you win. Either way, you win." And the scene where Jake adjusts the TV and accuses Joey of cheating with Vickie: "Maybe you don't know what you mean." The dialog reflects the Little Italy of Scorsese's childhood, as when Jake tells his first wife that overcooking the steak "defeats its own purpose."

The fight scenes took Scorsese ten weeks to shoot instead of the planned two. They use, in their way, as many special effects as a science-fiction film. The sound track subtly combines crowd noise with animal cries, bird shrieks, and the grating explosions of flash-bulbs (actually panes of glass being smashed). We aren't consciously aware of all we're listening to, but we feel it.

The fights are broken down into dozens of shots, edited by Schoon-maker into duels consisting not of strategy, but simply of punishing blows. The camera is sometimes only inches from the fists; Scorsese broke the rules of boxing pictures by staying inside the ring, and by freely changing its shape and size to suit his needs—sometimes it's claustrophobic, sometimes unnaturally elongated.

The brutality of the fights is also new; LaMotta makes Rocky look tame. Blows are underlined by thudding impacts on the sound track, and Scorsese uses sponges concealed in the gloves and tiny tubes in the boxers' hair to deliver spurts and sprays of sweat and blood; this is the wettest of boxing pictures, drenched in the fluids of battle. One reason for filming in black and white was Scorsese's reluctance to show all that blood in a color picture.

The most effective visual strategy in the film is the use of slow motion to suggest a heightened awareness. Just as *Taxi Driver*'s Travis Bickle saw the sidewalks of New York in slow motion, so LaMotta sees Vickie so intently that time seems to expand around her. Normal movement is shot at twenty-four frames a second; slow motion uses more frames per second, so that it takes longer for them to be projected; Scorsese uses subtle speeds such as thirty or thirty-six frames per second, and we internalize the device so that we feel the tension of narrowed eyes and mounting anger when Jake is triggered by paranoia over Vickie's behavior.

The film is bookmarked by scenes in which the older Jake LaMotta,

(279)

balding and overweight, makes a living giving "readings," running a nightclub, even emceeing at a Manhattan strip club. It was De Niro's idea to interrupt the filming while he put on weight for these scenes, in which his belly hangs over his belt. The closing passages include Jake's crisis of pure despair, in which he punches the walls of his Miami jail cell, crying out, "Why? Why? Why?"

Not long after, he pursues his brother down a New York street, to embrace him tenderly in a parking garage, in what passes for the character's redemption—that, and the extraordinary moment where he looks at himself in a dressing-room mirror and recites from *On the Waterfront* ("I coulda been a contender"). It's not De Niro doing Brando, as is often mistakenly said, but De Niro doing LaMotta doing Brando doing Terry Malloy. De Niro could do a "better" Brando imitation, but what would be the point?

Raging Bull is the most painful and heartrending portrait of jealousy in the cinema—an Othello for our times. It's the best film I've seen about the low self-esteem, sexual inadequacy, and fear that lead some men to abuse women. Boxing is the arena, not the subject. LaMotta was famous for refusing to be knocked down in the ring. There are scenes where he stands passively, his hands at his side, allowing himself to be hammered. We sense why he didn't go down. He hurt too much to allow the pain to stop.

GoodFellas

NOVEMBER 24, 2002 (RELEASED 1990)

As far back as I can remember, I always wanted to be a gangster. To me, being a gangster was better than being president of the United States.

So says Henry Hill in the opening moments of Martin Scorsese's *GoodFellas*, a movie about the tradecraft and culture of organized crime in New York. That he narrates his own story—and is later joined by his wife, narrating hers—is crucial to the movie's success. This is not an outsider's view, but a point-of-view movie based on nostalgia for the lifestyle. "They were blue-collar guys," Hill's wife explains. "The only way they could make extra money, real extra money, was to go out and cut a few corners." Their power was intoxicating. "If we wanted something, we just took it," Henry says. "If anyone complained twice they got hit so bad, believe me, they never complained again."

At the end of the film, Henry (Ray Liotta) still misses the old days. His money is gone, most of his friends are dead, and his best friend was preparing to kill him, but after he finds safety in the federal witness protection program, he still complains. "We were treated like movie stars with muscle," he remembers. "Today, everything is different. There's no action. I have to wait around like everyone else."

The rewards of unearned privilege are at the heart of *GoodFellas* (1990). There's an early scene introducing Henry's partner Jimmy Conway (Robert De Niro), and he enters the shot in a sort of glowing modesty; his body language says, "no applause, please." Henry's other partner is Tommy DeVito (Joe Pesci), who makes the mistake of overexercising his clout instead of letting it go without saying. In one of the great buildups and payoffs in movie history, he believes he's going to become a "made" man, realizes his mistake too late, and says "Oh, no" before being shot in the head. He never learned to relax and enjoy his privileges. He always had to push things.

The early scenes of *GoodFellas* show young Henry Hill as a gofer for the local Brooklyn mob, which has its headquarters in a taxi garage right across the street from his house. (A shot of Henry looking out the window mirrors Scorsese's own childhood memories from Manhattan's Little Italy neighborhood, and so does a following sequence which uses subtle slow motion for close-ups of the mobster's shoes, ties, hair, rings, and cigars.) In a movie famous for violence that arrives instantly, without warning, the most shocking surprise comes when Henry is slapped by his father for missing school. He had to "take a few beatings" at home because of his teenage career choice, Henry remembers, but it was worth it. Violence is like a drumbeat under every scene.

Henry's joy in his emerging career is palpable. He sells stolen cigarettes out of car trunks, torches a car lot, has enough money at twenty-one to tip lavishly. In the most famous shot in the movie, he takes his future wife, Karen (Lorraine Bracco), to the Copacabana nightclub. There's a line in front, but he escorts her across the street, down stairs and service corridors, through the kitchen area, and out into the showroom just as their table is being placed right in front of the stage. This unbroken shot, which lasts 184 seconds, is not simply a cameraman's stunt, but an inspired way to show how the whole world seems to unfold effortlessly before young Henry Hill.

There is another very protracted shot, as Henry introduces us to his fellow gangsters. Henry leads the camera through a crowded club, calling out names as the characters nod to the camera or speak to Henry. Sometimes the camera seems to follow Henry, but at other times it seems to represent his POV; sometimes he's talking to them, sometimes to us. This strategy implicates us in the action.

The cinematographer, Michael Ballhaus, did not get one of the film's six Oscar nominations, but was a key collaborator. Following Scorsese's signature style, he almost never allows his camera to be still; it is always moving, if only a little, and a moving camera makes us not passive observers but active voyeurs.

The screenplay by Nicholas Pileggi and Scorsese is based on Pileggi's book about Hill, *Wiseguy: Life in a Mafia Family*. It is equally based, probably, on Scorsese's own memories of Little Italy. It shows a mob family headed by Paul Cicero (Paul Sorvino), who never talks on the phone, dislikes group conversations, disapproves of drugs (because the sentences are too high), and sounds like a parish priest when he orders Henry to return home to his wife. That doesn't mean he has to dump his mistress; all the guys seem to have both a wife and a mistress, who are plied with stolen goods of astonishing tastelessness.

GoodFellas is unusual in giving good screen time to the women, who are usually unseen in gangster movies. Karen Hill narrates her own side of the story, confessing that she was attracted to Henry's clout and fame; after she tells Henry the guy across the street tried to hit on her, Henry pistol-whips him and then gives her the gun to hide. She tells us: "I know there are women, like my best friends, who would have gotten out of there the minute their boyfriend gave them a gun to hide. But I didn't. I got to admit the truth. It turned me on." It is reasonable to suggest that *The Sopranos* finds its origin in the narrations in *GoodFellas*, especially Karen's.

Underlying the violence is a story of economic ambition. Henry and Karen come from backgrounds that could not easily lead to Cadillacs, vacations in Vegas, and fur coats, and she justifies what he has to do to pay for the lifestyle: "None of it seemed like crimes. It was more like Henry was enterprising and that he and the guys were making a few bucks hustling, while the other guys were sitting on their asses waiting for handouts."

The story arc follows Henry's movement up into the mob and then down into prison sentences and ultimate betrayal. At first the mob seems like an opening up of his life, but later, after he starts selling drugs, there is a claustrophobic closing in. The camera style in the earlier scenes celebrates his power and influence with expansive ease. At the end, in a frantic sequence concentrated into a single day, the style becomes hurried and choppy as he races frantically around the neighborhood on family and criminal missions while a helicopter always seems to hover overhead.

What Scorsese does above all else is share his enthusiasm for the material. The film has the headlong momentum of a storyteller who knows he has a good one to share. Scorsese's camera caresses these guys, pays attention to the shines on their shoes and the cut of their clothes. And when they're planning the famous Lufthansa robbery, he has them whispering together in a tight three-shot that has their heads leaning low and close with the thrill of their own audacity. You can see how much fun it is for them to steal.

The film's method is to interrupt dialog with violence. Sometimes there are false alarms, as in Pesci's famous restaurant scene where Tommy wants to know what Henry meant when he said he was "funny." Other moments well up suddenly out of the very mob culture: The way Tommy shoots the kid in the foot, and later murders him. The way kidding around in a bar leads to a man being savagely beaten. The way the violence penetrates the daily lives of the characters is always insisted on. Tommy, Henry, and Jimmy, with a body in their trunk, stop at Tommy's mother's house to get a knife, and she insists they sit down at 3 AM for a meal.

Scorsese seems so much in command of his gift in this film. It was defeated for the best picture Oscar by *Dances with Wolves*, but in November 2002, a poll by *Sight & Sound* magazine named it the fourth-best film of the past twenty-five years (after Coppola's *Apocalypse Now*, Scorsese's *Raging Bull*, and Bergman's *Fanny and Alexander*). It is an indictment of organized crime, but it doesn't stand outside in a superior moralistic position. It explains crime's appeal for a hungry young man who has learned from childhood beatings not to hate power, but to envy it. When Henry Hill talks to us at the opening of the film, he sounds like a kid in love: "To me, it meant being somebody in a neighborhood that was full of nobodies. They weren't like anybody else. I mean, they did whatever they wanted. They double-parked in front of a hydrant and nobody ever gave them a ticket. In the summer when they played cards all night, nobody ever called the cops."

The Age of Innocence

AUGUST 14, 2005 (RELEASED 1993)

"It was the spirit of it—the spirit of the exquisite romantic pain. The idea that the mere touching of a woman's hand would suffice. The idea that seeing her across the room would keep him alive for another year." So Martin Scorsese told me one autumn afternoon, as we drank tea in the library of his New York town house, a house like the ones inhabited by the characters in his film *The Age of Innocence*.

He was explaining why the director of *Taxi Driver* and *Raging Bull* had made a film about characters defined by the social codes of New York society in the 1870s. We had both read the Edith Wharton novel, and so really no explanation was necessary. We understood that passion and violence can exist in places where absolute decorum rules; that Jake LaMotta, smashing his fists into the walls of his cell in *Raging Bull*, found a release that Newland Archer could not discover anywhere in the sitting rooms and dinners and nights at the opera that defined his life in *The Age of Innocence*.

Archer was a man who loved one woman and married another, because it was the right thing to do. Or, more accurately, because everyone in his world thought it was the right thing to do, and made sure that he did it. The film employs a narration (read by Joanne Woodward) that reflects the way Wharton addresses us directly in the novel, telling us how Archer was trapped. Listen to her: "They all lived in a kind of hieroglyphic world. The real thing was never said or done or even thought, but only represented by a set of arbitrary signs."

Those words could also describe the world of the Mafia in Scorsese's films. Scorsese told me that in reading Wharton's novel, "What has always stuck in my head is the brutality under the manners. People hide what they mean under the surface of language. In the subculture I was around when I grew up in Little Italy, when somebody was killed, there was a finality to it. It was usually done by the hands of a friend. And in a funny way, it was almost like ritualistic slaughter, a sacrifice. But New York society in the 1870s didn't have that. It was so cold-blooded. I don't know which is preferable."

The Age of Innocence is one of Scorsese's greatest films, improperly appreciated because, like *Kundun* (1997), it stands outside the main line of his work. Its story of a man of tradition who spends a lifetime of unrequited love resembles one of Scorsese's favorite films, Michael Powell's *The Life and Death of Colonel Blimp*.

The story: Newland Archer (Daniel Day-Lewis) is planning a proper marriage to the respectable society virgin May Welland (Winona Ryder). Then the Countess Ellen Olenska (Michelle Pfeiffer) returns to New York, and her presence stirs him beyond all measure. Ellen is an American, May's cousin, who unwisely married a Polish count. The count took her fortune and mistreated her; she left him and has fled back to New York—where in the movie's opening scene she joins her relatives, including May and May's mother, in their box at the opera.

This causes a shock in society circles; the Wellands are boldly and publicly standing by the countess in the face of malicious gossip, and Newland Archer admires it. Observe how Scorsese sets up the dynamic of the film before a word has been spoken between Newland and May or Ellen. It involves a point-of-view sequence, and Scorsese told me: "We look through his opera glasses, seeing what he sees. But not just in regular time. We did stop-frame photography, exposing one frame at a time and printing each frame three times and then dissolving between each three frames. It looks sort of like what you see when you look through an opera glass, but with heightened attention. He scans the audience and then backs up and stops on her. With all the different experimenting we did, that took almost a year to get right."

Archer prematurely announces his engagement to May, perhaps

because he senses the danger in his attraction to Ellen. But as he sees more of Ellen, he is excited not only physically but especially by her unconventional mind and tastes. In Europe, she moved among writers and artists; in New York, Newland has a library where he treasures his books and paintings in solitude, because there is no one to share his artistic yearnings. He has a safe job in a boring law office, and only in his library, or during conversation with the countess, does he feel that his true feelings are engaged.

She is attracted to him for the same reason: in a society of ancient customs and prejudices, enforced by malicious gossip, she believes Archer to be the only man in New York she could love. Ellen tells him, "All this blind obeying of tradition, somebody else's tradition, is thoroughly needless. It seems stupid to have discovered America only to make it a copy of another country." Again, later: "Does no one here want to know the truth, Mr. Archer? The real loneliness is living among all these kind people who ask you only to pretend."

I recently read *The Age of Innocence* again, impressed by how accurately the screenplay (by Jay Cocks and Scorsese) reflects the book. Scorsese has two great strengths in adapting it. The first is visual. Working with the masterful cinematographer Michael Ballhaus, he shows a society encrusted by its possessions. Everything is gilt or silver, crystal or velvet or ivory. The Victorian rooms are jammed with furniture, paintings, candelabra, statuary, plants, feathers, cushions, bric-a-brac, and people costumed to adorn the furnishings.

These people always seem to be posing for their portraits, but Scorsese employs his invariable device of a constantly moving camera to undermine their poses. The camera may be moving so subtly we can hardly tell (unless we watch the sides of the screen), but it is always moving. A still camera implies an observation, a moving camera an observer. The film's narrator observes and comments, and so does the camera, voyeuristically. Occasionally, Scorsese adds old-fashioned touches like iris shots to underline key moments. Or he'll circle an area in brightness and darken the rest, to spotlight the emotion in a sea of ennui.

His second strength is a complete command of tone. Like her

friend Henry James, Edith Wharton seldom allowed her characters to state bluntly what they were thinking. They talked around it, inhibited by society and perhaps afraid of their own thoughts. Wharton, however, allows herself a narrator who does state the plain truth. At a key point in the story, May, now Archer's wife, makes comments that reveal how frankly she views the world, and then quickly returns to her tame and naive persona. The narrator tells us what Archer cannot, that he wonders "how such depths of feeling could coexist with such an absence of imagination."

Consider the most crucial passage in the film. Archer has decided to take a decisive step, to break away from his flawless but banal wife, be with the countess and accept the consequences. Then the prospects of the countess change dramatically, and his wife tells him something he did not expect to hear. He is an intelligent man and realizes at once what has been done, how it cannot be undone, and what as a gentleman he must do. His fate is sealed. As he regards the future, the narrator tells us what cannot, in this world, possibly be said in dialog:

> He guessed himself to have been, for months, the center of countless silently observing eyes and patiently listening ears. He understood that, somehow, the separation between himself and the partner of his guilt had been achieved. And he knew that now the whole tribe had rallied around his wife. He was a prisoner in the center of an armed camp.

The film ends with a sense of loss, sadness, and resignation, reminding me of the elegiac feeling in Orson Welles's *The Magnificent Ambersons*. The final scene, on a park bench in Paris, sums up not only the movie but Scorsese's reason for making it; it contains a revelation showing that love is more complex and secret than we imagine. Archer's son, Ted, says his mother told him his father could be trusted because "when she asked you to, you gave up the thing you wanted most." Archer replies, "She never asked me." We reflect, first, that she never did, and second, that she never needed to.

Index

(295)

NEW YORK UNIVERSITY

School of the Arts
Institute of Film and Television
Undergraduate Program

65 SOUTH BUILDING
WASHINGTON SQUARE, NEW YORK, N.Y. 10003
AREA 212 598-3703

3/12/70

Dear Roger:

A note to remind you That
I will be sending a copy of the
Other script "Jerusalem, Jerusalem"
which is the last (or middle, it doesn't
matter) part of the "Knocking" trilogy
along with "Season of the Witch" which
you should have now. The two
scripts ("WITCH" is a 1st draft) are the
ones we spoke about in N.Y.C. in
regard to the Two projects which
will probably never be made but